MILAT

Other books by
Clive Small and Tom Gilling

Smack Express: How organised crime got hooked on drugs
Blood Money: Bikies, terrorists and Middle Eastern gangs
Betrayed: The shocking story of two undercover cops

MILAT

INSIDE AUSTRALIA'S BIGGEST MANHUNT

A DETECTIVE'S STORY

CLIVE SMALL

AND TOM GILLING

This edition published in 2016
First published in 2014

Allen & Unwin
83 Alexander Street
Crows Nest NSW 2065
Australia
Phone: (61 2) 8425 0100
Email: info@allenandunwin.com
Web: www.allenandunwin.com

Cataloguing-in-Publication details are available
from the National Library of Australia
www.trove.nla.gov.au

ISBN 978 1 76029 330 7

Internal design by Design by Committee
Typeset by Midland Typesetters, Australia
Printed and bound in Australia by Pegasus Media & Logistics

15 14 13

The paper in this book is FSC® certified.
FSC® promotes environmentally responsible, socially beneficial and economically viable management of the world's forests.

EU Authorised Representative: Easy Access System Europe, Mustamäe tee 50, 10621 Tallinn, Estonia, gpsr.requests@easproject.com

Dedicated to the victims
and to the families and friends of the victims
of Ivan Milat, and to the members of Task Force Air,
whose efforts put him in gaol for life

'Amazing police work. Amazingly painstaking.'

—Mark Tedeschi, Senior Crown Prosecutor,
commenting on the work
of Task Force Air

CONTENTS

PART 2: BEYOND BELANGLO

IMPORTANT DATES IN THE BACKPACKER INVESTIGATION

1989

30 DECEMBER	Deborah Everist and James Gibson last seen
31 DECEMBER	James Gibson's camera found at Galston Gorge, near Hornsby

1990

15 JANUARY	Deborah Everist and James Gibson reported missing
25 JANUARY	Paul Onions flees from abductor on Hume Highway, near Bowral
13 MARCH	James Gibson's backpack found at Galston Gorge

1991

20 JANUARY	Simone Schmidl last seen
25 JANUARY	Simone Schmidl reported missing
26 DECEMBER	Gabor Neugebauer and Anja Habschied last seen

1992

30 JANUARY	Gabor Neugebauer and Anja Habschied reported missing
18 APRIL	Joanne Walters and Caroline Clarke last seen
29 MAY	Joanne Walters reported missing
EARLY JUNE	Caroline Clarke reported missing via Interpol
19 SEPTEMBER	Body of Joanne Walters discovered at Belanglo State Forest, near Bowral
20 SEPTEMBER	Body of Caroline Clarke discovered at Belanglo

1993

5 OCTOBER	Remains of Deborah Everist and James Gibson found at Belanglo
6 OCTOBER	Clive Small appointed to head investigation into the Belanglo murders
18 OCTOBER	Alex Milat interviewed
1 NOVEMBER	Remains of Simone Schmidl found at Belanglo
4 NOVEMBER	Remains of Gabor Neugebauer and Anja Habschied found at Belanglo

1994

26 FEBRUARY	Ivan Milat placed under surveillance
5 MAY	Paul Onions identifies Ivan Milat as his abductor
22 MAY	Police raid Milat family properties and Ivan Milat arrested
24 OCTOBER	Ivan Milat's committal—on seven charges of murder, attempted abduction and related charges—begins

1996

11 MARCH	Trial of Ivan Milat begins
27 JULY	Ivan Milat convicted and sentenced to seven life sentences for murder and six years for 'detention for advantage'

2010

29 AUGUST	Remains of 'Angel' found at Belanglo
20 NOVEMBER	Matthew Milat and Cohen Klein murder David Auchterlonie at Belanglo
8 JUNE 2012	Matthew sentenced to 43 years and Klein sentenced to 32 years for murder

ACKNOWLEDGEMENTS

Our sincere thanks to those who have helped directly or indirectly with the writing of this book. Thanks also to the journalists who over the decades have contributed to the solving of crimes through their reporting on the backpacker murders, unsolved murders and the 'disappearance' of missing persons.

Special gratitude to Tim Everist, Janet Fife-Yeomans, Bob Godden, Frank Goodyer, Olga and Guenther Habschied, Martha Jabour, Frank and Angela Klaassen, John Laycock, Rod Lynch, Robert May, Graham McNeice and Graham McNeice Productions, Neil Mercer, Dr Rod Milton, Manfred and Anke Neugebauer, Alex Pollock, Kim Shipton, Candy Sutton and Ray and Gillian Walters for their support and advice.

ABOUT THE AUTHORS

In 2008 Clive Small and Tom Gilling published the best-selling book *Smack Express: How organised crime got hooked on drugs*, which exposed the growth and transformation of organised crime in Australia since the late 1960s. They followed this up two years later with *Blood Money: Bikies, terrorists and Middle Eastern gangs*, and later with *Betrayed: The shocking story of two undercover cops*.

CLIVE SMALL is a 38-year New South Wales Police veteran. Much of his time was spent in criminal investigation. He was awarded several commendations. From 1977 to 1980 he worked as an investigator with the Woodward Royal Commission into Drug Trafficking. During 1987–88 he was an investigator on Strike Force Omega, which reinvestigated the 1984 shooting of Detective Michael Drury. In the early 1990s Small led the backpacker murder investigation, which resulted in the conviction of Ivan Robert Milat for the murder of seven backpackers in the Belanglo State Forest, south of Sydney, between 1989 and 1992. In 2001, as head of the Greater Hume Police Region, he helped dismantle the Vietnamese street gangs that had made Cabramatta Australia's heroin capital. After retiring from the police he joined the New South Wales Independent Commission Against Corruption as the executive director of operations. Since March 2007 he has been writing full time.

TOM GILLING's first two novels, *The Sooterkin* (1999) and *Miles McGinty* (2001), were both shortlisted for major awards and chosen as notable books of the year by *The New York Times*. They have been translated into several languages. His third novel, *Dreamland* (2008), has been published in Australia, Britain and the United States. As a journalist he has worked for numerous publications including *The Sydney Morning Herald*, *Rolling Stone*, *The Guardian* (UK), and *The New York Times*. Before *Smack Express* he co-wrote two non-fiction books, *Trial and Error* (1991), about the Israeli nuclear whistleblower Mordechai Vanunu; and *Bagman: The final confessions of Jack Herbert* (2005), about the events that led to the Fitzgerald Inquiry into police corruption in Queensland.

PREFACE

On 27 July 1996 a jury found Ivan Milat guilty of murdering seven backpackers and of abducting another, Paul Onions, who would surely have been Milat's eighth victim had he not managed to escape.

Other books have been written about the groundbreaking investigation that led to the arrest and conviction of Milat. This book will tell the story from a unique perspective, drawing on unpublished sources and operational insights available to me as the original commander of Task Force Air. But the book tells a much broader story.

First, I want to show how the crimes of Ivan Milat have left a profound mark on all of us, so that twenty years after his capture the very words 'Milat' and 'Belanglo' still cause a collective shudder. Second, by recounting the events that led to Milat's capture from my own point of view at the head of the investigation, I want to demonstrate how the techniques and systems pioneered by Task Force Air have transformed the investigation of major crime in New South Wales.

As the title suggests, Ivan Milat and the murders he committed (as well as others he may have committed but has never been charged with) are the focus of this book. At a deeper level, however, the book is a study not just of the backpacker murders but of all murders, of how they affect us as individuals and as a society, and of the never-ending challenge faced by the police to bring the killers to justice.

Clive Small

PART 1
THE ROAD TO BELANGLO

1
MISSING

Between 1989 and 1992 seven backpackers—three couples and one woman travelling alone—were reported missing in Australia. All seven had been last seen in Sydney or its suburbs. These reports would trigger one of Australia's biggest ever manhunts.

On 15 January 1990 Deborah Phyllis Everist and James Harold Gibson, both nineteen years old, were reported missing by their mothers at the Frankston Police Station in suburban Melbourne. James and Deborah had left Melbourne on 28 December 1989 and hitchhiked to Sydney to visit friends of James in the inner-city suburb of Surry Hills. They then left for Walwa, on the Victorian side of the Murray River, to attend the Confest conservation festival. It was thought they would catch a train to Liverpool, in Sydney's south-west, before hitchhiking the rest of the way. They never reached Walwa.

James lived with his family in Moorooduc, a Melbourne suburb on the Mornington Peninsula. Deborah lived with her parents in Frankston. She was a green activist and during the late 1980s had travelled the east coast of Australia to take part in anti-logging protests. She planned to start university in 1990. The pair met in mid-1989 at a concert.

On 13 March 1990 Wendy Dellsperger was driving along the narrow and winding Galston Road at Galston Gorge, about 36 kilometres north-west of Sydney, when she saw a red backpack on the side of the road. Thinking it might have been lost, Dellsperger stopped and put the backpack into her car. That night she examined it. The top, where a name might have been expected to be written, had been cut off, but inside she saw the name 'Gibson', a Victorian address and a phone number. The next day she called the number. James Gibson's mother, Peggy, answered. The next morning Dellsperger took the backpack to the Hornsby Police Station and showed police the spot where she had found it, but little more was done. On 27 March the Hornsby *Advocate* ran a story about the discovery of the backpack and the missing hikers, mentioning James Gibson's Ricoh camera. The story was seen by Michael James who, while cycling through Galston Gorge early on the morning of 31 December 1989—a day after James and Deborah were last seen—had found a similar camera. He still had the camera and immediately took it to Hornsby Police Station. It was James's.

In early April 1990 police divers searched the river that runs through the gorge and on 29 April, 140 police and support personnel, including members of the State Emergency Services and Rural Fire Service, began a search that extended for

3 kilometres along the road from the small wooden bridge at the bottom of the gorge. James's father and brother were present during the search, but nothing belonging to James or Deborah was found.

■ ■ ■

On 25 January 1991 Erwinea Schmidl reported her 22-year-old daughter, Simone, missing to Russell Street Police Station in Melbourne. Erwinea had flown to Australia from her home in Regensburg, Germany, to catch up with her daughter in Melbourne, but Simone failed to arrive. Erwinea reported Simone as a missing person and appealed to the media for help, but returned to Germany without knowing what had happened to her daughter.

Simone Loretta Schmidl was born in 1969 in Regensburg, at the confluence of the Danube and Regen rivers. She began her travels in 1987 when she visited Yugoslavia. Two years later she travelled to Canada and Alaska. Simone arrived in Australia on 1 October 1990 and stayed in Sydney before hitchhiking with a friend to Melbourne and then travelling to Queensland. Always on the move, Simone and her friend returned to Sydney and again visited Melbourne before returning to Sydney and leaving for New Zealand on 20 November 1990. They travelled around the country for two months before returning to Sydney on 19 January 1991.

That night Simone and her companion slept at a friend's place at Guildford in Sydney's west. The next morning Simone left with the intention of catching a bus to nearby Liverpool, from where she intended to hitchhike to Melbourne. She was never seen again.

On 30 January 1992, 22-year-old Gabor Kurt Neugebauer and 21-year-old Anja Susanne Habschied were reported missing to the Special Branch, Australian Federal Police, by the Embassy of the Federal Republic of Germany. They had been due to return to Germany on 24 January 1992. Anja's father, Guenther, had gone to Munich Airport to meet them, but after they failed to arrive he checked and found they were not on the plane. There was no record of them having boarded it. Guenther rang the Neugebauers and told them Gabor and Anja had not arrived, and over the next few days the parents made unsuccessful efforts to contact their children before reporting them missing.

Gabor was born in 1970 in the town of Sulz on the Neckar River, Germany, but the family moved several times because of his father's position in the West German Air Force, before settling in Heimerzheim, about 20 kilometres west of Bonn. During 1991 Gabor and his girlfriend, Anja, who was born in 1971 in Munich, visited several countries in Europe. Later that year they visited Indonesia, staying only a few weeks before flying to Darwin in November 1991. From Darwin they travelled to the North Queensland coast and made their way to Sydney, arriving a few days before Christmas and staying at the Original Backpackers Hostel in Kings Cross. On the morning of 26 December they left by road for Adelaide en route to Darwin, where they had pre-booked a flight to Indonesia on 1 January 1992. It was the last time they were seen alive.

Two months after reporting their son missing, Manfred and Anke Neugebauer were in Kings Cross searching for answers. They stayed in Sydney's eastern suburbs with some family friends, Frank and Angela Klaassen. The Klaassens asked their long-time friend, German-born Rita O'Malley, to help look after the Neugebauers while they were in Australia and later observed, 'Rita became invaluable in helping the police with translating documents and making phone calls to Germany.' With the Sydney inquiries exhausted, the Neugebauers hired a campervan and spent three weeks travelling up the east coast to Queensland, across to Darwin, down to Alice Springs, Port Augusta and Broken Hill, contacting backpacker hostels and other places where Gabor and Anja might have stayed. Recalling the trip, the Klaassens observed, 'Unfortunately the trip was to no avail, but we must say it was an incredible feat; having to adjust to driving on the other side of the road, acclimatising to the extreme temperatures and coping with the desperation of not finding any evidence of Gabor and Anja.' A reported sighting of the two backpackers in South Australia gave the Neugebauers a sense of hope, but that hope was dashed when the sighting was found to be false.

On 29 May 1992 Joanne Lesley Walters, a 22-year-old British backpacker, was reported missing to North Sydney Police Station by a former employer for whom Joanne had worked as a nanny at Kirribilli on Sydney's lower north shore. The report had been prompted by Joanne's worried parents in the United Kingdom. A short time later, Joanne's travelling companion, 22-year-old Caroline Jane Clarke, was reported missing to the New South Wales Police Missing Persons Unit, via Interpol. Caroline's parents, Ian and Jacquie, in England, made the report.

Joanne's parents, Ray and Gill, had been concerned about their daughter's safety within weeks of her leaving Kings Cross. She had not contacted them for a while and, unusually, had missed Father's Day. Ray made inquiries of a number of his daughter's friends in Australia, only to be told they had not heard from her either. Ray and Gill knew their daughter was travelling with Caroline Clarke and from information their daughter had given them, they were able to track down Caroline's parents. The Clarkes hadn't heard from their daughter since early April. Both families agreed to contact the police.

Joanne Walters was born in 1970 in the small town of Maesteg, South Wales. In 1990 she visited and worked in Greece, Italy and Sardinia, before flying to Australia in June 1991 with a friend she had met during her travels. After spending a short time in Sydney the pair made their way up the Queensland coast, picking up part-time work as they went, before returning to Sydney and settling in Kings Cross.

Caroline Clarke was born in 1970 and raised in Surrey, England. In August 1991 she left to explore the world with a friend, 23-year-old Noel Goldthorpe. They travelled around Europe before Goldthorpe returned to England, leaving Caroline to fly on alone to Australia. Arriving in Sydney on 19 September, she found accommodation at the Original Backpackers Hostel at Kings Cross where, about two months later, she met Joanne Walters.

After visiting Adelaide to spend Christmas 1991 with a friend she had met in Europe, Caroline returned to Kings Cross in early January 1992. In February, Caroline, Joanne and two of their flatmates went to Mildura to pick grapes. They caught a train to Liverpool before splitting into pairs to hitchhike the rest of the way. In a letter to Gill Baker, a close friend from England, Caroline wrote, 'I'm no longer in Sydney, but actually in Victoria in a place called Mildura for 6 to 8 weeks.

I'm doing grape picking . . . the money's not bad, about 40 pounds a day. I'm not paying rent so it's even better . . . [W]e all get on really well and have a good laugh in the evening.'

The girls returned to Kings Cross in late March, but Caroline and Joanne were back only a few days before they and two friends left for Tasmania, hitchhiking from Liverpool to Melbourne and catching the ferry to Tasmania. A fortnight later Caroline and Joanne decided to return to Sydney, but before they did Caroline and Steve Wright, one of their companions, swapped tents. Caroline's was a small one-person tent while Wright's was a three-person tent that she and Joanne could share. The pair made their way back to Kings Cross, where they booked into the Bridge North Apartments. Within weeks they were on the move again, bound for Mildura, but they would never arrive.

By late July 1992 the New South Wales Police Missing Persons Unit had identified six foreign backpackers who had disappeared in broadly similar circumstances: Caroline Clarke and Joanne Walters, Gabor Neugebauer and Anja Habschied, Simone Schmidl and a young woman who had disappeared from the Gold Coast several years earlier. The head of the Missing Persons Unit, Sergeant Peter Marcon, told *The Sydney Morning Herald*, '[W]e've got nothing at this point to suggest they've been killed, but we've had a massive media campaign and we haven't been able to come up with anything positive.'

It was the first time Simone's name had been mentioned alongside those of Caroline and the others. At this stage the missing Victorians, James Gibson and Deborah Everist, had not been connected with the others.

2
TWO BODIES

People go missing in New South Wales every day, often by choice. The head of the Missing Persons Unit, Sergeant Marcon, told *The Sunday Telegraph* in July 1992 that 'there were 861 people regarded as long-term missing in New South Wales and about a further 400 more recent cases being investigated'. But media interest both in Australia and England, generated especially by the father of Caroline Clarke, pressured senior police to take seriously the disappearance of the foreign backpackers.

Kings Cross–based Detective Sergeant Neville Scullion was given the job of investigating the disappearances of Caroline Clarke and Joanne Walters. It was an unfortunate choice, as Detective Scullion's main interest was in enriching himself through corruption—a fact revealed some years later by the Royal Commission into the New South Wales Police Service.

Nevertheless, growing media attention and speculation of foul play forced Scullion to spend the following weeks chasing leads and, in some cases, taking statements from seemingly credible witnesses who claimed to have seen Caroline and Joanne since their disappearance. Few leads provided results; most fizzled out after a cursory investigation.

After about two months Scullion was convinced that Caroline and Joanne were dead, but he had no idea where, how or why they had been killed, or who had killed them. Police interest in the case began to wane. But Caroline's parents refused to give up and they continued to speak to the newspapers. In August 1992 Joanne's parents, Ray and Gill, came to Sydney. They spoke to Scullion, who told them privately that he believed both girls were dead. Despite Scullion's advice, Joanne's parents continued hunting for information about their daughter in Kings Cross and elsewhere, even travelling to Mildura to visit the vineyard where Joanne and Caroline had picked grapes.

Ray and Gill Walters were still in Sydney on Saturday 19 September when an unidentified body was found in the Belanglo State Forest, about 140 kilometres south of Sydney, near the town of Bowral and about 12 kilometres west of the Hume Highway. Keith Siely and Keith Caldwell had been on an orienteering training exercise in the forest when they noticed a bad smell. It came from a nearby rocky overhang about 95 metres south-west of the Longacre Creek fire trail. Under the overhang and covered by dry sticks and leaves they saw a bone, a boot and some clothing. They had discovered a body.

Two others on the orienteering course soon joined them. They rang Bowral Police who, along with Senior Constable Andrew Grosse of the Goulburn Police Crime Scene Unit, arrived and began an examination that continued into the night. The female body was badly decomposed, but it was soon clear that it had been subjected to extreme violence. There was evidence of at least fourteen stab wounds to the neck, chest and back, cutting ribs, spine and cervical vertebrae. What appeared to be a garrotte lay on the ground near the victim's neck.

The next morning, as police scoured the surrounding bush, another female body was found hidden under branches and other forest debris beneath a fallen tree about 30 metres away from the first. The second was also badly decomposed. An examination revealed ten bullet entry wounds to the skull from five different angles: the back, front, each side and top of the skull. Ten .22 calibre Winchester cartridge cases were found clustered on the ground about 3 metres from the body. A red cloth had been wrapped twice around the head, apparently before the shooting. There were also a number of stab wounds to the upper body and multiple slashings of the clothing.

Except for the clothing and jewellery worn by the victims at the time of the attack, few other personal items were found at either scene or in the surrounding bush.

The first crime scene yielded little additional evidence, but at the second police found six cigarette butts. Five were later identified as being Longbeach, the brand smoked by Caroline Clarke; the sixth was not identifiable. All cigarettes were believed to have been smoked by Caroline. This suggested the killer had spent half an hour or more at the scene before killing Caroline.

Ten fired Winchester cartridge cases were found about 3.5 metres from the head of Caroline Clarke. It was a position where the cartridges would be expected to have landed after being ejected from a rifle used to shoot Caroline Clarke in the head in the area where her body was found. Three bullets were recovered in the ground under the head of Caroline Clarke and seven were later recovered from her skull during the autopsy. It appears that her head was moved at least three times and further shots were fired each time. Sergeant Gerard Dutton of the Forensic Ballistics Unit said that eight of the bullets were consistent with having been fired from a Ruger 10/22 rifle while two of the bullets were too damaged to identify the weapon from which they had been fired.

Dr Peter Bradhurst, a forensic pathologist, and Dr Christopher Griffiths, a forensic odontologist (dental expert), came to the forest to inspect the bodies. The remains were then taken to the morgue at Glebe, where a detailed examination was carried out and the findings photographed and documented. Both girls appeared to have been sexually attacked.

Before the bodies were removed from the bush, the first had been tentatively identified as that of Joanne Walters and the second as that of Caroline Clarke. Detective Scullion was contacted by investigators and told of the finds and the provisional identifications. Among other things, a distinctive ring on the finger of the first body convinced investigators and examiners that the first body was Joanne's. Scullion contacted her parents and met them at the Opera House, where they were sightseeing. In a public place crowded with tourists and local visitors, Scullion told Joanne's parents the news they had hoped never to hear: their daughter was dead. Her body and the body of her friend Caroline had been found in the Belanglo State Forest. They had been murdered.

Gill Walters broke down while her husband, Ray, tried in vain to console her. Ray would later say of the news, 'The miracle we'd always hoped for just didn't occur. We have cried so much since she went missing. Now we're too numb to take it in.'

Scullion also passed the news to an English police officer who had been acting as liaison with the Clarke family. The Clarkes were devastated to hear that Caroline was dead, but at the same time they felt some relief from knowing at last what had happened to their daughter. Now they wanted to know who was responsible.

Detective Inspector Bob Godden, head of the South West Region Homicide Squad, and squad member Detective Sergeant Steve McLennan were called in to take over the investigation. Godden and McLennan were both long-serving detectives, with experience of numerous murder investigations, but the level of violence still took them by surprise. Another odd feature was the amount of time evidently spent at the crime scene by the killer or killers, indicated by, among other things, the time it would have taken to smoke the cigarettes. While robbery did not appear to be a primary motive, there was no sign of the personal property backpackers would be expected to be carrying, such as tents, sleeping bags, backpacks, clothing and identification documents. If these items had been kept as trophies then they might lead police to the killer or killers.

Godden and McLennan studied the few leads they had: the recovered spent bullets, the cigarette butts and the bodies themselves. With luck, forensic analysis back at the laboratories would yield further clues. But one thing they knew for sure: there would be no quick arrest.

Over the next seven days some 40 police searched an area 300 metres around the crime scenes and along the Longacre Creek fire trail towards the highway for a distance of about 3 kilometres, but nothing was found.

Media reporting of the discovery of the bodies brought another flood of information and sightings. Investigators trawled through files of missing persons in the hope of finding a link, but came up with nothing.

In October Caroline Clarke's body was returned to England, where she was farewelled by her family and friends at the village of Slaley in Northumberland. A few days later the Clarkes flew to Australia where they met Gill and Ray Walters. They would stay in Sydney while Gill and Ray accompanied the body of their daughter back to Maesteg in South Wales.

Over the following weeks Godden and McLennan briefed a forensic psychiatrist, Dr Rod Milton, on the Belanglo murders and took him to the crime scenes. Milton was well known to both Godden and McLennan, and over the years had worked for the police as a profiler on several big cases. At the forest they were joined by Detective Andy Grosse from the Crime Scene Unit.

From what he had seen and heard, Milton drew several conclusions: the killer or killers were familiar with the forest; the victims had been killed for pleasure; because they had been killed in different ways with different weapons, and because two victims had been abducted and killed together, there were likely to have been two killers, probably brothers. The older brother, probably in his late twenties to mid-thirties, was dominant. The younger one was rebellious and not very bright, but submissive to the elder. The younger brother was more sexually inclined; the older one was the shooter. It was likely that they lived locally and belonged to a local gun club. They were probably involved in hunting and were not very sociable. The shooter showed signs of needing to be in control. They probably lived in isolation in the bush. Neither would have talked much to their victims. Milton stressed that his conclusions were not science but informed guesswork. That did not mean they were not true.

In November the New South Wales Government offered a $100,000 reward for information leading to the arrest and conviction of the killer or killers. The offer included the possibility of a free pardon to any accomplice who had not committed the actual crime.

Despite further forensic and ballistics analysis, and potential leads from police records and the public, the investigation petered out. Meanwhile, police were no closer to explaining the disappearances of James Gibson and Deborah Everist, Gabor Neugebauer and Anja Habschied, and Simone Schmidl. By Christmas 1992 the murders of Caroline Clarke and Joanne Walters seemed unlikely to be solved without a major breakthrough.

That breakthrough happened ten months later with the discovery of two more bodies in the Belanglo State Forest.

3
A POISONED CHALICE

Wednesday, 6 October 1993 started out as a typical day at the Liverpool Local Area Command: thefts and other crimes were being reported; several people arrested during the night were in the cells waiting to be processed; detectives were investigating cases or preparing to give evidence in court; uniformed police were patrolling the streets.

The previous afternoon I had been told that the remains of two unidentified bodies had been discovered in the Belanglo State Forest. Newspaper headlines were now screaming that a serial killer was on the loose and that the police had botched the investigation; how many more bodies were buried at Belanglo? It was bad news, the sort every area commander dreads, and I was relieved that it wasn't on my patch.

About 10.30 a.m. the phone on my desk rang. The caller was my district commander, Chief Superintendent Dennis Gilligan.

'You've heard about the bodies?' he asked. 'Get down there now and find out what's going on. The boss [Assistant Commissioner Bill Galvin, South West Region commander] wants you to get down there and give us an assessment. You'll probably have to take it over. We're out at Broken Hill for a few days.'

As I drove to the forest I listened to commercial radio, which was in a frenzy over the discovery of the bodies. Trying to manage a criminal investigation in the full glare of the media was always difficult, and I had been in the police long enough to know what could happen when media coverage began to influence the way an investigation was run.

My mind raced back four and a half years to another case that had dragged me into the spotlight: Harry Blackburn, a former police superintendent, had been arrested and charged with thirteen counts of sexual assault and twelve related charges of assault, robbery and detaining for advantage. The charges related to two sets of attacks, more than fifteen years apart, on a total of sixteen women. Blackburn's arrest had been stage-managed for the TV news cameras. He was employed at the Australian War Crimes Commission and footage of the arrest was accompanied by archival film of Nazi troops saluting Hitler. When the senior detective involved in the Blackburn investigation was seriously injured in a car accident, I was instructed by Police Headquarters to take on the case. I drafted two more detectives, Detective Ron Shaw and Detective Jackie Plotecki, to join the original investigation team. I was assured that all the investigative work had been done and that all I would have to do was 'put the brief of evidence together'.

Within days I knew we were in trouble. There was no brief of evidence or even partial brief of evidence, no recording or tracking system of documents or exhibits; formal statements had not been obtained, and several that had been obtained were of dubious quality and value; procedures that led to the identification of Blackburn were questionable—during one attack the offender had at all times been wearing a balaclava, but was identified by a victim; and evidence had been tampered with and, in some cases, obtained illegally. In other cases, exculpatory evidence had been excluded.

As I studied the evidence, the investigative team became defensive and I began to hear rumours. A conspiracy theory was circulating within the police and among politicians and the media about a so-called fight for control of the New South Wales Police. According to this theory, the forces of evil ('black knights' or 'the barbecue set', of which I was supposedly a member) were locked in a bitter struggle with the forces of good ('white knights', led by Assistant Commissioner, later Commissioner, Tony Lauer). Supposedly, Blackburn was actually guilty but I had somehow ripped the evidence out of the case against him to discredit the white knights and enable the black knights to take control.

Amid this climate of suspicion and accusation, the briefs of evidence were served on the Office of the Director of Public Prosecutions, which quickly dropped all charges against Blackburn. The government bowed to calls for a royal commission under His Honour Mr Justice Lee, which reported in mid-1990 that not only was there insufficient evidence to convict Blackburn, the evidence exonerated him. His Honour said:

> Mr Small had done all that any man could have done to get the senior police to recognise the appalling predicament in which Mr Blackburn had been placed at the hands of the investigating police, but the senior police clung tenaciously and blindly to the hope that Mr Small might be wrong, and they did so without either really acquainting themselves with the fine print of the evidence in the brief, or treating the evidence with objectivity, as every competent investigator into crime knows he must do.

Blackburn received around $1 million in compensation, a sum the government was willing to pay in order to make the embarrassment go away. Professionally, it was a gratifying result for me, but one that would not make the police executive happy.

Assistant Commissioner Tony Lauer, who had 'executive oversight' of the original Blackburn investigation, was promoted to commissioner. (Justice Lee found that 'the word "oversight" provides an excuse to claim no responsibility and should not be used'. Four years later Lauer dismissed calls for a royal commission into the New South Wales Police. He told the press, 'We have dealt with institutionalised corruption.'

Lauer resigned in 1996 as the royal commission was about to release its first report. Superintendent Col Cole, who also had an 'oversighting role' in the arrest and charging of Blackburn, was promoted to assistant commissioner in charge of Police Internal Affairs. (A short time later he was boarded out of the police medically unfit after the botched reporting of a corruption investigation.) A number of senior detectives involved in the original Blackburn investigation were discharged medically unfit on full pensions. The only person ever criminally charged over the Blackburn matter was the most junior officer on the team, Constable Kevin Paull. In 1993, after a trial without a jury, Paull was acquitted of perverting the course of justice.

As I listened to the flurry of rumour and speculation on talkback radio about the bodies in the Belanglo State Forest, I could only hope that Police Headquarters had learnt its lesson about the dangers of playing to the media.

I arrived at the police base in the forest around mid-afternoon and found a situation of organised chaos. The large—and growing—media contingent was clamouring for interviews with investigating detectives, pictures of the crime scenes, responses to speculation about the possible killer or killers and about the number of bodies that might still be in the forest, not to mention exclusive 'leaks'. Some also wanted to carry out their own search of the forest.

Amid the hysteria, crime scene examiners were quietly getting on with their jobs, retrieving the bodies and searching for clues, thoroughly documenting everything as they went. Others continued their search of surrounding areas, while investigators assessed the needs and operational priorities for the immediate search and for the wider investigation.

The first police officers I met in the forest were Detective Inspector Bob Godden, whom I had known for many years, and Detective Sergeant Steve McLennan. Talking to them eased my fears of a repeat of the Blackburn fiasco. I spent the next few days inspecting the crime scenes and receiving briefings from investigators, specialist and support police in the field, and local police.

Many of the immediate priorities were obvious: we urgently needed more detectives and more police to carry out the search of the forest, as well as office space in both Bowral and Sydney (a temporary incident room had already been established in the Bowral Police Station). Longer term priorities included a system of data collection, management and retrieval that ensured nothing was lost or missed; a plan to 'manage' the media; and ongoing local motel accommodation to handle the stronger police presence. Critically, we would also need to insulate the task force from political and media pressures, as well as from Police Headquarters itself, to ensure that we could do the job properly and were not rushed into decisions that could jeopardise the investigation.

At the back of my mind, however, was the fear that we might already be too late. The lack of progress into the murders of Joanne Walters and Caroline Clarke highlighted the problems we faced. The fact that Joanne and Caroline were from overseas meant they had few, if any, ties in Australia. The length of time between their disappearance and the discovery of their remains, the remoteness of the crime scene and the damage caused by the weather were all factors that counted against our hopes of solving the crime.

I doubt I was the only person who felt that in being put in charge of the backpacker murder investigation I had been handed a poisoned chalice.

4
TASK FORCE

The second pair of bodies belonged to the missing Victorian backpacker James Gibson, whose property had been found three and a half years earlier in Galston Gorge, and his friend Deborah Everist. It seemed inconceivable that their deaths were not linked to the murders of Joanne and Caroline. The location, the methods and violence of the killings, the way the bodies had been hidden, the fact that both sets of victims were backpackers who had been hitchhiking, and the absence of backpacks and other personal property all suggested a connection.

Bruce Pryor, a local potter who lived in the town of Bundanoon, had spent plenty of time in the nearby forests, including Belanglo, collecting firewood. He felt that the police could have spent more time in Belanglo looking for other bodies after the discovery of Caroline's and Joanne's remains, and had searched the forest himself on a number of occasions but found nothing.

On the morning of Tuesday, 5 October, Pryor set out for Nowra, about 70 kilometres south-east of Bundanoon, but halfway there he changed his mind, turned around and drove to Belanglo instead. He followed a number of different fire trails until he came to a small clearing near the Upper Long-acre Creek fire trail, an area he had not searched before. Within minutes he spotted what he thought was a human bone. After examining it, he put it back on the ground where he had found it and continued searching. About half an hour later he saw a human skull that showed signs of violence. Pryor realised he had found another victim and another crime scene, but wasn't sure what to do. He didn't have a phone and the police were in Bowral. Should he leave the skull or take it with him? Having decided to take it, Pryor wrapped the skull in a jumper. He was about to leave the forest when he saw a man repairing an old hut used by orienteers. Pryor borrowed a phone to report his discovery to the police at Bowral, who were quick to arrive. After showing them the skull, he took them to the spot where he had found it.

At the base of a large gum tree, partially covered in forest debris, lay the skeletal remains of a person. The bones had been scattered by animals and several were missing, but the skull and upper part of the body showed signs of multiple stabbings and fractures. Among the remains were a crucifix and two bracelets. Some partly degraded women's clothing was found close to the body. The clothes had numerous cut and slash marks, apparently made by a sharp knife, indicating that the victim had been wearing them at the time she was murdered. Four lengths of insulation tape—two yellow and two red—were recovered nearby.

It did not take long for police to find the remains of a second body. About 20 metres from the first, near the base of a large tree, were the remains of a person lying in a foetal position against a log and covered by forest debris. There were signs of multiple stab wounds to the chest and back. The body was clothed.

While the police realised they had the remains of one female and one male, they did not have a positive identification of either. The media were already speculating: were these the bodies of James Gibson and Deborah Everist, Gabor Neugebauer and Anja Habschied, or some other missing persons?

It was an agonising time for the four families. Police phoned Peggy Gibson and Patricia Everist and warned them to prepare for the worst. It took several days before the bodies could be formally identified as those of James Gibson and Deborah Everist. The families had to endure the horror of knowing their children had been murdered and that the killer or killers were still at large, but at least they would be able to put those children to rest. The Neugebauer and Habschied families still had no idea whether their missing children were alive or dead.

Once again, forensic pathologist Peter Bradhurst and forensic odontologist Christopher Griffiths carried out preliminary examinations of the bodies before the remains were taken to the morgue at Glebe. They were assisted by the local coroner, Ian McRae.

Examination of the crime scenes took several days. About 400 metres from the bodies, investigators found a tree trunk with nine bullets embedded in it. Eight had been damaged beyond identification. The ninth was identified as a .22 calibre bullet.

On 7 October a community meeting organised by Detective Godden took place at Bowral. The discovery of two more bodies had cast a pall over the town. Around 200 people came to the meeting, together with a large number of journalists. Godden, McLennan and I gave a broad outline of progress on the Clarke and Walters investigation and a summary of recent developments. We couldn't share many details. Our most important message was that we, the police, were there to stay. We were redoubling our efforts and were appealing for help from the community. Any scrap of information, however seemingly insignificant, could be crucial in helping us solve these murders. People at the meeting were clearly worried, and had every right to be, even though the killer or killers did not appear to be targeting locals.

With four bodies already discovered, and perhaps more still to be found, I knew our only hope of success lay with the creation of a large, well-resourced task force, and I quickly called for it to be formed.

The first recruits were Detectives Godden and McLennan, and other investigators and analysts who were already in the forest. Detective Inspector Rod Lynch, a very capable, experienced and meticulous investigator, was appointed deputy commander. I had known Rod for many years and had great respect for him. From the outset I saw him not as a deputy but as an equal partner.

The then State Crime Command assigned names to task forces. We were told verbally that the backpacker task force was to be called 'Air' and assumed the usual spelling. (Having informed the media of the task force and its name, I was startled to receive paperwork spelling it as 'Eyre', as in Lake Eyre in South Australia. I could picture the newspaper headlines if we tried to correct the spelling: 'They can't get the name of the task force right, what chance have they got of catching the killers?' We decided to stick with 'Air' and not mention the error, but it didn't remain secret for long.)

Task Force Air began with fifteen detectives and two intelligence analysts assisted by forensic investigators. Over the next three months the task force grew until it had a total of 33 detectives, eleven analysts and an administrative officer, supported by ballistics, crime scene and other forensic investigators. (See Appendix 4 for a complete list of task force members.)

There was great pressure on print, television and radio journalists to get a daily story, preferably an exclusive. We knew many of the journalists personally. Their approach was always the same: 'What's really going on?', 'What are you doing tonight—can we buy you dinner?', 'Can we get the first interview tonight?' Some would speculate in the hope of getting a response. Refusal only encouraged them to try their luck with another investigator.

How to manage the media was a key question from the first days of the task force. I was convinced the media would play an important role in the investigation and that it might be vital in solving the case. At the same time, wild speculation by journalists could result in the waste of valuable time and resources, and unguarded 'leaks' could seriously damage both the investigation and the chances of a successful prosecution. In deciding what information to give to the media, we had to take into account the priorities and needs of the whole investigation, not just parts of it.

To make this work we had to put in place a strict media protocol. There would be no leaks or unofficial briefings to the media. There would be no 'quiet' drinks or meals with members of the media. All media releases would be handled by me unless otherwise authorised.

The complexity of the case, as well as the intense media interest, made a 'single voice' approach essential, both to ensure consistency of information and to minimise disruption to the investigation. There would be one briefing in the morning and one in the afternoon. That meant two stories a day, unless there was a breaking story that required a special briefing, or some other special circumstance. The timing of the briefings would be determined by the journalists to enable them to meet their deadlines. Each night we expected to be left alone to have dinner. If a journalist wanted to join us afterwards, he or she would be welcome, but it would be a social meeting and there would be no discussion of the investigation. Inevitably, there was some disappointment among journalists eager for scoops, but they all agreed it was a fair arrangement. Most nights we ended up at the Bowral Hotel.

Due to the remoteness of the search area, we decided to allow the media access to police facilities (including the canteen) without cost.

Once the media realised there would be no leaks, nights at the hotel became more relaxed. We knew there was a killer out there who had to be stopped, but the pressure to catch him was intense and we needed somewhere to unwind.

5
SERIAL KILLER

After the discovery of two bodies in 1992 there had been an extensive search of Belanglo State Forest. The discovery of two more bodies, just thirteen months later, was a serious embarrassment. Now the task force set about searching the forest again. The new search would be led by Detective Chief Inspector Bob May of the Tactical Support Unit; it would have to be more extensive, more thorough and more painstaking than last time. When we left the forest we had to be certain there were no more bodies waiting to be found.

Before beginning the search we had to develop a detailed plan to ensure nothing was missed. We used satellite images of the forest to identify changes in the density of vegetation between the late 1980s and 1993 that could affect vehicle access, to identify possible burial sites and to help us plot individual search areas. We estimated the search would cover about 78 kilometres of tracks and fire trails, extending up to 150 metres either side of the track (depending on the terrain)—a total of around 24 square kilometres.

The search team was increased from 40 to 300, using police seconded from several regions. The searchers would sleep at the Police Academy in Goulburn and be bussed to and from the forest command post each day.

For the period of the search the command post would be staffed around the clock. It had communications support, including radio contact with searching groups. GPS would be used to plot sites where human remains and other significant items were found. This data would then be plotted on search progression maps.

Searchers worked in teams of about 40, moving through the forest in single lines. When an item of interest was found, the whole team stopped and the team leader was informed. The finding officer's details were recorded and the command post was contacted. Crime scene personnel, including forensic officers, would be called in. Photographs of locations and items found, together with detailed information, would be logged with the command post. In the case of major finds, such as human remains, the site would be guarded until all crime scene investigations had been completed.

Two specially trained cadaver dogs with handlers searched selected areas of the forest. Because the terrain was so rugged we had to have special 'boots' made to protect the dogs' feet. Police search teams scoured some areas on their hands and knees, used metal detectors and sieved the soil.

On 1 November searchers found the skeletal remains of a fifth body, which we later identified as that of Simone Schmidl.

The skull and part of the upper body were visible, despite an attempt to hide the still-clothed body under a pile of dried wood, sticks and other forest debris. Other clothing, jewellery and backpacking equipment were found nearby. A red T-shirt with the front cut open was found about 50 metres from the body. Preliminary examinations by Drs Bradhurst and Griffiths revealed multiple stab wounds to the chest and back. A length of soft wire tied in the shape of a noose, as though it had been used as a restraint, was found nearby. As with the other victims, there was no sign of Simone's backpack. Items found by forensic investigators were bagged, labelled and taken away for further examination, while Simone's body was taken to the Glebe morgue.

Before we could contact her, Erwinea Schmidl heard news of the discovery of her daughter's body on the radio in Germany.

Three days later searchers found a brown leather sandal with a broken strap. About 15 metres away the skeletal remains of a human body, later identified as that of Anja Habschied, were found buried under sticks and other forest debris. Anja appeared to have been wearing a pink top at the time she was killed. The top showed signs of multiple stabbings and slashings. Her spine had been severed by a knife, but the skull was missing. Anja wore a ring on one finger. A wrist watch and wrist bands or ankle bands were found close to the body, along with a 4.5-metre length of blue and yellow rope, doubled over with tied loops at both ends.

Fifty metres from Anja's remains, searchers found the skeletal remains of a seventh body, together with decomposed clothing, covered in debris beside a log. The skull had six bullet holes in it. A cloth had been tied over the mouth as a gag. Four fired bullets were later found in the skull and another in the upper chest. Four were identified as .22 calibre Winchester bullets; the others were too badly damaged to identify. Airline tickets in the name of Gabor Neugebauer were found in a clear plastic bag 5 metres from the remains. Seventy metres away, searchers found the remains of a Jack Wolfskin–brand money belt containing Neugebauer's and Habschied's International Student Cards, five American Express travellers' cheques and some cash. A black plastic adjustable tie, a length of black insulation tape wound into two wrist-sized loops, a length of cord and a 1-metre leash with a catch at each end were discovered 20 metres from the money belt. The leash and cord were wrapped around the insulation tape and tie. Searchers also found several other pieces of black electrical tape.

After a preliminary forensic examination, the bodies of Anja and Gabor were taken to the Glebe morgue.

Nearly 200 metres from the site where Gabor's body was discovered, searchers found other vital pieces of evidence: a weathered green cardboard ammunition packet with the words 'Winchester brand, Winner model, .22 calibre cartridge', and a partial batch number, '. . . CD . . . CF2' (the first and fourth letters or numbers were illegible); a black plastic cartridge holder for 50 bullets; an ammunition packet for 50 Eley Subsonic hollow-point .22 calibre bullets, batch number 'J23CGA' or 'J26CGA'; and a pair of pink jeans later identified as belonging to Anja Habschied.

Altogether, forensic investigators found 47 fired .22 calibre Winchester cartridge cases and 46 fired .22 calibre Eley cartridge cases. Fragments of six .22 calibre bullets were found in two tree trunks 30 and 50 metres away. The same calibre bullets had been used to murder Caroline Clarke.

Detective Godden made the phone calls to the Neugebauers and Habschieds in Germany and told them the news.

After the discovery of Gabor's and Anja's remains, we continued searching the forest for another twelve days, until I finally called a halt on 16 November.

Although Galston Gorge had been searched in April 1990 after James Gibson's backpack and camera were found, I wanted the whole area combed after the discovery of James's body. Between 16 and 19 November police boats and divers searched the full length of Berowra Creek from Crosslands to Galston Road, while the area from the upper Berowra Creek to the junction of Galston Creek was searched on foot. Eighty police, supported by members of the State Emergency Service, then spent three days conducting a shoulder-to-shoulder search of an area up to 100 metres on either side of the Benowie Walking Track and Galston Road, but nothing was found.

By now talk of a serial murderer preying on young backpackers was beginning to have a serious effect on local communities that depended on tourism, adding to the pressure we all felt to make an arrest. Public meetings, rather than reassuring people, were reported by the media in ways that served only to fuel the growing panic about the killer at large.

In the first few weeks our media briefings had tended to focus on the search of the forest, allowing us to deal in facts and avoid vague speculation about the identity of the killer. But our refusal to speculate did not stop the media from speculating. By mid-November I realised I would have to give them what they wanted. Yes, I told them, we were looking for a serial killer. No, we did not have a prime suspect or suspects for the killings, but 'I believe we are getting a better picture of what happened, a better picture of the direction in which we should be going and to that extent we are making progress.' I made it clear that the investigation would not be wound down once we left the forest; we had plenty of leads to pursue.

While our search of the forest was over, the process of evaluating what we had found had only just begun. Detailed forensic studies of more than 200 exhibits, including clothing and other personal effects, would have to be carried out by units specialising in crime scene analysis, forensic ballistics, mapping, photogrammetry, fingerprints, document examination and videos. Our own forensic examiners were being helped by outside agencies including the Forensic Services Division and the Firearms and Ballistics Branch of the Australian Federal Police, the South Australian State Forensic Science Laboratory and the School of Materials Science at the University of New South Wales.

By the time we left the forest, several trends or 'facts' had begun to emerge. The abductions and killings had all occurred between 30 December 1989 and 18 April 1992. The seven victims were all hitchhikers. Liverpool was a common point in their travels, and the likely area where they had been picked up. All of the bodies had been stabbed multiple times. Two of the bodies had also been shot multiple times; the same weapon, a .22 calibre Ruger rifle manufactured between 1964 and 1982, had been used, and the bullets fired were Winchester Winner. The shooter or shooters appeared to be familiar with and to have a degree of expertise in the use of firearms. There appeared to be an increase in the ritualistic nature of the murders. The abductions and killings appeared to have been well planned. More and more time was being spent at the crime scene: the murders themselves were taking longer to commit. Bindings were found at or near five of the crime scenes, indicating that the victims had been bound and the binding had been removed before 'burial'. In several cases evidence suggested that the victims had been sexually assaulted, although sex did not seem to dominate the killer or killers' behaviour. In each case, the victim's backpack and other personal items they might have been expected to be carrying were missing. Since these items were of little monetary value, robbery was unlikely to be the motive. Were souvenirs being taken and, most importantly, kept? The killer or killers knew the Belanglo State Forest well. Given the rough terrain that had to be travelled in the forest, it was likely a 4WD had been used to pick up the victims and drive them to their fate.

On 11 November 1992 the New South Wales government had approved a reward of $100,000 for information leading to the arrest and conviction of the person or persons responsible for the murders of Caroline Clarke and Joanne Walters. No one had tried to claim it. Twelve months later, following the discovery of five more bodies, the government increased the reward to $500,000 (at the time the largest reward ever offered in Australia) for information leading to the killer's conviction. A free pardon was also offered to any accomplice not involved in the murders who would give the killer up.

Within 24 hours of phone lines being set up, 5100 calls from around Australia were logged. Dealing with such a volume of information created enormous problems of its own, but the scale of the response convinced me that if we were going to catch the killer, it would be with the public's help.

6 TOO MUCH INFORMATION

Detective Inspector Rod Lynch had worked on plenty of major task force investigations during his time as a detective, but he was taken aback by what he saw when he arrived at Air. 'I was tasked with setting up an office in Sydney at the former Technical Services building, known as the Old Hat Factory, at the corner of Smith and Campbell. The building had been occupied by several police units, including the Criminal Investigation Branch until it was disbanded in the mid-1980s, and the building had seen little use since. The conditions were shocking.'

The office area was derelict and the whole building was very run-down. Police Properties was quickly brought in and asked to fix it up. That meant not only cleaning the building from top to bottom, but installing furniture and upgrading electricity and electronics for computer networking and security. While this was being done Rod was busy recruiting investigators, analysts and support staff. He also visited the forest to get a first-hand feel for the needs of the investigation.

It was clear from the outset that one of our biggest challenges would be information management. The case had already generated six different investigations: four after the initial disappearances; a more general inquiry by Kings Cross Patrol into missing persons from that area; and a murder investigation by the South West Region Major Crime Squad after the bodies of Caroline Clarke and Joanne Walters were found in 1992.

Information had been treated differently in each case. Some had been recorded in hard copy and kept locally; some had been entered on police databases that could not be cross-referenced with other databases; the murder investigation used the department's Task Force Information Management System, which was designed as a stand-alone. The murder investigation itself had logged more than 7500 inquiries and questioned more than 500 people.

After the bodies of James Gibson and Deborah Everist were discovered in early October 1993, the information base exploded. We quickly realised the systems we had were hopelessly inadequate: not only did they lack the capacity to handle such a mass of information, but they were also incompatible with each other, making it impossible to cross-check between systems or to retrieve information as and when we needed it. Quality control was either poor or non-existent.

The Task Force Information Management System had been developed by the police in 1990 to manage information during the investigation of major crime. While the system had been widely used since then, it was not designed to handle an investigation of the size and scope of Task Force Air. Furthermore, as a stand-alone system, it couldn't be used to search records or retrieve information provided by government departments, interstate police agencies and the Australian Federal Police.

The only solution was a more sophisticated computerised information management system, devised and implemented by the police themselves. Working closely with intelligence analysts from the State Intelligence Group as well as police data-management and computer experts, we outlined the kind of system we would need and how we would use it. By combining elements from about a dozen different software packages, some developed internally and others bought off the shelf, they were able to put together a package that allowed us to record, mine and cross-reference data from a variety of sources. Crucially, the task force office in Sydney was networked with Bowral and with the Criminal Research Bureau of the State Intelligence Group, enabling us to update information constantly, and ensure nothing was lost between systems.

Essential as it was, this re-engineering came at a cost. Since the old systems were no longer usable, all the data they contained had to be re-entered into the new system. Inevitably, this took time and caused frustration among task force members who were temporarily unable to access information. But the prize, once it was finished, was a fully integrated system in which every item of information could be logged and retrieved, and the chances of missing a vital clue would be drastically reduced. During the period the system was being developed and put into operation, the investigation depended on the ability of individual detectives to maintain a strong and detailed picture of what was occurring.

Our problems with information management were one issue I decided not to share with the media. I could imagine the sort of headlines we could expect if the newspapers found out about the mess we had inherited. However, when news of the new information system broke in March 1994, the tone was positive. Under the headline 'High tech tool speeds up backpackers' murder probe', *The Australian Financial Review* reported: 'Criminal investigators working on the backpackers murder case are sieving through more than a million items of information with the help of a powerful Australian high-tech tool . . . The technology, known as NetMap, is helping them probe far deeper than with traditional methods and could save hundreds of man hours as it digs for clues . . . Names, addresses, vehicles, times of day, locations all make up a mountain of information from which the system "mines" similarities and connections. It massages the information, transforming it into a multi-dimensional, graphical representation.'

The report also mentioned the use of a tool called Farm Image, a remote-sensing package for interpreting satellite images of the Belanglo State Forest to identify changes in the light intensity of vegetation on the dates the backpackers were last seen, and changes between dates, and to attempt to locate possible burial sites by identifying areas of new growth in the forest.

While the task force was getting to grips with NetMap, Sergeant Dutton at the Forensic Ballistics Unit was painstakingly examining the fired cartridges and bullets. Analysis of the 47 Winner cartridge cases found 165 metres from Gabor Neugebauer's remains confirmed that several had been fired from the same Ruger 10/22 model .22 calibre rifle that had fired four of the six bullets found in two nearby trees as well as the cartridge cases found at the Clarke murder scene. The 46 fired .22 calibre Eley cartridge cases found in the same area and two of the spent bullets recovered from the tree trunks were found to have been fired by an Anschutz .22 calibre bolt-action rifle. Dutton was certain the bullets had come from the Winner and Eley cartridge boxes found at the scene.

Detective Sergeant Royce Gorman went to the Winchester factory in Geelong, Victoria. The manufacturer was able to identify the Winner cartridge packet stamped with the partial batch number '. . . CD . . . CF2' as batch 'ACD1CF2'. The batch had comprised 320,000 bullets. Working through its records, the company was able to calculate the total stock of .22 calibre bullets on hand at the time the batch was manufactured. It concluded that the batch had been sold to 55 outlets, mostly gun shops, across Australia between 2 June 1988 and 30 November 1988, a year before the first known disappearance. Twenty-seven of those outlets were in New South Wales.

The manufacturer of the Eley bullets clarified the partly unreadable batch number on the Eley cartridge box as 'J23CGA', a batch manufactured on 23 March 1979 and distributed to retailers well before the first known disappearance. Unfortunately, the company had no record of which outlets had bought the bullets.

Dutton identified the weapon used in the killings as a .22 calibre Ruger 10/22 model self-loading rifle with a ten-round rotary magazine. It suggested that the killer or killers had fired a full magazine into Clarke. Tens of thousands of such weapons had been imported into Australia. Dutton, however, was able to narrow the search. The fired cartridge cases bore the impression of a firing pin that left an upward indentation. This was a manufacturer's fault in Rugers made between 1964 and 1982. The fired cartridges had other common features that could help identify the rifle used, while the bullets themselves all had gouge marks along their length caused by a silencer.

The Australian Federal Police (AFP) had built a significant database on Ruger rifles after the 1989 murder of Colin Winchester, an assistant commissioner in the AFP responsible for the Australian Capital Territory. Winchester had been shot twice in the head with a Ruger 10/22 .22 calibre semi-automatic rifle fitted with a silencer as he parked his police car in the driveway next door to his house in Deakin. (David Eastman was eventually arrested and convicted of the murder.) In the course of the investigation the AFP test-fired more than 500 Ruger rifles, the results of which were given to the task force. We also benefited from the advice of Detective Superintendent Ian Prior, head of the AFP's Firearms and Ballistics Branch, who had been in charge of the forensic ballistics analysis in the Winchester investigation.

The US manufacturer was able to tell us that about 55,000 Rugers of the suspect type had been imported into Australia between 1964 and 1985. Starting with the manufacturer's and AFP's records, we set out to build a database of those 55,000 Rugers.

The first task was to rule out Rugers that had come into police possession by way of seizure or other means, and were either still in police possession or had been destroyed before September 1992, the time of the first killing known to have involved a Ruger. Once that was done we could start checking gun shop records (both sales and repairs), along with the records of licensed firearm dealers and holders, to identify individual owners.

During December 1993 task force investigators visited 27 firearm dealers across New South Wales, checking records for both Winner cartridges and Ruger rifles. In fact, we checked the records of several different types of .22 calibre rifle, not wanting to draw attention to Rugers in the initial stage of our investigation, as we were concerned that the killer or killers would get rid of the weapon if alerted that the task force was looking for a particular type and model.

As in other aspects of the investigation, we adopted two strategies in our search for the Ruger rifle, one macro and the other micro. We wanted to trace every Ruger rifle manufactured between 1964 and 1985 that had been imported into Australia. At the same time we would check the records of gun shops, gun owners and gun clubs, and test-fire individual weapons where necessary, in order to eliminate as many Rugers as possible from the investigation.

Working from the top down and from the bottom up would, we hoped, enable us to identify both a number of unaccounted-for Rugers and a number of people who could not account for their Ruger. The two-pronged strategy ought to expose omissions and highlight mismatches, while allowing us to narrow the focus to specific geographic areas and to individual gun-owners who could not be eliminated.

It was laborious and time-consuming, but we were not in a race.

7
HOTLINE

On Saturday, 16 October 1993, Detective Sergeant Kevin Hammond and a colleague visited the Belanglo Pistol Club during a competition shoot to ask whether anybody had seen anything suspicious or unusual, or had any information that might be useful to the investigation. Hammond had been seconded to the task force from his job as head of the Bowral detectives' office. Bill Ayres, from nearby Buxton, suggested to Hammond that he should speak to another member, Alex Milat, who might have some information that would interest him. After speaking to Alex at the club, Hammond arranged for him to be interviewed at Bowral Police Station.

Two days later, 52-year-old Alexander 'Alex' Milat told Hammond that around 4 p.m. on Sunday, 26 April 1992, he and Bill Ayres had left the pistol club after a day's shoot. They were in Alex's Holden Rodeo 4WD, with Ayres driving and Alex in the passenger's seat. They were travelling down the unsealed Belanglo Road towards the Hume Highway, said Alex, driving slowly to avoid hitting any of the wombats or kangaroos that often crossed the road in the late afternoon. As they approached an intersection with a track that led into Belanglo State Forest, Alex saw two vehicles coming towards them, the leading vehicle signalling its intention to turn right into the forest. After passing the intersection Ayres moved to the right-hand side of the road, causing the oncoming cars to pass on the passenger's side. According to Alex, the first vehicle was a chocolate-brown 1980-model Ford Falcon sedan and the other a 4WD dual-cab utility, either a Holden Rodeo or a Nissan Navara, beige on the bottom and brown on the top.

Alex said that as the cars passed each other, he noticed that the driver of the Falcon had what appeared to be a tattoo on the fingers of his left hand. '[H]e appeared to be a tall person . . . a Caucasian of medium complexion . . . thin build . . . about 100 kilograms in weight, aged in his mid-twenties . . . [with] . . . a prominent nose and Adam's apple . . . a flat top hair style and . . . "mutton chop" style side levers. His hair was coloured orange, red colour . . . [and] . . . he had acne spots or marks on the cheeks of his face.'

Alex went on to describe the physical characteristics of the Falcon's male passenger in similar detail, before adding that he was 'holding what appeared to me to be a shotgun 410 model. He had hold of its barrel which was pointing upwards towards the roof of the vehicle and the stock appeared to be on the floor beside him.' In the rear passenger seat, Alex claimed to have seen a woman aged in her twenties:

> with shoulder length or slightly longer mousy coloured hair, a Caucasian or fair complexion and she appeared not to be a heavy build. I saw what appeared to me to be a 'gag' which consisted of a length of honey coloured material which was wrapped around her head across her mouth. Outside the mouth the material appeared to be knotted a number of times . . . I saw that this female was looking at me and she appeared to sit up in the back seat with her arms by her side as if she was trying to attract my attention.

According to Alex, the woman was sitting between two men, although he could not describe either of them.

As the second car passed, he saw two men in the front and another man in the back, who was sitting next to a woman. The woman 'had a "gag" consisting of a piece of honey coloured material', though it was a different colour to the material he had seen wrapped around the woman in the Falcon. It was, Alex said, 'wrapped around her head across her mouth . . . and as we were driving past she also sat up in the seat and looked at me with her eyes wide open as if she was frightened . . . this female was aged in her twenties, a Caucasian of fair complexion . . . a heavier build than the female I had seen in the Falcon [and had] dark brown hair'.

According to Alex, the only man in the second car he was able to describe was the one in the back seat next to the woman: '[He] appeared to be aged in his middle twenties, a Caucasian, fair complexion with brownish coloured hair which was neatly groomed and cut to the ears and neatly trimmed around the sides to the rear. He was clean shaven and appeared to be well dressed. From memory he was wearing an off white coloured collar style long sleeve shirt.' As we 'became closer and almost level', Alex said, 'this person raised his left hand and placed it beside his face so it blocked my view of him. At this time I noticed his hands were not rough as if he was an office worker as opposed to a labourer and his hands were clean.' Alex claimed to have written down the registration number of the second vehicle on a piece of cardboard he had now lost, but to the best of his recollection, 'the following letter combinations and numbers have some significance to me. They are ALD-537, ALO, DAL and ACL.'

After he was shown pictures, Alex identified Caroline Clarke and Joanne Walters as the women in the two cars. He explained his earlier failure to report the matter to police by saying:

> I was of the opinion that it was just some young blokes taking some girls into the forest to have a good time and I didn't give much thought to it being anything more than that. I didn't wish to get involved so I didn't contact the police and inform them what I had seen. From my knowledge and experiences in that area I am aware of countless times when young men and women are observed driving around the forest looking like they are lost or looking for somewhere they can have a good time and I didn't think that this incident was any different.

Alex said he had seen the Ford Falcon 'on at least two prior occasions in the forest area'. On one occasion there were five men in the car 'and all but one had possession of a rifle which were [sic] protruding from the vehicle through the windows'.

At least two of the rifles were '.22 calibre', Alex said. One 'was a Winchester, as I have one of these weapons myself, and the other one appeared to be a Ruger rifle'. On the second occasion, 'I saw one male occupant who appeared to have an SKS type rifle without the bayonet connected in his possession which was visible through the front passenger side window and a male passenger in the rear nearside seat also had possession of a rifle.' The sightings were said to be close in time and about nine months before April 1992.

Bill Ayres was then interviewed. Despite having recommended the task force speak to Alex, Ayres gave only very qualified support to Alex's claims. He had been driving Alex's vehicle at the time, he said, and while he remembered seeing the two cars turning into Belanglo, he saw 'nothing else'. However, he added, 'If Alex says there's fifteen bullet holes in a signpost, there'll be fifteen bullet holes in it.'

Given he had been looking through the window of a moving vehicle, the level of detail in Alex's statement was extraordinary, not to say bizarre. Another anomaly was the eight-day gap between when the girls were last seen leaving Kings Cross and when Alex claimed to have seen them. While, like every member of the task force, I hoped for the miracle breakthrough that would lead us to the killer, there were too many things about Alex's statement that did not ring true.

Questions began to pile up in my mind. Was it a complete fabrication? If so, what was Alex's motive? Was Alex involved in the murders and playing a game with the task force? Did Alex know something about the murders and was he trying to tell the task force something without coming out directly and providing that information? Why would he have involved

Ayres if he hadn't expected Ayres to support his story? Were the claims an attempt to distract the task force from the real killer or killers? (When their bodies were found, Caroline had a sloppy-joe-type top wrapped around her head and Joanne had a cloth gag covering her mouth. This information had been widely reported and Alex could have read it in the newspapers.)

The statement also raised some chilling questions about Alex himself. Having claimed to have seen the bindings on the women and the fear in their eyes, how could he explain it away by saying he was 'of the opinion that it was just some young blokes taking some girls into the forest to have a good time'? Did he regard the abduction and rape of women as harmless fun? Was Alex the backpacker killer? If so, why would he draw such attention to himself?

Despite the macabre level of detail in Alex's statement, the most crucial piece of information—a complete or near-complete car registration number—was missing. The 'letter combinations and numbers' he claimed to remember (ALD-537, ALO, DAL and ACL) were so vague as to be virtually useless. All in all, Alex's statement offered no tangible leads that could be pursued using normal investigative techniques. Would hypnosis help him remember the car registration and other information? It would be an unusual tactic, as evidence obtained under hypnosis would have little or no credibility, and evidence contaminated by information gleaned from hypnosis risked being thrown out by the courts. On the other hand, we had already obtained a signed statement from Alex and this would not be contaminated by hypnosis. In my view, it was worth the risk. A short time later Alex was hypnotised.

Nothing was gained or lost, but lingering questions over Alex's motives remained.

Around the time Alex made his statement, Lyn Butler contacted detective Ewhen Hreszczuk of South Region Major Crime Squad, whom she knew, with information related to missing backpackers and the Belanglo State Forest. A week earlier, on 11 October 1993, Paul Douglas had dropped into the Albion Hotel, Parramatta, for a drink with Lyn's husband, Des. Douglas and Des were workmates at Boral Australian Gypsum Ltd. They began to talk about the bodies found in Belanglo and media speculation that there might be other victims. Both men were troubled by comments made to them by another Boral workmate, Paul Thomas Miller, over the past twelve months.

Sometime around Easter 1992—before any of the bodies had been found, but while there was widespread media coverage about missing backpackers, including Gabor Neugebauer and Anja Habschied—Miller had said to Butler, 'I know who killed the Germans.' The comment came out of the blue. Immediately after saying it, Miller had changed the subject.

Five months later, on 21 September, Douglas and another workmate, Nick Collins, were discussing the discovery of Clarke's and Walters' bodies when Miller joined the conversation and said, 'There's more bodies out there. They haven't found them all yet.' Later the same day, during another conversation about the bodies, Miller said, 'You could pick up anybody on that road and you'd never find them again. You'd never find out who did it either.'

A few weeks later, Miller said to Douglas, 'There are two Germans out there they haven't found yet.' During yet another conversation, this time about the sentences imposed by the courts on rapists, Miller said to Douglas, 'Stabbing a woman is like cutting a loaf of bread.' (Three of the four bodies discovered by this time were women. All had stab wounds although one, Caroline Clarke, had also been shot.)

Douglas and Butler knew that while Miller used that name at work, he also had another name: Richard James Milat.

Miller had spoken to his workmates about coming from a large family of brothers, some of whom were wild and violent, and of having a violent relationship with his partner. Miller often came to work drunk or high on cannabis. Some workmates regarded smoking cannabis as Miller's full-time occupation.

Believing Miller was affected by cannabis when he spoke about the missing Germans and the forest, Douglas and Butler didn't take him seriously at first. But when Miller repeated his claims they began to feel uneasy, especially as they were aware of the propensity of some of his brothers for violence.

Miller's habit of altering his appearance also aroused suspicion. He was constantly changing the colour and style of his hair. He regularly grew, and then shaved off, a goatee beard. His moustache varied in style from one that sat neatly above his top lip to a Merv Hughes–style handlebar moustache. His side levers also changed, sometimes stopping halfway down his ears and at other times growing down to his beard.

Then there was his use of two names, Paul Thomas Miller and Richard James Milat, and two driver's licences, one in each name.

Suspicion followed Miller, even after he accepted a redundancy package and left Boral at the end of 1992, having worked there for about three years. The company became aware that he had been using false tax file numbers. It was also common knowledge at Boral that Miller had a brother, William Milat, who had worked at Boral for a year from late 1988.

After listening to Paul Douglas and her husband discussing Miller, Lyn Butler joined the conversation. The three of them agreed that Miller's behaviour was too weird to ignore. Des Butler decided to ring the Crime Stoppers hotline. A few days later Lyn Butler contacted detective Ewhen Hreszczuk.

When Hreszczuk and his partner, Detective Brett Coman, did a name check they found that Miller had convictions dating back to 1972, when he was sixteen. His record comprised convictions for break, enter and steal; theft; possessing and smoking cannabis; and driving offences under the name Richard Milat. They contacted detective Godden at the task force and passed on their information. (Coman was later seconded to Air.)

Early in the investigation Richard and Ivan, another brother, had been separately mentioned as suspects, often because of the family reputation rather than for anything they were known to have done. There was a common view that 'the Milats are strange', 'they have been in trouble with the police', several of the brothers were 'gun nuts', and so on.

As thousands of pieces of information continued to pour in, the police hotline received a call from a woman we will call Mary, who lived in south-west Sydney. Mary said that in 1977, as eighteen-year-olds, she and her then friend Therese had been hitchhiking from Liverpool to their home in Canberra when they accepted a lift from a man in his 'early 30s' with 'black straggly hair'. Just south of Mittagong, where he had stopped to buy petrol, he turned right off the Hume Highway, telling them 'it was a shortcut to Canberra'. A few minutes later he turned onto a dirt track and stopped the car. 'I forgot to go to the toilet back at the garage,' he said. He opened the boot and bonnet, then grabbed Mary by her arms and said, 'Okay, girls, who's first?' Mary said she punched the man and that she and Therese ran into the bush. They found a spot to hide and lay in the bushes for several hours before the man gave up looking for them and left.

Mary and Therese walked back along the road until they found a farmhouse. After hearing their story, the occupants offered to drive Mary and Therese to Bowral Police Station. They didn't report the matter, but accepted a lift back to the highway and hitchhiked on to Canberra. On the same day that Mary contacted the backpacker hotline, Therese, who lived in western Sydney, independently rang the hotline. Both women told the same story, which they later confirmed in statements.

During March 1994 Mary and Therese were separately shown a series of pictures by police that included Ivan Milat and his brother Richard. While Mary did not select anyone from the photographs, Therese pointed to photograph 4 (Ivan) and said, '[His] eyebrows are similar and shape of face is similar.' She then pointed to photograph 11 (Richard) and said, 'At first glance, most similar, triggered some memory.' Neither amounted to a positive identification that could be used in court, but they added to the suspicions that were building around the Milat brothers.

The same month Therese, who was employed by SBS, appeared on a *Four Corners* program about the unsolved backpacker killings. When the program went to air, the name

'Milat' appeared in the corner of a blackboard in the background of one of the scenes. It had gone unnoticed during both the filming and editing, but was noticed by Alex when it was screened. He reported it to the ABC, who deleted it from any further showing of the program. The slip could have proved catastrophic, but Alex did not appear to have told other members of the Milat family about the reference. Fortunately, nothing further came of it.

On 9 November 1993, a week after Mary and Therese had rung the hotline, a call was received from Joanne Berry of Canberra. Berry said that in January 1990 she had been driving along the Hume Highway to Canberra when, just outside Berrima, she saw a 4WD car on the side of the road and a man running towards her, chased by another man. She stopped and the first man called out, 'Help me, he's got a gun.' Berry let him into her car and drove him to Bowral Police Station, where he reported the incident. The man told her his name was Paul Onions, he was English, and he had been hitchhiking when the man chasing him had offered a lift. Onions had become suspicious when the man stopped the car. When he produced a gun, Onions leapt out and ran.

Two days after Joanne Berry made her report, the hotline received a phone call from England from a man who said his name was Paul Thomas Onions and that he had visited Australia between December 1989 and June 1990. In January 1990, he said, he had caught a train to Liverpool, from where he intended to hitchhike to Melbourne. He got a lift with a man he described as being 'in his early 40s who was fit looking, about 5'10" tall . . . [and had] . . . a Merv Hughes moustache with black hair' driving a 'white Toyota Land Cruiser 4WD with woolly seat covers'. Onions remembered them driving for about an hour before the man pulled over to the side of the road and 'pulled out a black revolver. I jumped out of the car and ran. He chased me and I jumped in front of a car. The lady driving stopped the car and she took me to Bowral Police Station'. Onions explained to the Bowral police that he had left his backpack with all his property, including his passport, in the car when he fled.

On 24 November analysts began to examine the records of the Police Modus Operandi Unit and extract all records of abductions and kidnappings since 1985. Inexplicably, there was no record of the incident described by Berry and Onions.

Among the hotline calls was another from a local woman who said she 'didn't know if she could help', but was suspicious of a man who lived in the area. He drove a 4WD, owned lots of guns and was into shooting. His name was Ivan Milat. She had no other information about the man, but hoped her call might be of some assistance.

8 BREAKTHROUGH

Between October 1993 and February 1994 Strike Force Air tripled in size, from thirteen investigators and two analysts to 33 investigators and eleven analysts, supported by ballistics and other forensic officers. With the increased resources, no more daily media briefings and a slowdown in the flow of information from the public, we were able to restructure the investigation around a number of broad investigative strands: Ruger rifles; the ammunition found in the forest; the statement by Alex Milat; known users of the Belanglo State Forest; three persons of interest (not including the Milats); a series of murders on Sydney's north shore; and a number of other unsolved murders. While following up these leads, we would compile a brief of evidence for the coroner that, in the event of an arrest, could be converted to a criminal brief.

At this time the Milats were clearly a family of interest. Although there was no admissible evidence against any particular member of the family, we had enough information to suggest that one or more of the brothers might well have been involved in the murders.

The hotline had provided us with our strongest lead yet: Paul Onions' story of being given a lift by a man with a gun. We knew Ivan Milat owned a vehicle similar to the one described by Onions, that he often used the name 'Bill' and that another brother had the name 'Bill'.

A thorough investigation of the Milat family was a priority, but not one we could afford to pursue at the expense of every other lead. We now had a list of more than a dozen missing persons suspected of having been murdered, together with six unsolved murders and five people nominated by members of the public as possibly connected with the backpacker murders. Any one of these might have led us to the killer. Nevertheless, I assigned a team of six detectives under Detective Sergeant Royce Gorman, who had a couple of priority lines of investigation, to turn his attention to the Milat family.

On 6 February 1994 Detective Sergeant Rex Little of Bowral Police took a statement from Joanne Berry in which she repeated her story of having rescued Paul Onions from a man with a gun just outside Berrima and taken him to Bowral Police Station. After speaking to Berry, Little searched the archives of Bowral Police Station for any record of Onions' original report. Eventually he found a typed 'Occurrence Entry' relating to the incident, which had also been recorded in the notebook of a constable attached to the police station. The information provided by Onions had never been followed up.

Five of the seven backpackers had been murdered after Onions had reported the matter to Bowral Police.

Around 20 February I asked Detective Paul Gordon to check the criminal histories of all members of the Milat family, particularly Ivan. A day or so later Gordon told me, in front of Rod Lynch and others, that the Milat family, including Ivan, had little or no criminal history. I asked Gordon if he had carried out a thorough check and he told me he had. We had been told by a number of sources, however—including then Superintendent John Laycock who had lived near the Milat family in Guildford for many years—that Ivan and some of his brothers had criminal records for armed hold-ups and related offences going back to the 1970s, and that Ivan had been involved in an abduction and sexual assault. I asked Gordon whether he had checked the criminal histories held on microfiche. He hadn't. In 1984 the police had switched to a computerised system, but pre-1984 records still had to be checked manually at the Central Records Office. I would have expected even the most junior detective to have been aware of this, since fingerprint checks were so central to a detective's work. I told Gordon to go and check those records. A day or two later Gordon returned to the task force office with a smile on his face and declared, 'He's our man. He did it.' I replied, 'A big call, tell us all about it,' and he went on to outline Ivan's arrest for rape in 1971.

Ivan had a criminal record dating back to 1964, when he was convicted of break, enter and steal. The following year he was convicted of stealing a car, and two years later of being an accessory to the theft of a car. In 1971 he had been arrested with others and charged with armed robbery, and later the same year with rape. Bailed, Ivan did not hang around. He fled to New Zealand, where he lived for about two years before returning to New South Wales following trouble with the New Zealand Police (we could never identify what the 'trouble' was). Sometime after his return to New South Wales, Ivan was arrested over the outstanding charges. In 1974 he beat the robbery charge, but his brother Michael and others were convicted and gaoled. The same year he beat the rape charge at trial, but the detail in the court file convinced Gordon that Ivan was our man.

The court file revealed that on 10 April 1971 Ivan had picked up two eighteen-year-old female hitchhikers, Margaret and Greta, at Liverpool and offered to drive them to Canberra. Near Goulburn he took them to a secluded spot. At first, Ivan said that he wanted to 'make love' to both women, but when they rejected him, he threatened them with two knives, saying, 'You know what I'm going to do, I'm going to kill the both of you. You won't scream when I cut your throats will you? Either one of you has sex with me or I will kill you both.' Greta pleaded with Ivan to drive away and leave them alone. Margaret then agreed to have sex with him if he didn't carry out his threat to kill them. Ivan untied Margaret's feet and raped her, telling Greta, 'Don't watch us, look out for any cars coming.' Afterwards, Ivan drove to a service station. When he stopped, the women escaped and reported the rape to police. Not long after, Ivan was arrested after a high-speed chase and charged with rape. According to Ivan the sex had been consensual and he had dropped them off at the service station.

Our inquiries revealed it had been an ugly trial. Ivan claimed that Margaret had agreed to have sex with him. Ivan's lawyer,

John Marsden, accused both women of being lesbians who were receiving psychiatric treatment and taking prescription drugs. Margaret was very confused about her sexual orientation and admitted that she was involved in the 'camp scene', that she and Greta used to go to gay bars together, and that she had lesbian friends and homosexual male friends. Asked about having sex with Ivan, Margaret blamed herself for the incident. She said that Ivan had raised the subject and that she had agreed to have sex with him. She said, 'I don't really enjoy being camp; I can't seem to make a decision about sexual identity . . . He made the decision [to have sex], I didn't have to make it.'

Greta, on the other hand, was in no doubt about what had occurred and who was responsible. Ivan had brandished a knife and threatened to cut their throats if they resisted and then he had raped Margaret.

Marsden's tactics would probably not be allowed in a court today. In his 2004 book, *John Marsden: I am what I am*, he wrote:

> Juries in those days were extremely prejudiced against gays and lesbians, and on top of that, we had put into their minds the possibility that the sex may have indeed been consensual.
>
> I am not proud of my conduct that day, but as a solicitor operating in a court-room environment at that time, I had no choice but to go down that path. I had to act according to the ethics of the profession. That said, I don't believe I should receive any praise for the win. I had a job to do and I did it.

Greta's allegations against Ivan went further, although some were not admitted into the court proceedings. Greta recalled that after Ivan had raped Margaret, Margaret asked him whether he had done this before, to which Ivan replied yes. He said that he often picked up hitchhikers and always carried knives and ropes in case an opportunity arose.

The details of the 1971 rape charge and Greta's further allegations looked bad for Ivan, but did not represent evidence against him for the backpacker murders. By paying too much attention to them we risked closing our minds to the possibility that Ivan had not committed the murders, and that somebody else had. Our suspicions were focused firmly on Ivan but we had to keep looking for evidence that either proved or disproved his guilt. For example, had any of the attacks taken place on a day when Ivan was outside the state and could not have committed them? Had he used a credit card that showed he could not have been the killer or one of the killers? Alternatively, could we find evidence to prove that Ivan was in the vicinity of Belanglo when the victims were murdered? Had he been caught on a speed camera?

It seemed to me that Gordon had already made up his mind that Ivan was the killer, forgetting that there are two sides to every investigation—the inculpatory and the exculpatory—and that both sides must be thoroughly explored. I said to Gordon, 'Tell me if there is any reason why Ivan could *not* be our killer.'

Gordon seemed to interpret my comments to mean that I thought Ivan was innocent; I didn't, but nor did I think we had sufficient evidence to prove beyond doubt that Ivan was guilty. To me, it seemed that Gordon was getting into the mindset of the Blackburn investigators, in which everything that looks bad is proof of guilt, while everything inconsistent with guilt is ignored. We couldn't afford to make the same mistake with Ivan.

A few days later, on 26 February 1994, Ivan was placed under surveillance. There were insufficient grounds to justify an application for a phone intercept or listening device in his home.

Meanwhile, a search of traffic records revealed that on 16 January 1991 a red-light camera had caught Ivan driving a silver–white Nissan 4WD, and that he owned that vehicle until September 1992. It matched the vehicle described by both Berry and Onions.

Gordon continued to make inquiries about several of the Milat brothers, but especially Richard and Ivan. Richard no longer worked at Boral, but employee records showed that he had a watertight alibi for the day Gibson and Everist were last seen: he was at work. Ivan had worked at the Roads and Traffic Authority (RTA) since 1977. (In January 1989 the Department of Main Roads, Department of Motor Transport, and the Traffic Authority were amalgamated into the RTA.) Gordon was told to be discreet and to speak only with senior management about Ivan and his work record, but after convincing himself that Ivan was the murderer, Gordon became indiscreet and spoke with a broader group of people at the RTA, including a number of Ivan's workmates. It became known that Gordon was investigating the backpacker murders and that Ivan was a suspect. Word spread and soon Ivan was aware of Gordon's—and, therefore, the task force's—inquiries.

Yet Ivan appeared unconcerned. From what we knew already this did not surprise us. Ivan always believed that he was in absolute control. He was the sort of criminal who believes he cannot be caught and that, if he *is* caught, he will not be convicted. Dr Rod Milton was convinced that the backpacker killer or killers would keep mementos of the killings—items belonging to the victims such as clothing, jewellery and hiking equipment—through which he or they could relive the sex attacks and killings, enjoying the moment again and again. But this was supposition at best and we were worried that leaks of information might prompt Ivan—if he was guilty—to get rid of any mementos or other items that connected him to the murders.

The leaks, as a result of Gordon's indiscreet questions at the RTA, were becoming such a concern that we had to back off our inquiries, as we were nowhere near ready to interview, let alone arrest, any member of the Milat family, nor did we have enough evidence to obtain search warrants for their homes. As a precaution, our surveillance of Ivan was called off, at least for the time being. On 22 April, eighteen days after suspending our surveillance of Ivan, we reassessed the risk and made the decision to resume it.

Meanwhile, arrangements were being made for Paul Onions to travel from London to Sydney. We hoped he would be the 'smoking gun' we were looking for.

In late 1993, during discussions with members of the State Intelligence Group, I raised the issue of setting up an informal group of academics whose expertise could be useful to the investigation. I wanted to include Dr Rod Milton, who had been brought into the investigations shortly after the discovery of the bodies of Caroline Clarke and Joanne Walters, and whom we had approached again after more bodies were found in late 1993. Milton knew that the profiling of suspects was a 'best guess', but he was right more often than he was wrong and had been of value to police in a number of major investigations. Three others were invited to join the group: Dr Robert Young, Dr Michael Bailey and Dr Richard Basham, all of Sydney University. We met on a number of occasions between January and April 1994. (Dr Young subsequently produced a paper, 'Some thoughts on investigative data management and analysis' which, three years later, was crucial to the development of a new computerised information management system for major criminal investigations known as E@gle.i —see Chapter 15.)

By this time we believed that the killer (or killers) had good local knowledge, was comfortable in the forest and had probably been raised in the area. At school he was likely to have stood out as 'different', a 'loner' with a propensity for violence, a 'future worry', or to have come from a family that stood out. We decided to visit all government and non-government schools in the Southern Highlands and interview teachers and former teachers with a view to identifying pupils of interest who had attended school between the mid-1950s and 1985. While this strategy would not provide us with evidence against the killer (or killers), we hoped it would point us in the right direction and lead to other inquiries that would provide evidence. Another benefit of such a strategy was that it would quickly come to the notice of the media and would reinforce the message that the task force was leaving 'no stone unturned' in its hunt for the murderer.

Paul Onions arrived in Sydney on 2 May 1994. Two days later he accompanied Detectives Stuart Wilkins and Graeme

Pickering to Liverpool where, in January 1990, he had got off the train and walked along the Hume Highway as far as Casula, trying unsuccessfully to hitch a ride. At Casula, Onions had gone into the newsagency to buy a drink before accepting a lift from a man with a Merv Hughes moustache. Onions pointed out the spot where the man's vehicle had been parked, then took Wilkins and Pickering to a place about 900 metres north of the turn-off to Belanglo State Forest, where the attempted abduction had occurred.

In his statement to police, Onions said that he had left England in early December 1989, gone to India and stayed in New Delhi for about a week before flying to Singapore. After staying in Singapore for a few days, he flew to Australia for a six-month holiday, arriving in Sydney a couple of days before Christmas. On the morning of Thursday, 25 January 1990, he caught a train from Central Station to Liverpool, intending to hitchhike down the Hume Highway. After buying a drink at the Casula newsagency, Onions was approached by a man he described 'as five foot ten to six foot tall, about 40 years old, fit-looking in appearance, dark short-to-medium length hair, a black moustache similar to the one worn by Merv Hughes but not as thick, wearing black sunglasses, possibly a green T-shirt and dark coloured shorts'. Asked if he needed a lift, Onions said yes.

> He said, 'Where are you headed?'
> I said, 'To Melbourne.'
> He said, 'Will Canberra do you?'
> I said, 'Yeah, great.'

He said, 'That's my vehicle over there. I'm going to get a drink', indicating a silver-coloured 4WD which was in the car park for the shops.

Onions said he waited near the vehicle, which he identified as a Nissan or Toyota 4WD with chrome-plated side steps, large tyres with a spare tyre on the back, and a bull bar on the front. It had bucket front seats with lamb's-wool seat covers, and he thought it had two doors. When the man returned, they both got into the vehicle and Onions threw his backpack onto the back seat. As they drove south, the driver introduced himself as 'Bill'. During their conversation, Onions said that he came from Birmingham.

Bill asked, 'How long are you here for?'
I said, 'I'm just on a working holiday.'
Bill asked, 'What do you do for a job?'
I said, 'I'm an air-conditioning engineer and have just finished service in the navy.'
Bill asked, 'Did you ever serve in the Special Forces or Northern Ireland?'
I said, 'No.'
Bill asked, 'Do you have any family in Australia?'
I said, 'No.'

After some general conversation, Onions asked Bill where he worked and Bill replied, 'I work for the Roads [sic] at Liverpool but I travel around a bit.'

After about 45 minutes Onions said, 'I'm surprised at how many Japanese there are in Sydney.' He was caught off guard by Bill's response: 'We shouldn't have all them in the country . . . It's the same with you Brits, you shouldn't be in Northern Ireland either.' They had a brief conversation about immigration, during which Bill became increasingly aggressive. After Bill fell silent. Onions said that about fifteen minutes later, 'I started to see him continually look in his rear vision mirrors and he started to slow down.'

Onions became suspicious of Bill, who explained that the radio faded at this distance from Sydney and that he wanted to pull over and get some tapes from under the seat. This made Onions more apprehensive, as he could see several tapes lying between the front seats. Bill pulled over and got out, then started 'messing about' under the driver's seat. Onions decided to get out of the vehicle. Bill suddenly got agitated and shouted, 'Why are you getting out of the vehicle?' Onions replied that he was just stretching his legs and returned to the vehicle in an attempt to placate Bill, who then got back in the driver's seat and said, 'I'll just have a look under the driver's seat one more time.' After getting out of the car, Bill reached under the driver's seat and pulled out a black revolver, which he pointed straight at Onions.

> I asked, 'What are you doing, Bill?'
> Bill said, 'This is a robbery.'
> I said, 'Calm down, calm down.'
> Bill said, 'Do you know what this is?'
> I started taking off my seatbelt and Bill said, 'Put that fucking seatbelt back on.'

At this point, Onions said, Bill appeared to panic and pulled a length of rope from under the seat, so 'I bolted out of the car'.

Bill shouted, 'Stop or I'll shoot, stop or I'll shoot!' and Onions heard a single gunshot.

> I never looked back. I just legged it north up the highway running in a zig zag motion. I started running across the roadway and three and four cars swerved to miss me but nobody would stop. I looked up and didn't see any cars coming and I turned around for the first time and there was Bill chasing me. He was yelling at me, 'Get back in the car, get back in the car.' He clutched at me as we reached the centre grass area of the roadway and he grabbed my right sleeve and tore my shirt. He couldn't get a grip on me and at that point I made one last effort to get away from him and I ran directly onto the eastern side of the highway. I was going to stop the next car whatever happened and I saw a van approaching over the rise and I stood right in front of it. I held my hands out and the woman had to brake or run me over. The van stopped in front of me and I ran to the passenger side which had a sliding door and opened it. I got in the vehicle and locked the door. I said to the woman driver, 'He's got a gun, he's got a gun.'

Onions said that he saw Bill stop chasing him, and as the woman did a U-turn Bill went back towards his 4WD, got in and drove off along the highway towards Canberra.

After reporting the incident to Bowral Police, Onions caught a train back to Sydney. Five months later he later returned to England. In 1992 he read newspaper stories about the British backpackers who had gone missing. When he learnt that bodies had been discovered in the forest near Bowral, he called the New South Wales Police hotline.

On 5 May 1994 Onions was taken to the Sydney Police Centre and shown thirteen photos on a video. He identified picture 4 as Bill. It was a picture of Ivan.

With the other corroborative evidence, including Joanne Berry's statement and RTA details of the vehicle Ivan owned at that time, we now had enough to charge Ivan with the attempted abduction of Onions and to have him held in custody, bail refused, while other charges could be considered.

Based on Onions' identification of Ivan, a phone intercept was placed on the phone at his home in Eagle Vale, which he owned and shared with his sister Shirley Soire. We also considered installing listening devices, but to do this we would have had to get inside the house, and surveillance had disclosed a complex electronic security system, which Ivan turned on whenever he left the house. Having concluded that the system could not be bypassed, we had to abandon the idea of installing listening devices.

9
ALADDIN'S CAVE

Paul Onions' identification of Ivan Milat as his attacker had been a major breakthrough, but it also created some dilemmas for the task force. By itself Onions' evidence was not enough to charge Ivan with the backpacker murders. If Ivan was charged with the attempted abduction, what impact would that have on the murder investigations? Would other investigative avenues close down? Ivan already knew we had been making inquiries about him. Would he destroy any evidence that connected him to the backpacker murders? Was he likely to run?

Once Ivan had been charged, the media would seize on his identification by Onions and the link with Belanglo to ask whether Ivan was the backpacker murderer. Any indiscreet or unguarded word from the task force could prove disastrous for a successful prosecution, as Milat would be certain to argue that he had been denied a fair trial.

We had been able to observe Ivan's response when he discovered in April that we were asking questions about him. He had continued to behave like a man who believed he was in control. This seemed to confirm Rod Milton's assessment that the crimes exhibited significant elements of control by the offender or offenders, and that belief in control was likely to be even stronger if there was only one killer. Milton never wavered in his belief that the killer would have kept mementos of his victims and his acts, hidden in plain sight so that he could enjoy looking at them in the presence of other people, reliving the thrill of his victims' helplessness while they were under his control.

At the same time, Milton remained convinced there was more than one killer, the older stronger and dominating the younger. The use of different types of weapons—guns and a knife—supported the idea that there were two killers.

By now our opportunities for covert inquiries were largely exhausted; the only way to find the evidence we needed to prove Ivan was the killer was to go in and search every inch of his house and other properties belonging to members of the Milat family—to pull them apart if we had to. A large number of police would be required, and the planning alone would take several weeks. We couldn't afford to make mistakes.

Security and the avoidance of any leaks were critical to the operation's success. At the same time, we had to be careful not to make the media suspicious that we were planning a major operation. When we arrested Ivan for the attempted abduction of Onions, there was to be no comment whatsoever about the backpacker murders.

Meanwhile, I felt that we owed it to the families of the victims to let them know something big was about to happen, even if we couldn't tell them what it was. (For a start, we could not risk compromising their role as witnesses in any future court proceedings.) We told them we would keep them informed as far as we could, but asked them to say nothing to the media.

Over the next few weeks, together with Rod Lynch and other senior members of the task force, I drew up a list of people of interest and of properties to be raided. We decided to make Campbelltown Police Station the command post. Search warrants were to be obtained for seven properties, while police would also visit four other properties (two in Queensland) that did not justify the issue of search warrants. The raids called for around 300 police, led by members of the task force, backed by patrol support groups from locations across south and western Sydney, the South West Region Major Crime Squad, State Protection Group personnel, the Physical Evidence Section, the Dog Squad and the Radio Electronics Unit, as well as lawyers. Police Media staff would be attached to the task force for the duration of the raids, and ambulances and the local hospital were warned to be on standby.

The operation was to be split into three parts: Queensland (Alex Milat's home in West Woombye, in the Sunshine Coast hinterland, and Michael Milat's home in Nanango); North (properties at Eagle Vale, Kearns and Guildford), to be led by Detective Senior Sergeant Bob Benson; and South (Richard Milat's house at Hill Top and other properties owned by various members of the Milat family at Hill Top, Bargo, Buxton and Wombeyan Caves), to be led by Detective Inspector Bob Godden.

To ensure the search teams knew exactly what they were looking for, we prepared a list of more than a hundred items of property belonging to the victims, and more than twenty items—including ammunition, firearms, ropes, plastic ties and other items—identical to those used during the murders.

Most of the searchers were to be housed in the Police Academy at Goulburn on the Friday, for what they were told was to be an 'exercise' to be carried out over the weekend. They would be briefed at the academy on Saturday night and taken direct to their search locations early on Sunday, 22 May. Others were told to report direct to Campbelltown.

The movement of so many police from a range of commands and specialist areas was certain to arouse curiosity, no matter what cover story we told. As it was going to be impossible to prevent leaks to the media, we decided to give confidential press briefings to tell senior media executives that Task Force Air was going to carry out raids on Sunday. We emphasised the need for secrecy and made it clear that no media outlet would be allowed to get a jump on the others. Anyone breaching the arrangements would be excluded from future briefings. Journalists were invited to come to Campbelltown Police Station on Sunday morning, where they would receive a more detailed briefing once the raids were underway, but only if they stuck to the deal to keep the operation secret.

With the raids only days away, we made an important change to the schedule. Our original plan had been to complete the New South Wales end of the operation before visiting the houses in Queensland. Instead, we decided to send Detectives Bob Benson, Stuart Wilkins and Tony Roberts to West Woombye in Queensland to interview Alex Milat on Saturday, 21 May, the day before the raids in New South Wales. Ivan's phone was being intercepted and we had him under observation. If Alex rang Ivan to warn him we would know.

Detective Roberts had worked as a miner in a colliery with Alex Milat before joining the police. We hoped that his presence would make the interview seem more casual and relaxed. The pretext for their visit was Alex's earlier statement about seeing two bound girls, whom he had identified as Caroline Clarke and Joanne Walters, in Belanglo State Forest, in two cars in the company of several young men.

In fact, Alex didn't add anything significant to what he had told us already, but a bombshell awaited the three detectives as they chatted to Alex and his wife, Joan.

When Benson asked Alex whether he owned any ammunition, Alex produced a large amount, some of which was Winchester Winner .22 calibre ammunition—the same type as that found near the bodies of Gabor Neugebauer and Caroline Clarke. Benson said nothing and turned to another subject. 'What about backpacks or stuff like that?' Benson asked casually. Joan said they had a backpack: it was in the shed in the backyard. Alex took the police to the shed, unlocked it and showed them a Salewa-brand backpack. 'Where did you get it?' Benson asked. Joan replied, 'Ivan gave it to me.' She explained that Ivan had given it to them before they had moved to Queensland. According to Ivan it had belonged to a friend 'who was going back to New Zealand and she didn't want it, so I could have it'. The detectives were stunned: they recognised it as Simone Schmidl's backpack. Alex also willingly provided a mouth swab for DNA testing before the detectives left with the backpack.

Benson could not wait to ring Rod Lynch in Sydney. We all sat there as we listened to the news, excited but somewhat bemused. What on earth had induced Joan to tell us about the backpack, and why had Alex been so willing to give it to us? In response to Benson's inquiry about ammunition, why had Alex showed them his arsenal of .22 calibre bullets? It seemed inconceivable that Alex did not have some suspicions about his brother Ivan, but if he did he showed no sign of it to Benson and his colleagues. Nothing in his behaviour indicated that Alex realised the significance of what he had just done: that is, provide us with the first concrete evidence linking Ivan with the backpacker murders.

Back in Sydney, a preliminary examination of the backpack confirmed that it belonged to Simone, boosting our hopes of finding further mementos during the Sunday raids.

The interception of Ivan's phone revealed another surprise: Alex made no attempt to tip off his brother about either the police visit or the backpack. Was Alex himself innocent after all—and if not, what was he up to?

The same day that Benson and his colleagues visited Alex Milat and his wife in West Woombye, Detectives Royce Gorman, Mark Feeney and Brett Coman drove to Bargo, about 100 kilometres south-west of Sydney, to speak to Bill Milat. Bill wasn't there, but was said to be staying in a caravan at Lake Tabourie on the south coast. Soon after the three detectives left, Bill's daughter, Debbie, phoned Ivan and told him police had been asking about a silver 4WD vehicle similar to the one he owned. Luckily for us, Ivan dismissed Debbie's warning. We weren't sure whether he was just trying to give Debbie the impression of a clear conscience, or whether he suspected his phone might be intercepted and was trying to convince the police he had nothing to fear, or both.

When Gorman and his colleagues reached the lake, they spoke to Bill and asked him why Ivan's car was registered in his name. Bill replied, 'Because the registration and insurance was cheaper if you live in the bush.' Gorman had told Bill they were making inquiries about armed hold-ups. About 2 a.m. the next morning, Bill rang Ivan and told him he had been visited by detectives asking questions about his car. Once again, Ivan seemed unconcerned. Our surveillance of his house showed no sign of movement: Ivan still believed he was in control and had not been panicked into getting rid of incriminating evidence.

Meanwhile, on Saturday night, Detective Inspector Bob Godden was at the Goulburn Police Academy briefing teams for the next morning's raids. More than 200 officers would be involved; they would be taken to their target areas before dawn, and all of them would be in place by 6.15 a.m.

Detective Benson's North group comprised a force of 60, including 21 investigators, two dogs and handlers, four trained negotiators and 26 heavily armed members of the State Protection Group (eight of whom would remain on standby at Campbelltown Police Station).

Police began arriving at Campbelltown Police Station around 3 a.m. on Sunday. The command post was already operating. Some bleary-eyed journalists also started to gather. They all wanted to know what was going on.

The command briefing began on time. I could see the expectation in the faces of everyone present. The pressure on all of us had been intense. After months of painstaking investigation, we were finally ready to act. My message was short and simple:

> We're here to arrest Ivan Milat over the attempted abduction and attempt to shoot Paul Onions. Milat is considered a violent and dangerous person. He is believed to be well armed. We don't know what to expect and are not taking any chances. We will also be executing search warrants on seven properties and visiting and interviewing people at another four properties (two in Queensland) relating to the backpacker murder investigations. Operational discipline is critical. Ensure your team leaders are kept informed of all developments at all times. In turn, they will keep the command post informed. The integrity of the operation is vital. Any property to be seized will be secured by the designated exhibit officer at each location. Team leaders have a list of property we are looking for. We will not leave a property until we are satisfied there is nothing left to be searched, no matter how long it takes. Team leaders will brief you with respect to specific properties.
>
> Not until Ivan Milat's home at Eagle Vale is secured and we have Ivan in custody will there be any move on any other property.
>
> Do not make any comment to the media. Command will make any comment that is required or will at least approve all comments. The media is not to be allowed on any property being searched.
>
> We have one shot at this. Let's do it right, no matter how long it takes.

Rod Lynch then addressed the group, providing a more detailed operational overview. He finished with a warning:

'Milat is dangerous. Don't take any chances and keep the command centre informed. The entire investigation rests on what happens during the next couple of hours.'

Rod and I received a briefing from Bob Godden by phone. He was at the Police Academy and would soon be taking his teams out to the search locations.

I decided to give the journalists at the police station an 'off-the-record' briefing. Task Force Air, I said, was preparing to execute a number of search warrants during the course of the day. There would be no interviews with task force police; all inquiries could be made through two Police Media staff attached to the command post. The media staff would have to follow strict task force instructions before releasing any information, to ensure the operation was not compromised. No further information could be provided at this stage, but as the day progressed we would do all we could to cooperate with the media. Reluctantly, the media agreed. They understood that this operation was about more than headlines; it was about protecting the community. As professionals, they were also shrewd enough to know that if they did the right thing by us, there would be no shortage of opportunities for photographs and stories in the days and weeks to come. And just to make sure, I left them in no doubt that breaching the arrangements would result in a complete media blackout.

As dawn approached, the State Protection Group, negotiators and support team left Campbelltown Police Station in convoy for Eagle Vale. At a nearby intersection a few doors up from Ivan's home, we set up a local command centre. Uniformed police formed an outer perimeter preventing access to the street and ensuring the safety of local residents.

The houses on either side of Ivan's were both occupied. Behind his property was a vacant block. Teams of police dressed in black, with bulletproof vests and armed with shotguns and submachine guns, were sent in to secure the perimeter to Ivan's property. At 6.36 a.m., Detective Sergeant Wayne Gordon (no relation to Detective Paul Gordon), the lead negotiator with the State Protection Group, phoned Ivan's number.

'Mr Ivan Milat, is it?'
A male voice answered, 'No.'
'Is Ivan Milat there?'
'No, he's not here at the moment.'

Gordon knew it was Ivan's voice. Surveillance had put Ivan and his girlfriend, Chalinder Hughes, in the house the previous night, and since then no one had left or entered.

'Is that the premises at . . . Street, Eagle Vale?' Gordon asked.
'Yep.'
'I'm a negotiator with the State Protection Group.'
'Mmm.'
'I want you to come outside for the safety of yourself and whoever's in the house with you. Now what I want you to do is to come out the front door. I want you to turn left, go through the front gate. I want you to walk with your arms out, exposed from your body . . . '
'Mmm.'
'You'll be met by some State Protection Group police who'll be dressed in black. They will be armed and

> I want you then, at their direction, to lie face down on the ground.'
>
> 'Okey dokey.'

Negotiations continued for a short time, during which Ivan confirmed that his girlfriend, Chalinder Hughes, was the only other person in the house. He agreed to come out, leaving the front door open, and to follow Gordon's instructions, once he had 'put me pants on'. Gordon hung up.

The door remained closed. Noise and movement was heard in the house. A few minutes went by. Gordon rang the house again. It was answered by Hughes. She didn't know what was going on; Ivan hadn't told her who was on the phone. Gordon introduced himself and explained what he wanted. She put Ivan on the phone and Gordon repeated his direction for Ivan (and now Hughes) to leave the house. Ivan sounded calm and told Gordon he thought it was 'someone from work' ringing up for a joke.

Gordon assured Ivan that it was no joke and that there was a warrant to search his house over an armed robbery. Milat laughed and told Gordon he had looked out of the window but couldn't see any police. While Gordon repeated his instructions Ivan went on laughing, ignoring the instructions and trying to take control of the situation. When Gordon suggested that he leave the house first, followed by Hughes, Ivan replied, 'I think we'll just walk out together.'

Again, Ivan hung up and the police outside heard movement in the house. A car door in the garage could be heard opening and closing. For a few moments Gordon and the police surrounding the house worried that Ivan might try to make a run for it—not that he could get far. If he was on foot he would be stopped by the perimeter teams. If he tried to break out in his vehicle, as he seemed to be preparing to do, he would be blocked at the outer perimeter.

Still the front door did not open. At 6.48 a.m.—twelve minutes after Gordon had made his first phone call—he rang for the third time and spoke with Hughes, who told him they were about to come out. Gordon waited . . . and finally Ivan emerged.

Being confronted by men in black, pointing shotguns and machine guns at him, was not quite what Ivan had expected. When they ordered him to 'Get down!' he quickly obeyed. Detectives Steve Leach and Paul Gordon, who were to interview Ivan, approached. As the handcuffs were being put on Ivan, another team of men in black rushed past him and into the house, securing it one room at a time.

Hughes had followed Ivan out of the house, but the two had been quickly separated by the police. She seemed bewildered by the scale of the raid, believing there must have been some mistake. After a short conversation she was taken to the Campbelltown Police Station.

Back at the command centre, we had been kept informed at each step of the operation. I'm sure I was not alone in wishing I could have been present when Ivan was arrested, but at the same time I knew that standing back was the only way I could maintain an overview of the entire operation. I had absolute faith in the skills and judgement of the people I had entrusted with leading the raids; my job was to see the broader picture, to make sure each strand of the investigation came together and to minimise the risk of mistakes. After all, the raids were not an end in themselves, but a crucial step in the larger operation to successfully prosecute the killer or killers. That said, all of us in the command centre felt an overwhelming sense of relief at the news that Ivan had been arrested and the house in Eagle Vale secured without incident. With Ivan safely in custody I gave the order for search warrants to be executed on the other properties.

Detective Leach told Milat we were investigating the abduction and armed robbery of Onions and cautioned him that he was not obliged to answer any questions, to which Milat replied, 'I understand that, but I don't know what you're talking about.' Milat was also shown and had explained to him the warrant to search his house. Told he would also be asked questions about the backpacker murders, Milat again replied, 'I don't know what you're talking about.' Even with detectives milling around his doorstep, Milat still seemed to believe he could bluff it out.

Milat was taken into his house, where he showed Leach each of the rooms and told him what they were used for. He denied having any guns in the house or owning any guns.

The search began and it was not long before the police started finding incriminating material. In Ivan's bedroom police found a postcard that began, 'Hi Bill'—the name used by Ivan when he picked up Onions. When shown the card by Leach, Ivan denied ever using the name Bill and said, 'It must have been a mistake.' The writer of the postcard asked whether 'Bill' would be visiting New Zealand soon; if he was, the writer said he would 'see a guy about deer shooting'. The writer was later identified as a friend of Ivan. Some New Zealand dollars were also found in his room, which Ivan explained by saying that he had 'been to New Zealand'. (Ivan had fled to New Zealand in 1971 while on bail for rape and armed robbery charges. In 1974 he returned to Australia and was acquitted of all charges.) The postcard was dated 22 April 1992, four days after Caroline Clarke and Joanne Walters had disappeared.

Ivan explained 38 .22 calibre bullets found in the wardrobe of his bedroom by saying, 'I used to go shooting at my brother's place,' referring to Alex Milat's property at Buxton. Some of the cartridges were Winchester Winner, the type found at the Clarke and Neugebauer crime scenes in the forest. The police also found some Indonesian currency in the bedroom; Ivan had never travelled to Indonesia, but Gabor Neugebauer and Anja Habschied had spent time in Indonesia immediately before coming to Australia. Two rolls of black electrical tape similar to that located near Gabor's and Anja's bodies were also found. Searchers also discovered a driver's licence with Ivan's photograph and the name 'Michael Gordon Milat'. When Ivan was asked by Leach whether he had ever been to the Belanglo State Forest, Ivan replied that 'he had driven up a dirt track that goes past it [in the mid-1980s]'.

Several items of interest were also found in the spare bedroom, including a camouflage knife similar to the one described by Onions; four boxes of Eley .22 calibre cartridges of the same batch number as those found near Gabor's body; a broken barrel band from a Ruger rifle; a Ruger 10/22 instruction manual; various gun parts; 50 Winchester cartridges, including Winner cartridges like those found at or near the Clarke and Neugebauer crime scenes; a range of ammunition for .22, .32, .38 and .45 calibre guns; and a green water bottle and pouch similar to one belonging to Simone Schmidl.

In the bedroom used by Ivan's sister Shirley, searchers found a green sleeping bag similar to that used by Deborah Everist, and a Salewa sleeping bag like that used by Simone Schmidl.

Suspicious or incriminating items continued to be found in almost every room of the house. On the coffee table in the family room was a photograph album with pictures of Ivan's girlfriend, Chalinder Hughes, wearing a green and white striped Benetton top like that owned and worn by Caroline Clarke. The photograph was dated '92' (Caroline had disappeared in April of that year). In the hall cupboard, they discovered part of a Ruger 10/22 rifle, coloured with camouflage paint, and a map of the Southern Highlands, which included the Belanglo State Forest. A camera, cooking set, stove and cups similar to those owned by Simone were found in the kitchen, while a .32 calibre Browning pistol and ammunition were found under the washing machine in the laundry.

Asked to explain some of these items, Ivan usually responded with a shrug and some form of denial: 'I don't know', 'I've never seen it', 'It doesn't belong to me', or 'I don't understand.'

The searchers moved on. A Salewa sleeping bag cover, a green tent and tent cover, tent frame and related items believed to belong to Simone; a silencer that would fit a .22 calibre rifle; ammunition; black electrical tape and cable ties similar to those found at the Neugebauer and Habschied crime scenes; a pillowcase; and several blood-stained sash cords were found in the garage. Items found inside the red Holden Jackaroo included .22 calibre ammunition; a 1989 English 20-pence coin (Paul Onions, Caroline Clarke and Joanne Walters all left the United Kingdom after 1989); and a threaded barrel cap that could be used on an Anschutz rifle. Ivan had previously told Leach that he had not owned a car during the previous six years. Asked about the red Holden Jackaroo in the garage, he said, 'It's me brother's.' The Jackaroo was registered in the name 'W. Milat', but Ivan later admitted it belonged to him.

Detective Senior Constable Peter O'Connor was one of the team that searched the garage. Using a ladder, O'Connor climbed through a manhole and began searching the roof cavity of the house, pulling out the insulation batts and shining a torch into the cavity between the inner and outer walls. After searching for some time without finding anything, O'Connor spotted a plastic bag lying on a piece of timber inside the wall cavity, but the bag was out of reach. Using a stick he had taken from the garage, O'Connor groped in the cavity until he managed to hook the bag and pull it out. Inside were some rags and what looked like parts of a gun, including a trigger mechanism.

Ballistics expert Gerard Dutton immediately recognised the parts as a complete breech bolt assembly, a complete trigger assembly and a Ram-Line magazine from a Ruger 10/22—the model Dutton had previously identified as having been used in the murders. Using a magnifying glass, Dutton could make out two features—a crescent-shaped firing pin and two small burrs on the bolt face—that matched the impressions on several of the fired cartridge cases recovered from the forest.

Leach was called to the garage and shown the parts. Ivan was then brought in and asked, 'What's this?' Ivan casually replied, 'Looks like something out of a gun,' and denied ever having seen the parts before.

Knowing Rod Milton's assessment of Ivan, Rod Lynch and I were reasonably confident of finding some small 'memento'

—a piece of jewellery, for instance, or a personal item—in Ivan's house, but neither of us had expected the avalanche of calls that began within moments of the search teams entering the house. From our point of view it was an Aladdin's cave of evidence, a fantastic and, frankly, unbelievable vindication of the careful detective work we had been doing behind the scenes for months.

Around 8 a.m. the other teams began searching the other properties on our list.

Rod Lynch and I couldn't wait any longer; we decided it was time to make an onsite assessment. When we arrived at Ivan's house the street was still closed off; the search wasn't finished yet. The media had been allowed into the yard but not inside the house.

We found Ivan sitting in the living room, handcuffed and guarded by a police officer. Ivan showed no sign of being aware of the consequences of what was happening around him. After speaking to some of the searchers, Rod and I looked at some of the items that had been recovered. As I walked from room to room a thought struck me: the house was jointly owned by Ivan and his sister, but the way Ivan's things—including weapons, ammunition, clothing and other property apparently linked to the backpacker murders—were strewn around the property made it look as if the house was Ivan's alone. I left the house convinced that Rod Milton had been right in his assessment that control, possession and domination were the driving forces behind Ivan's life.

Satisfied that the search teams at Eagle Vale had all the equipment they needed, Rod and I returned to the command centre, where information had already begun to come in from the other properties.

Steve Leach now decided it was time to take Ivan to Campbelltown Police Station. Newspaper reporters and TV camera crews crowded around as Ivan—handcuffed and with a jacket over his head to hide his face—was led out of the house and taken to a police car. Questions were flying—What was Ivan being arrested for? What had been found in the house?—but it was too soon for them to be answered.

Meanwhile, O'Connor was still searching the roof and wall cavities. A call came through asking for permission to cut a hole in the lounge room wall in order to retrieve something hidden in the cavity: it turned out to be a rotary magazine for a Ruger rifle. Cadaver dogs and metal detectors were brought in to search the backyard. Every item found was photographed and logged with a description, location and the name of the finder.

Back at Campbelltown Police Station, Chalinder Hughes was told the allegations against Ivan. Although clearly in a state of shock and disbelief, she consented to police searching her home at nearby Kearns. Nothing that incriminated Ivan or any other person was found.

■ ■ ■

Margaret Milat, the 76-year-old family matriarch, was, as always, protective of her sons, refusing to assist the police in their search of the family home at Guildford. Rather than open a padlocked locker behind the house, she forced the police to break it open. Inside the locker they found a .22 calibre rifle and rifle sight with the name 'Ivan' engraved on it. In the garage, police recovered a Hallenstein T-shirt similar to one owned by Simone Schmidl; a Next shirt similar to one owned by Paul Onions; and a piece of rag similar to the gag used on Joanne Walters. A cavalry sword was found in a bedroom used by one of Ivan's brothers, 35-year-old David, who had lived with his mother since losing an arm and suffering severe brain damage in a car accident.

Richard Milat's property at Hill Top comprised about a hectare. He and his partner lived in two caravans that had been joined together, although they had plans to build a house on the property. The caravans were also joined to a number of sheds, inside one of which police found an Ultimate sleeping bag, a bed roll and a blue tent, each similar to those owned by Caroline Clarke, and a blue Caribee Blaze sleeping bag like that owned by Joanne Walters. In Richard's car, an old Datsun registered in his mother's name, police found a length of rope similar to that found near the body of Gabor Neugebauer, three rifles, a shotgun and a crossbow. Richard was later convicted of drug and firearms offences.

At Walter 'Wally' Milat's property, also in Hill Top, a High Sierra day pack similar to the one owned by Simone Schmidl was found in an alcove under the house. Ammunition, including 36 Winchester Winner .22 calibre cartridge packets and twelve packets of Eley .22 calibre cartridges, both of the same batch number as those found near the Neugebauer murder scene; an Anschutz rifle and bolt; a Winchester 30/30 repeating rifle; an unused Ruger 10/22 .22 calibre rifle; a .33 calibre revolver; a pump-action shotgun; a Ruger Mini-14 .223 calibre self-loading rifle; a self-loading shotgun; and parts of various weapons, some painted with camouflage paint, were found in and around the house. In total, searchers found about a quarter of a tonne of ammunition as well as 400 grams of cannabis.

Like Richard, Walter was later convicted of drug and firearms offences.

Richard told police that one night in March 1994 he received a phone call from Wally, who asked him to go to Ivan's house and 'pick up some things'. Richard said that he and Wally arrived there about the same time, and that they took 'guns and ammo' from the garage and roof of the house. Ivan told them he wanted the guns moved because 'the police might come to investigate'. Richard said they then took the guns and ammunition to Wally's house, where it was stored and later found by police. Richard also said that he understood Shirley had been complaining and wanted the guns moved. Wally confirmed Richard's story.

In Buxton, at a property previously owned by Alex Milat, a team of around 80 police spent six days excavating a homemade 'rifle range', while another team searched a 450-acre property near Wombeyan Caves, owned by Richard and Walter Milat and used by Ivan and other members of the Milat family for shooting practice. At both properties, police recovered thousands of spent cartridge cases and spent bullets.

At William Milat's property in Bargo, a family photograph album was found. It was later used to identify camping equipment Ivan had souvenired from his victims.

Meanwhile, in Queensland, police returned to Alex's West Woombye property with a search warrant, and seized a quantity of Winchester Winner .22 calibre ammunition with the same batch number as that found near the body of Gabor Neugebauer.

As the searches continued, Ivan was interviewed twice at Campbelltown Police Station by Detectives Leach and

Gordon. The detectives did most of the talking, with Ivan denying any knowledge of the items found. The second interview ended about 11.40 a.m.

After the interviews, Rod Lynch and I went to see Ivan in the interview room. Given everything we now knew, it was a strange experience. Ivan gave the impression that he was enjoying the attention and that he knew exactly what was going on and why he was there, but that he still believed he was in charge and would soon be going home.

On the afternoon of Ivan's arrest, the local lawyer, member of the Police Board and openly gay civil libertarian John Marsden was hosting a barbecue at his home for the board of directors of the Sydney Gay and Lesbian Mardi Gras when the phone rang. The caller was Ivan's sister, Shirley Soire, who told Marsden that Ivan had been arrested by the backpacker task force and was at Campbelltown Police Station.

Marsden hurriedly left the party but asked his guests to continue without him. Although he had represented Ivan on the 1971 rape charges, we didn't know that Marsden planned to represent Ivan this time until he turned up at the police station.

Marsden and I knew each other through his role on the Police Board. We didn't always agree, but we shared a mutual respect. When he arrived at the police station, he asked Rod Lynch and I whether I had any problems with him appearing for Ivan. I didn't. Marsden was there in his capacity as Ivan's solicitor, not as a member of the Police Board. In any case, the board wasn't involved in operational matters, although due to the media interest it had received some general briefings. At the station Marsden never asked for any special privileges and none were offered.

We explained that Ivan would be charged with the armed robbery of Paul Onions and some firearms offences, but at this stage no charges relating to the backpacker murders would be preferred. We also told Marsden that a large quantity of property we believed to be related to those murders had been seized and that the next day we would be seeking an adjournment while we made further inquiries. Bail would be opposed. Marsden was then taken to see Ivan. They spoke for some time before Marsden returned to tell us that Ivan insisted he had done nothing wrong and that he would not be answering any further questions. I told Marsden I wasn't concerned whether Ivan said anything or not and Marsden, looking somewhat surprised, asked, 'You're not?'

'No,' I said.

'You're telling me you think he's fucked,' said Marsden.

'I'm just telling you I don't care whether he says anything or not.'

Marsden looked at me and said, 'Okay,' before turning and walking away.

After Marsden had gone, Rod and I talked over our plan. Ivan would be charged with the robbery of Onions. That would be enough to ensure that his bail was refused. There would be no mention of the backpacker victims to the media or to the courts, not least because the searches of Ivan's house, the firing range at Buxton and the Wombeyan Caves Road property were not yet complete.

While the material gathered appeared to be overwhelmingly against Ivan, there was much to be done to verify the ownership of the exhibits; connect the seized ammunition and weapons with the murders; and assemble this information in a way that would enable us to present a cogent and compelling case to the courts. One mistake, such as an incorrect identification of property or an inaccurate forensic finding, could have serious implications in court.

Later that afternoon, Ivan Robert Marko Milat was charged with the armed robbery of Paul Onions at Berrima on 25 January 1990. While the media had photographs and footage of the operation, as well as comments from people living near the raided properties, they were smarting at the lack of official comment from the task force. There had been no police briefings since before the raids began, and there had been no leaks. Every journalist was being harassed by his or her editor for a scoop. All they could report, however, was that the backpacker task force, supported by heavily armed police, forensic specialists, cadaver dogs and the Airwing (the police aerial unit) had carried out a series of raids; that a large quantity of property, including firearms, had been seized; and that three people had been arrested. But for what?

We all knew the headline they were after—'Man charged with backpacker murders'—but they couldn't run it without getting confirmation from the police, and we had no intention of giving it to them.

As darkness fell I spoke briefly with the media in the yard of the Campbelltown Police Station. I told them we had executed search warrants at seven locations. 'One man has been arrested and charged with armed robbery and discharging a firearm south of Berrima on 25 June 1990. He will be appearing in court tomorrow morning. Two other men have been arrested and charged with firearm and drug offences. Our inquiries are continuing. I can't say any more at this stage.'

It was pretty much what they already knew. They had learnt the names of those arrested from the neighbours. There was a barrage of questions, but they all amounted to the same thing: 'What about the backpacker killings?', 'Is the man going to be charged with the backpacker killings?', 'Can you at least say the robbery charge today is linked to the killings?'

I could understand their frustration. My concern, however, was not for tonight's or tomorrow's headlines, but for a successful prosecution. That meant leaving nothing to chance, and resisting the pressure to rush into things before we were ready. The media had their agenda and we had ours. What we needed was time, and sleep. Like several of my colleagues, I had slept little during the past week. I had to be back early in the morning to prepare for Ivan's court appearance, and all I wanted to do right now was go home and sleep. It had been an extraordinary day, but the media went home dissatisfied.

Usually, a preliminary court appearance and adjournment are formalities lasting only a few minutes, but that was never going to be the case with Ivan. As it happened, John Marsden couldn't be in court (he was attending a New South Wales Police Association biennial conference in Wollongong), so Ivan was represented on that first morning by Marsden's brother, Jim, a member of the same legal firm. Jim arrived at the police station early and had a lengthy conversation with Ivan in the cells. Jim then went directly to the court to wait for Ivan.

Campbelltown Court was packed. Few of those who had come to see the man arrested by the backpacker task force were able to get inside. Those who did were frisked for weapons by security staff. Meanwhile, a large crowd gathered outside the court, hoping to catch a glimpse of the defendant.

The court opened at 10 a.m. Ivan was well down the list and he had to wait while a string of mostly minor matters came before the magistrate, Kevin Flack. Then, about 11.30 a.m., Ivan's name was called. He was brought into the court through a side door, surrounded by security guards. After acknowledging his solicitor, Ivan sat motionless and expressionless as the police prosecutor read out the fact sheet containing the allegations against him. Paul Onions' name was suppressed by the magistrate. Journalists scribbled furiously while sketch artists tried to capture Ivan's looks and features.

The fact sheet was long and detailed but it was four words—'Belanglo State Forest turn-off'—that grabbed the media's attention. Those words were a red light to Jim Marsden. While asking for bail, Jim said, 'Two words make it [the case] a bit emotive. They are "Backpackers" and "Belanglo" . . . [Ivan] is only charged with one incident relating to something that occurred four years ago.' Jim asked the magistrate to discount these words when considering the question of bail. But Mr Flack refused bail, citing the seriousness of the charges and the possibility of further offences being committed.

Ivan was remanded to appear again at Campbelltown Court on 31 May 1994.

10
THE MILATS

Task Force Air had been in operation for only a matter of weeks when it started receiving information about Ivan and the Milat family, but most of it consisted of broad suspicions about 'that family' and 'those boys'. Fear of alerting Ivan made it difficult to follow these up. It was not until after Ivan's arrest that we could openly investigate the Milat family.

Ivan's father, Stiphan, was born on 26 December 1902 in the town of Blato, on the Croatian island of Korcula in the Adriatic. He was one of 22 children, only four of whom survived infancy. At the age of 24, Stiphan migrated to Australia. He worked as a miner in Queensland before settling in Sydney, where he had various jobs. Stiphan (who later was also known as Stephen) was working as a wharf labourer when, in 1934, he met fourteen-year-old Margaret Piddlesden, who lived with her parents in western Sydney. Two years later they married and moved to Milsons Point on the north shore of Sydney Harbour.

The family moved between Sydney and Newcastle as Stiphan sought work, mostly on the wharves. By the early 1940s they were living in a large shed on a property in Sydney's western suburbs, and within a few years Stiphan was growing vegetables for the family and the markets. At other times he worked as a stonemason and a labourer. Between 1936 and 1962, Stiphan and Margaret had fourteen children. The fifth, Ivan, was born on 27 December 1944. In the late 1960s the family moved to Guildford, which would be the family home until Margaret died in 2001. (Stiphan died, aged 81, eighteen years earlier.)

A hard worker and heavy drinker, Stiphan could be a brutal father, although some described him as 'strict but fair'. Margaret, on the other hand, was permissive and protective towards the children. As Stiphan could never earn enough to support his large family, the children had to leave school early to find jobs.

Ivan went to Patrician Brothers High School at Liverpool and left school at fifteen. By this time he and some of his brothers had shown a deep interest in shooting and collecting guns. Ivan was said to have had the occasional run-in with local police, although his first recorded offences were in 1962 when, aged seventeen, he appeared before the Liverpool Court on charges of stealing from a house. He was released on probation until he turned eighteen, but the same year and while on probation he again appeared before Liverpool Court on a charge of break and enter with intent to steal. This time he was committed to an institution for six months. Two years later he again appeared before Liverpool Court on two charges of break, enter and steal, and was committed for trial at the Campbelltown Quarter Sessions. He was convicted and sentenced to eighteen months' gaol on each charge.

In 1964 Ivan began an affair with Marilyn, the wife of his older brother Boris. The following year Marilyn had a baby daughter, Lynise. It was an open secret among the family that Ivan was the father. Boris and Marilyn already had a daughter, but their marriage had been turbulent and was collapsing by the time Ivan became involved, although Boris had been trying to save it. While Boris did his best to treat Lynise as his own daughter, her birth marked the start of a long feud with Ivan.

In November 1965 Ivan was arrested and charged with stealing a motor vehicle and stealing electrical goods and a leather jacket. A year later he was sentenced to two years' gaol. He was released in April 1967, but four months later he was charged at Liverpool with being an accessory to stealing. In October 1967 he was convicted and sentenced to three years' hard labour.

In August 1971 Ivan's younger brother Michael, then 22, was interviewed over a recent robbery at the Bank of New South Wales in Canley Heights. Michael named his accomplices as John Powch, John Preston and Ivan. Wearing stockings over their heads and armed with .22 sawn-off rifles and a sawn-off single-barrel shotgun, they had stolen $360. Ivan's car, a gold Falcon, had been the getaway car. Powch admitted to the offence and, like Michael, implicated Ivan. Powch was interviewed about a second robbery at Revesby on 23 July and again implicated Ivan and the other two. Michael later confirmed Powch's story.

On 7 August Ivan was interviewed about the two robberies. Told that Michael had admitted to the Revesby robbery and had implicated him, Powch and Preston, Ivan replied, 'If your brother puts you in, it's not much good trying to get out of it. I was in it but it wasn't my idea.' He also admitted his involvement in the Canley Heights robbery and was charged at Sydney Local Court with assault and robbery while armed, and two counts of carrying an unlicensed pistol. Ivan's mother, Margaret, put up $1000 cash for his bail. While Ivan was on bail, a warrant was issued for his arrest on a charge of rape.

Ivan was 27 and had spent more of the past decade in gaol than out. Not wanting to risk another gaoling, he fled, causing his mother to forfeit her $1000 bail money. He was on the run until 25 April 1974. Ivan believed it was Boris who had turned him in. He told the police he had been working for the Water Board under an alias during his three years as a fugitive, but the truth was he had spent most of that time in Auckland, New Zealand, and had returned only after he got into trouble with the New Zealand Police.

Charged with two robberies and rape, Ivan had his application for bail refused. On 9 December 1974 he was acquitted in the Sydney District Court of the assault and robbery charges. Four days later, with John Marsden as his solicitor, Ivan was acquitted in the same court of rape.

In February 1972 Michael Milat had pleaded guilty to one count of armed robbery with wounding, and was sentenced to sixteen years' gaol and to twelve years' gaol on each of three counts of armed robbery. All sentences were to be served concurrently. A further five charges of armed robbery were taken into account. All nine offences were committed in south-west Sydney between 22 June and 3 August 1971. Michael's criminal record had begun at the age of fifteen when he was placed on a twelve-month good behaviour bond for stealing.

John Preston, who had a long criminal record for theft and street offences, pleaded guilty in 1972 to a series of armed robberies with Michael and was sentenced to eighteen years' gaol. John Powch pleaded not guilty, but was convicted and gaoled for eighteen years. He has spent most of his adult life behind bars, and in the early 1980s was named one of the state's ten most wanted criminals after escaping from Cessnock gaol in 1980. After teaming up with the notorious drug trafficker David Kelleher, Powch was arrested in 1985 and gaoled for 26 years for conspiring to import heroin, while Kelleher was sentenced to life in gaol. In 2004 Powch was gaoled for nine years and four months on three counts of sexual assault.

In October 1975 Ivan was living with his parents in Guildford and driving Mack trucks when he was introduced to seventeen-year-old Karen Merle Duck by her brother, Wayne, a truck mechanic. Ivan was 31 years old and had been out of gaol for less than a year after being acquitted of the armed robbery and rape charges. A fortnight later Karen and Ivan started going out. Karen didn't tell Ivan that she was six weeks' pregnant to another man. About a week later, Ivan stopped the car in which they were driving, walked around to Karen's side and, grabbing her by the throat, forced her to have sex with him. The violence of the assault was similar to that described in the 1971 rape allegation. Karen came forward in 1994 after Ivan's arrest and told police, 'he grabbed me by the throat and . . . I just sort of lay there and said he could help himself because I'd had it'. Later, Karen told Ivan that she was pregnant, but he claimed to have known already.

Despite Ivan's violence, Karen continued seeing him while she lived with her parents at Lurnea in Sydney's south-west. On 24 July 1976 Karen gave birth to a son, Jason. Karen remained at the family home for another two years before moving out to live with Ivan in a caravan in the yard of the family home at Guildford. It was during this two-year period that a man resembling Ivan attempted to rape two eighteen-year-old hitchhikers on a dirt track off the Hume Highway just south of Mittagong. (See Chapter 7 for a detailed account of this incident.) Although the evidence provided by the women in 1994 was insufficient for court purposes, it convinced me and other members of the task force that it had been another abduction and intended rape, if not an attempted rape and murder, by Ivan.

Ivan did not pay board while he and Karen lived at Guildford, but she helped with the housework and he did odd jobs and maintained the house. Karen described Ivan's father, Stiphan, as 'a nice person who kept very much to himself while Margaret was very permissive with the children'. Karen got on well with Margaret, although in disputes Margaret always took Ivan's side.

Karen described how Ivan behaved as a stepfather to Jason and spoiled him, 'buying him all sorts of presents'. During the pregnancy she had considered having an abortion, but decided not to. When she told Ivan he 'complimented' her on the decision. When Karen told Ivan she would like to have another baby, a girl, Ivan said he'd like a girl too, before suddenly changing his mind and telling her he'd shoot her if he ever found out she was pregnant.

To Karen, Ivan appeared to have settled down, staying out of trouble with the police and taking jobs that kept him close to home. But she didn't find it easy to live at the Guildford property in the caravan. There were ten in the house: Ivan's parents and his brothers Richard, David, Paul and George, and George's wife Patsy and their two girls. Jason couldn't play in the backyard because it was unfenced and the brothers left bits and pieces of cars scattered all over the yard.

In 1980 Ivan obtained a bank loan to enable him, Karen and Jason to move into a house at Blackett. Years later Karen heard that Ivan and his younger brother, Wally, had wanted to buy another property but the owner didn't want to sell; one night they went to the property and shot all the cattle. According to Karen, Ivan became abusive after they moved into the house at Blackett. He was very tight with money, refusing to give her any for anything but food, and he only ever used cash. He had no credit cards. Karen described Ivan as obsessive about cleanliness, criticising her if he found any dust in the house.

Once, in 1982, Ivan lost his temper and smashed a coffee table to pieces. He then gathered the fragments together on the floor and told Karen that if she threw them away he would wreck the whole house. The broken table was left there for a week to teach Karen not to challenge him.

During the same year Ivan and Karen stayed for a few days at Alex Milat's home at Yanderra, a village beside the Hume Highway near Bargo, where they lived during much of the 1970s and '80s. During their stay, Karen said, Ivan took her to the Belanglo State Forest so that he could shoot kangaroos. Even then he seemed to be familiar with the forest.

In 1983 Ivan's father died. That same year Ivan and Karen married, but their relationship was already on the slide and Karen left with Jason to stay with her mother, who had moved from Lurnea to the Central Coast. After several phone calls and letters from Ivan, Karen went back to him, claiming she 'loved him'.

Ivan enjoyed hunting and Karen described him shooting kangaroos and target-shooting in bush areas such as the Wombeyan Caves. During a visit by several of the brothers to Wally's property on Wombeyan Caves Road, Wally and Ivan amused themselves by shooting at rocks, trees and cans. Ivan also took Jason shooting, once shooting a kangaroo and cutting its throat, and another time shooting and skinning a deer.

Over the next few years Ivan regularly accused Karen of having an affair with the man next door; threw things at her if he found dust in the house; got angry if she spoke with the neighbours; and tried to stop her having friends, male or female. Several times Ivan threatened to throw hot coffee over Karen, and once he threw hot liquid near Jason when he would not take his asthma medication, causing the boy to faint. Whenever Ivan was away he would ring up at night to make sure Karen was home. Taking offence at something Karen's brother said to him while drunk, Ivan knocked him unconscious with a chair. On another occasion Ivan challenged Karen in front of a friend; when she returned the challenge Ivan took her outside, put a gun to her head and said he would shoot her if she ever did anything like that again. In Karen's opinion the abuse was less about physical violence than about wanting absolute control.

Sometimes Ivan spoke about doing violence to others. When Ivan saw a girl hitchhiking, he turned to Karen and asked what she thought would happen to the hitchhiker. 'She's going to get rooted,' Ivan told her. 'Killed and rooted.' (As Dr Rod Milton noted, 'If Ivan actually used those words in that order, it suggests he had memories or fantasies about sexual interference with bodies after death.') One day Ivan claimed to have picked up a female hitchhiker himself, telling Karen, 'She just got rooted and dropped off.' It was an apparent reference to the 1971 rape charge. He also claimed to have killed a man and left him in the bush. Once, when a car pulled out in front of Ivan, he grabbed his pistol and threatened to shoot the man. Guns remained a constant feature of Ivan's life. Karen knew that Wally Milat allowed Ivan to buy guns using his name, and that Ivan had driver's licences in several different names. (He did not obtain a driver's licence in his own name until 1981.)

Although Ivan continued to spoil Jason, he and Karen stopped talking. Feeling that she had become a prisoner in her own home, Karen threatened to leave, but Ivan told her she was staying whether she liked it or not. Karen suffered a nervous breakdown and was on heavy medication. In 1987, after a violent row during which Ivan threw a glass at the front door, just missing Jason, Karen and Jason left. She remembered it as 14 February: Valentine's Day.

A year later, there was a fire at the home of her mother and stepfather (Karen's mother had remarried) at East Lambton, a suburb of Newcastle. The fire had been deliberately lit, and destroyed the family car and garage and another car nearby. Karen believed the fire had been set by Ivan, who had demanded her mother tell him where she was living, and had threatened to burn the house down if she didn't. Ivan, who was by then working for the Department of Main Roads (DMR) in southern Newcastle, was interviewed by police but denied starting the fire. The fire was later investigated by Task Force Air.

According to family members, Ivan had a number of girlfriends after his split with Karen, but none of them mentioned that in early 1988 one of those girlfriends had been his brother Boris's wife, Marilyn. Ivan ran into Marilyn by chance at Gosford, on the Central Coast, where Boris, Marilyn and their children had been living for several years. Boris and Marilyn were now divorced, largely because Boris had been unable to accept Marilyn's earlier affair with Ivan. They had been estranged from the broader Milat family for around fifteen years.

In late 1988 Ivan left the DMR and got a job at the Boral plasterboard factory near Granville in western Sydney, using the name of his younger brother Bill in order to avoid paying maintenance to Karen. Aware that Karen was in the process of divorcing Ivan, Marilyn urged him to marry her, but Ivan wasn't interested and ended their relationship.

The divorce was finalised in October 1989. To Ivan, it was humiliating proof that he had lost control of Karen. As part of the divorce settlement, the house in Blackett was sold and Ivan returned to the Milat family home in Guildford. Once again, he responded to his marital upheaval by turning his attention to hitchhikers. Two months later James Gibson and Deborah Everist were abducted and murdered in the Belanglo State Forest. Over the next two and a half years another five backpackers would be abducted and murdered in the forest, and there would be an attempt to abduct—almost certainly with the intent to murder—a sixth: Paul Onions. On 19 September 1992, five months after the last murder, the body of one of the backpackers was found in the forest.

Ivan spent the years 1989–92 living at the Milat home in Guildford, but in mid-1992 he began building the house in Eagle Vale with his sister Shirley. She was a year younger than Ivan and in 1964 had married Gerhard 'Jerry' Soire. They had two children and lived at Liverpool before moving to Pleasure Point in south-west Sydney. After they divorced, the children did not stay with Shirley.

The intense publicity and police attention resulting from the discovery of the first two bodies brought an end to the Belanglo murders.

Around mid-1993 Shirley and Chalinder Hughes were working together at an accountancy firm. Shirley thought Chalinder, who had gone through her own divorce three years earlier, and Ivan would be good for one another and she introduced them. Within months they were in a serious relationship. After Shirley and Ivan moved into their new house in Eagle Vale, Chalinder was a regular overnight visitor, although she kept her own home at nearby Kearns. Her visits continued until Ivan's arrest in May 1994; after this Shirley moved in with Chalinder and stayed for a year.

11
COMMITTAL

With Ivan denied bail and the charges against him adjourned, Rod Lynch and I knew the next eight days would be critical to the success of the prosecution. We had literally hundreds of exhibits to examine, and we needed a clear understanding of exactly what evidence could be used with respect to each of the murders and the attempted abduction of Paul Onions.

Search teams continued to comb Ivan's house at Eagle Vale, Alex's former property at Buxton and the Wombeyan Caves Road property owned by Richard and Walter Milat. The media were still clamouring for information and comment, but the fact that Ivan was now before the courts had imposed certain legal restrictions on what both the police and the media could say. We had no intention of allowing Ivan's legal team an opening to argue that Ivan couldn't get a fair trial.

It was eight days before all three searches were finished. Altogether, we now had around 800 potential exhibits, almost all of which would need forensic examination and/or further investigation to establish beyond doubt what they were and to whom they had belonged. Some of these investigations would need to be conducted overseas—for example, with the family and friends of the victims, or the manufacturers of clothing and backpacking equipment. Thousands of cartridge cases and bullets recovered at the Buxton and Wombeyan sites required forensic analysis. Looming in the background was the question of whether Ivan had acted alone or whether other members of the family might have been involved; property believed to be linked to some of the murders had been found in the homes of various family members. Every item would need to be explained, although our suspicion was that all of it 'belonged' to Ivan or had been given by him to other family members. But despite the amount of evidence we had, it was all circumstantial and Ivan had not admitted to any crime.

By the weekend we were satisfied that we had enough evidence to justify charging Ivan with the backpacker murders. Knowing that the more time we had, the stronger our case would be, we decided to seek a further adjournment on the attempted abduction of Paul Onions before charging Ivan with the backpacker murders.

My confidence that we had everything under control was shattered when I picked up the *The Sun-Herald* on Sunday morning and saw an 'exclusive' by Martin Warneminde under the headline, 'Police breakthrough in Belanglo case'. Warneminde's story began, 'A lone investigation by a young detective has led police to believe the Belanglo Forest backpacker murders could be linked to a rape case more than 20 years ago . . . Sources close to the 38-strong Task Force Air which is seeking the serial killer said yesterday that credit for what could be a major breakthrough belonged to Detective Senior Constable Paul Gordon. He pursued a theory that Liverpool, the exit point from the city for hitchhikers heading south, could be the key to the Belanglo slayings mystery.'

According to Warneminde's story, Gordon had checked police files for reports of crimes involving hitchhikers who were picked up at Liverpool and found that, 'while no one was convicted, a man the two girls accused of rape could be connected with the backpacker murders'. An unnamed member of the task force was quoted as saying that 'he and many others considered it "clever lateral thinking by one of the actual guys [Gordon] at ground level"'. The task force member was reported to have said:

> What Paul Gordon has come up with is not the obvious. There is a lot of evidence and everybody has worked very hard to get it all together . . . But he thought we might be barking up the wrong tree . . . He decided that the total link in all this was just people who wanted to hitchhike. It was nothing to do with foreigners, it was nothing to do with backpackers, it was nothing to do with hostels. It was to do with how do you get out of Sydney when you hitchhike. He went off and checked his theory and sure enough some pieces have come together.

Gordon was said to have described his discovery of the possible link as being 'just lucky'.

Ivan was not named in Warneminde's article, but it was obvious to anyone who read the newspapers or had heard the news on radio or television that Ivan was the suspect being referred to.

I was furious and immediately rang Rod Lynch, who had just finished reading the story. We agreed that the article posed a significant risk to the investigation and would cause us problems in court the next day, its account of Gordon's role was both completely untrue and a betrayal of the team effort behind the arrest, and it contravened my explicit instructions about not talking to the media. After all our efforts to convince the media that everyone would be treated equally and no one would get the jump on their rivals, Warneminde's story risked starting a 'free-for-all' scramble for scoops.

After talking to Rod, I rang the Police Media Unit and asked them to prepare and distribute a media release stating that the story was inaccurate and potentially prejudicial. At the same time, we were realistic enough to know that it was too late to kill off the story. The damage had already been done.

Next I called Gordon and asked whether he had seen the story. He was evasive, seemingly unable to decide whether to admit to having seen it or not. When I asked when he learnt of the story, he denied knowing anything about it until he saw it in the paper. I asked whether he had spoken with Martin Warneminde or any other journalist about the story and again he was evasive, finally admitting that Warneminde had rung him, but claiming not to know how Warneminde had obtained his phone number. Later he claimed that Warneminde had the full story before speaking to him, and all he had told the journalist was that he had previously worked as a detective at Annandale. Gordon told me he thought the story was an accurate account of what had happened and he couldn't see anything wrong with it. He admitted disobeying my clear instructions not to have unauthorised contact with the media, and also admitted having made no attempt to inform me or any other senior officer on the task force about the story. I told Gordon I would speak with him the next day and reiterated that he was not to speak to the media.

Warneminde's story had put us in an awkward position. We now had no choice but to prefer the backpacker murder charges against Ivan on his next court appearance.

The tension at Campbelltown Police Station on Monday morning was palpable. Task force members were not sure whether to say anything about the *Sun-Herald* article or not, but they didn't have to wonder for long. When I spoke to Gordon he admitted that he had been less than forthcoming during our conversation the previous day, although he again insisted he could see nothing wrong with Warneminde's story. After initially denying that there were any inaccuracies in the story, he then claimed he had been 'set up' (he did not say how). He either did not understand, or would not admit to understanding, the potential legal problems created by the story.

This was not the first time Gordon had potentially harmed the investigation by his indiscretions and lack of professionalism. It was his careless inquiries at the RTA that had alerted Ivan to our interest in him. In addition, he had made basic errors in his research into the criminal histories of Ivan and his brothers, failing to look beyond the computerised records. I seriously regretted my decision not to get rid of him earlier. I couldn't risk any further setbacks.

I called a meeting of task force members and explained that as a result of the *Sun-Herald* article and the potential damage it had done to the investigation, I was removing Gordon from the task force. It is fair to say that most of the staff was shocked, but none expressed support for his actions. Several openly ridiculed the story's claims and Gordon's endorsement of them.

As we had predicted, Ivan's lawyer, John Marsden, arrived at Campbelltown Court the following morning determined to make the most of Warneminde's story. 'Clive,' he told me, 'you've got a serious problem. Releasing that story was stupid. My client can't get a fair go now and we will be having a fair bit to say in the court this morning. It won't be pleasant and we will be looking at getting the matter dismissed. Any further charges now will only make it worse for you. I can't believe you did it.'

'I didn't,' I said. 'The first I knew of it was when I read it in the paper. I'm as angry as you are.'

Marsden looked at me incredulously.

'Listen, John,' I said, 'the story about Paul Gordon isn't true and Gordon has already been sacked from the task force. We have strict rules about talking to the media and he broke them. As soon as I saw the story I contacted Police Media to try and have the story killed.'

Marsden knew me well enough to know I was telling the truth. But, as Ivan's lawyer, his job was to do anything he could to weaken the case against his client.

'Ivan will be charged with the backpacker murders in court this morning,' I said.

'He won't talk to you,' Marsden replied.

I shrugged. Ivan had told us nothing so far, so we weren't expecting him to start talking once we had charged him with the murders. None of us had any illusions about getting a confession.

The Crown was going to be represented at the hearing by the New South Wales senior Crown prosecutor, Ian Lloyd QC. It was rare to have a QC involved at such an early stage in the proceedings, but nothing about the backpacker case was ordinary.

Later that morning Marsden appeared in Campbelltown Court with his client. Ivan was under tight security as the Crown prosecutor read out the seven murder charges, disclosing publicly for the first time details of the violence of the crimes: the stabbings and shootings and the decapitation of Anja Habschied, whose head had not been found. 'An animal could not have carried it away,' Lloyd told the magistrate, Kevin Flack. Lloyd linked property seized during the raids a week earlier to the murdered backpackers and to Onions. The evidence was all circumstantial, but it made a strong case.

Marsden replied by stating that his client denied all the charges, emphasising that the charges consisted not of direct proof but of 'circumstantial innuendos and allegations'.

Marsden also raised the difficulty of Ivan getting a fair trial, particularly in light of the *Sun-Herald* article. To my surprise, however, he made no criticism of the task force. My decision to remove Gordon had convinced him that Gordon's behaviour was unauthorised and he directed his attack instead towards *The Sun-Herald* and the media generally.

While Lloyd described the violence of the murders, and again when Marsden attacked the media, I noticed a flicker of a smile on Ivan's face. Was he enjoying the attention, or the chance to relive the crimes? Or had he glimpsed in Marsden's robust defence the chance of escaping justice? I was left wondering as Kevin Flack adjourned the case for a month and Ivan was returned to the police cells, bail denied.

The hearing had lasted no more than half an hour, but Marsden was not finished. After leaving the court he spoke to the media and the public gathered outside. '[M]y client,' Marsden said, 'denies the serious allegations that have been made against him in court today . . . The outrageous allegations made in Sunday's media have already raised questions as to whether my client can receive a fair and just trial in the present climate.'

Within a day of the court adjournment I began receiving phone calls from journalists asking whether I thought Marsden had a conflict of interest. One suggested that Marsden, in his role on the Police Board, had been critical of me when I went before the board for promotion; another claimed that Police Headquarters wanted him to resign from the board. I knew some police were genuinely uncomfortable with Marsden representing Ivan, but my own feeling was that Marsden was entirely capable of fulfilling both roles. Marsden himself told the media, 'I don't see this is any different to any other case being handled by my office.' The government supported Marsden's position.

During the backpacker investigation I had been promoted from superintendent to chief superintendent. After Ivan's arrest, Police Headquarters was keen for me to take up my new position. I left the task force on 10 June 1994, and Detective Inspector Rod Lynch, who was promoted to acting detective superintendent, took over the same day.

More than 500 exhibits required examination by external agencies. The sheer number of exhibits made it impractical for every item to be taken overseas to be identified. Instead, detectives travelled to Germany and the United Kingdom with folders of photographs, which they showed to the victims' families as well as to manufacturers and distributors. In some cases property was formally identified when the witness came to Sydney to give evidence at the committal proceedings.

DNA profiling of various exhibits, including blood, hair and saliva, was conducted by forensic laboratories in South Australia and at Glebe and Lidcombe laboratories in Sydney. Selected items were also escorted to the Birmingham and Wetherby Laboratories of the Forensic Science Service, Home Office, United Kingdom, for further DNA examination. Among these exhibits were six lengths of sash cord and a pillowcase. DNA profiling disclosed that the blood on one length of cord and the pillowcase was 118,000 times more likely to come from a child of Caroline Clarke's parents than of any other parents taken at random from the population. The Forensic Science Service also re-tested hair found in Joanne's right hand that the Institute of Forensic Medicine in Glebe had concluded belonged to a man. The new DNA tests showed that the hair was consistent with being Joanne's. (This result was corroborated by subsequent profiling by the Institute of Forensic Medicine.)

In Sydney, Gerard Dutton, the ballistics expert whose role in the backpacker murder investigation began in September 1992 with the discovery of ten fired .22 calibre cartridge cases near the body of Caroline Clarke, was now carrying out detailed forensic examination of every weapon and piece of ammunition recovered. Dutton made his first breakthrough while searchers were still going through Ivan's house, confirming through a series of test firings that the breech bolt found in the wall cavity at Ivan's house was from the Ruger rifle that had been used to kill Caroline. He was 99 per cent sure the fired cartridge case found in Ivan's bedroom had also been fired from the same gun. Although none of the cartridge cases found near the body of Gabor Neugebauer could be conclusively matched to the breech bolt, some could be linked to cartridges used in Caroline's murder.

Eventually, Dutton found that of the thousands of .22 calibre fired cartridge cases and spent .22 calibre bullets found at the Buxton firing range, about 1500 cartridge cases and 500 bullets had been fired by a Ruger 10/22. After four of the .22 calibre cartridge cases were identified as having been fired by the Ruger rifle used to kill Caroline, we decided we had enough evidence and examination of the Buxton ammunition stopped. Dutton's analysis of the Eley cartridge cases found at the Neugebauer murder scene showed they had been fired from the Anschutz .22 calibre rifle owned by Ivan and found at Walter's house.

Significantly, having examined all the weapons found at various Milat properties, Dutton was able to link only two of them—Ivan's .22 Ruger 10/22 and Ivan's .22 Anschutz—with the backpacker killings.

Ivan's next court appearance was at Campbelltown on 28 June. Marsden had so far defied calls for him to stand down as Ivan's lawyer. But when he handed Ivan a piece of paper in the dock, Ivan threw it back at him, saying, 'Just get away.' Marsden returned to his seat for a few moments, then stood and addressed the magistrate, Mr Flack: 'I no longer appear for Mr Milat. I have been told he does not want me to represent him. He has chosen to represent himself.'

When an additional firearms charge was preferred against Ivan, Mr Flack asked whether Ivan wanted Marsden to act for him for the day's proceedings. 'I don't want him,' Ivan replied. 'Not today, I'll look after myself.'

Rejecting the offer of access to Legal Aid or a solicitor, Ivan addressed the court: 'I have been in gaol for six weeks. I have not seen a police brief of evidence or anything . . . I'm innocent.' A few minutes later he made a similar claim, 'I'm stuck in gaol and they [the police] don't have one iota of proof . . . they're making them up as they go along.'

The court had previously heard detailed allegations against Ivan and an outline of the evidence that would be presented by the prosecution, but in reply to Ivan's protests the prosecutor, Mr Lloyd QC, added a critical piece of evidence. A water bottle found at Ivan's house had been examined using infra-red photographic equipment. It disclosed the name 'Simi'—the nickname of the murdered backpacker Simone Schmidl—on the bottle. Someone had attempted to scratch off the name.

It would be three months before the police would be in a position to proceed with the charges, Lloyd told the court. The matter was adjourned for a week for Ivan to obtain legal advice. Bail was refused. As he was led from the court, Ivan shouted to Lloyd, 'I think you're framing me up.'

The realisation that he was in trouble and could be spending a long time in gaol seemed finally to be dawning on him.

In the months leading up to Ivan's committal hearings, Richard and Walter Milat appeared before the courts to answer charges arising from the police raids in May. Walter faced ten charges of possessing firearms, and cultivating and supplying cannabis. He pleaded guilty to eight charges and was fined a total of $2700, with four three-year good behaviour bonds. Richard faced five charges and pleaded guilty to two firearms charges, one charge of possessing cannabis and one charge of possessing a driver's licence in a false name (Paul T. Miller). He was fined a total of $500, with one three-year good behaviour bond. The firearms listed in the charges included SKS and SKK assault rifles, self-loading rifles, shotguns and a revolver.

Our problems with the media had not ended with the Warneminde story. The week after Ivan was charged with seven murders, a large picture of him appeared on the cover of *Who Weekly*, beneath a cover line that read: 'Backpacker serial killings: The accused.' Inside was a five-page story about the killings and the Milat family, and a smaller version of the same picture.

The then New South Wales attorney-general, Mr Hannaford, immediately charged *Who Weekly*'s publisher, Time Inc., with contempt of court and won an injunction in the Supreme Court preventing the sale of any further copies of the 13 June 1994 edition unless the two photographs of Ivan were obscured with irremovable stickers. Around 110,000 copies of the magazine had been distributed, and about half were estimated to have been already sold. Stickers were sent out and applied to the unsold copies, but the supposedly 'irremovable' stickers were found to be removable after all. New stickers were hurriedly issued.

On 16 September the Supreme Court found *Who Weekly* magazine guilty of contempt for publishing Ivan's photograph.

The magazine was fined $100,000 and its editor, Thomas Moore, was fined $10,000. The court found that the photograph was 'likely or calculated or had a tendency' to interfere with Milat's trial. The magazine indicated that it intended to seek special leave to appeal, but in February 1995 leave was refused by the High Court.

Having dismissed John Marsden, Ivan hired a new solicitor, Andrew Boe from Queensland. Boe had only six years' experience in criminal cases but owned two Porsches, attracting comment from some Legal Aid solicitors in Sydney.

The committal proceedings began on 24 October 1994 at Campbelltown Local Court before Mr Michael Price, with Boe instructing Brisbane barrister Catherine Holmes. The media, both inside and outside the court, outnumbered the public. Ian Lloyd QC, opened the prosecution case, observing that the brief of evidence against Ivan, although circumstantial, was strong. It included Paul Onions' identification of Ivan; Ivan's possession of property belonging to some of the victims; Ivan's possession of articles similar to those found at the crime scenes; his possession of ammunition identical to that fired at the crime scenes; his possession of firearms or firearm parts connected to fired cartridge cases and bullets discovered at the crime scenes; his possession of a sash cord and pillowslip marked with blood that had a very high probability of being that of Caroline Clarke; a modus operandi indicating that each murder was committed by the same offender(s); and opportunity by Ivan in all matters.

Minutes before the lunch adjournment, a bomb threat interrupted proceedings. The magistrate adjourned proceedings, although the threat turned out to be a hoax.

Witness after witness gave evidence for the prosecution, all of it damning of Ivan. Ivan's ex-wife described him as 'gun crazy'; after running around his brother's property shooting a revolver like a cowboy he gave himself the nickname 'Texas'. She said he often carried a loaded gun tucked inside his right sock, contradicting Ivan's claim never to have owned a firearm. Her evidence that Ivan liked to engrave his name, nicknames and initials on items he owned linked him to property belonging to the murder victims.

Ivan's barrister, Catherine Holmes, aggressively attacked the prosecution case, putting forward alternative explanations for the damaging evidence: some victims had been seen alive after being reported missing; Alex Milat had made a statement to police about Clarke and Walters that showed Ivan was not involved; and so on. Many thought she was doing a good job, given the overwhelming evidence against Ivan. Then, at the opening of the thirteenth day, Holmes abruptly informed the magistrate: 'Your worship, I no longer have instructions in the matter and I seek leave to withdraw.' With that, Holmes left the court: Ivan had sacked his second lawyer.

Andrew Boe sought a three-week adjournment to enable him to find another barrister. The application was refused, the magistrate telling Boe that seven witnesses from Germany were waiting to give evidence. (They included relatives of the three German backpackers, Anja Habschied, Gabor Neugebauer and Simone Schmidl.) 'These witnesses have come halfway around the world at the request of the defence,' he said. 'The defence wanted the opportunity to cross-examine these witnesses.' The prosecutor added that two Dutch girls were due to arrive in Sydney and were set down to give their evidence in the next two days. Boe was granted one day to prepare for his cross-examination of witnesses.

In the absence of a new barrister, Boe led Ivan's defence until the arrival of Brisbane barrister Terry Martin on 22 November. The problem was that Martin did not have a certificate to practise in New South Wales. When Martin's application to represent Ivan was refused, Boe again sought an adjournment, which was also refused. He then withdrew from the case and left the court, leaving Milat to defend himself.

Invited by the magistrate to sit at the bar table, Ivan complained, 'I can't defend myself . . . you've got all these charges on me and now you expect me to defend myself. I'm a road worker. Don't you read the newspapers, I'm not a solicitor.' Ivan then asked for an adjournment, but his request was refused. The court was in disarray, with Ivan still objecting and no one quite knowing what was going to happen next. After a short time, Boe returned to the court, declaring that Ivan would suffer 'extraordinary prejudice' if left to defend himself. A few days later Martin also returned, the problems of his practising certificate having been sorted out.

A month into the committal, I was called to give evidence. Boe began by asking some rather mundane questions about the investigation, the raids and the decision to arrest Ivan. We had always anticipated that one of the defence's tactics would be to cast doubt on which of the Milat brothers was guilty. Boe knew and we knew that being able to single out Ivan as the killer was critical. The incident that led us to focus on Ivan, I said, was the attempted abduction of Paul Onions: Ivan fitted both the personal background and physical description given by Onions, and Ivan's vehicle matched the vehicle described by Onions. Boe responded by pointing out that some of Ivan's brothers also fitted the description. I agreed that 'to varying degrees' Boe's suggestion was correct, but added, 'I don't believe any other member owned a silver four-wheel-drive with a white top and a red stripe down the side.'

As soon as I left the witness box the prosecutor announced that the Crown case was closed. While conceding that there was 'sufficient prima facie evidence' to commit Ivan for trial, the defence used Alex's evidence to argue that Ivan could not have killed Caroline Clarke and Joanne Walters; it claimed there had been sightings of the pair after they were supposed to have been murdered; that other people, perhaps including members of the Milat family, had been involved in the murders; and that Ivan had been framed by the police. An adjournment was sought so that at least ten witnesses who claimed to have seen the pair could be called, but the application was rejected.

On 12 December, after a 27-day hearing, the magistrate, Mr Price, observed: 'What this court has heard over recent weeks is but the prosecution's case as tested in cross-examination. The accused person is yet to stand his trial and have the factual issues determined by a jury of twelve.' With that, Ivan was committed to stand trial for the murder of seven backpackers and the attempted murder of Paul Onions.

During the hearing 172 witnesses—including around 30 from overseas—gave evidence; and 201 witness statements, 225 exhibits and nearly a thousand photographs were presented. The committal hearing produced almost 2000 pages of transcript.

Outside the court, Boe told the media he was concerned that Ivan wouldn't get a fair trial because of the media coverage that had been given to the hearing. The Milat case, he said, was a strong argument of 'untested allegations' that should not have received the 'degree of publicity and have this overbearing impact on the minds of potential jurors'.

Due to the large number of exhibits, all items had been recorded and stored in a dedicated exhibit room at Campbelltown Police Station. Once Ivan was committed for trial, the exhibits were transferred to a custom-built secure cage at the Sydney Police Centre.

12
TRIAL

After leading the prosecution of Ivan Milat through the committal proceedings at Campbelltown, the senior Crown prosecutor, Ian Lloyd QC, took a year's leave of absence to work in Cambodia with the United Nations, training Cambodian judges and prosecutors. He was replaced by an equally well-respected and capable lawyer, Deputy Senior Crown Prosecutor Mark Tedeschi QC.

Far from having ended with Ivan's committal for trial, the investigation continued for another seventeen months, almost up until the day Ivan's trial began. As a result of disclosures during the committal, a further 67 witnesses were interviewed and included in the prosecution case for trial.

During those seventeen months the defence made appeals to the Supreme Court, the Court of Criminal Appeal and the High Court in relation to various issues including: an application for each offence to be tried separately; the refusal of the director for Public Prosecutions to agree to a trial by judge alone; and the inadequacy of Legal Aid funding. The first two appeals were rejected; the third was partially resolved in favour of Ivan.

The trial of Ivan Milat began on 11 March 1996 under Justice David Hunt. At least one task force officer was in court at all times supplying information and managing the exhibits, and a response team was permanently on hand to conduct immediate follow-up investigations arising from the evidence given on any day.

The hearing began with two weeks of legal argument before the jury of eight men and four women was empanelled on 25 March. Tedeschi acknowledged that the prosecution case was circumstantial, but argued it was a strong case with fourteen 'circumstances upon which the Crown relies'. These were:

1. Ivan was in possession of a substantial amount of the deceased backpackers' property at his house at [Eagle Vale], among his own property in an alcove under Walter Milat's house, and at his mother's house at Guildford where he was living at the time of the murders.
2. Ivan owned the Ruger 10/22 that was used to shoot Caroline Clarke and Gabor Neugebauer.
3. Ivan was in Area A of the forest at the same time, or at much the same time, as Gabor Neugebauer when he was shot with Ivan's Ruger 10/22, because his Anschutz rifle was used there.
4. The Winchester Winner ammunition found with Ivan's property in the alcove under Walter's house

had the same batch number as that apparently used in Area A, where Gabor Neugebauer was shot, having been manufactured during a one-day shift at the Winchester factory at Geelong.

5. The Winchester Winner ammunition with an 'H' head stamp found in the accused's bedroom and in the spare room at [Eagle Vale], and the Winchester Subsonic ammunition with a 'W' head stamp found with the accused's property in the alcove under Walter's house, were consistent with cartridges and cartridge cases found in Area A, where Gabor Neugebauer was shot.
6. The batch number on Eley ammunition found with Ivan's property in the spare room at [Eagle Vale] corresponded with that on an Eley box found in Area A, where Gabor Neugebauer was shot.
7. The bullets recovered from and under the head of Caroline Clarke had a gouge mark, most likely from a silencer fixed to a rifle. Ivan had a handmade silencer in his garage at [Eagle Vale] and had stated an intention to buy a factory-made one.
8. Ivan left his Nissan with his neighbour, Mr El-Hallak, to repair the damage caused by a bullet having been discharged inside it, just over a week after Anja Habschied and Gabor Neugebauer disappeared.
9. Ivan was in possession of a piece of rope that was used in the murder of Caroline Clarke.
10. The components of the leash device at the Neugebauer scene were all available to Ivan at his home in [Eagle Vale].

11. Industrial recycled rags were used in the killings of Walters, Habschied, Neugebauer and Schmidl and in the storage of some ballistics.
12. Ivan carried a Bowie knife in his car that could have been used to stab the victims.
13. All seven murders followed the same pattern.
14. Ivan's attack upon Paul Onions was a thwarted attempt to take him into the Belanglo State Forest where he was to be killed.

(For a detailed 'Summary of circumstances implicating Ivan Milat in the seven backpacker murders and the abduction of Paul Onions', see Appendix 1.)

As a result of evidence given at Ivan's committal proceedings, his legal team made several admissions of fact, the most critical of which were:

- Nine items of clothing and backpacker equipment allegedly found at the Eagle Vale home shared by Ivan and his sister, Shirley, and one item of backpacking equipment allegedly handed to police by Elizabeth and Alex Milat at West Woombye 'were in the possession of Simone Schmidl at or immediately before her death'.
- Four items of backpacking equipment allegedly found at Richard Milat's property at Hill Top 'were in the possession of Caroline Jane Clarke at or immediately before her death', and one item of backpacking equipment allegedly found inside a garden shed 'was in the possession of Joanne Walters at or immediately before her death'.

- One camera and one item of backpacking equipment allegedly found at Galston Gorge 'were in the possession of James Harold Gibson at or immediately before his death'.

As a result of these and other admissions by the defence, the number of trial witnesses was culled to 150. Statements and depositions by a further 25 witnesses were tendered during the trial. More than 300 exhibits were tendered, many comprising numerous items. One exhibit, for example, comprised 180 pages and photographs. Numerous schedules were tendered by agreement, principally to assist the parties to follow the case.

Despite admitting that certain items of clothing and backpacking equipment belonged to four of the seven murder victims, Ivan denied any connection with the backpackers themselves. He variously claimed that the property found at Eagle Vale had been planted; that it came from the family home at Guildford; that it 'points to Shirley'; that it had nothing to do with him; and that a British coin 'possibly belongs to a relative of Chalinder Hughes'.

No admissions were made by Ivan or his lawyers about property owned by Paul Onions. His explanation for a shirt identified as belonging to Onions was that it had been found at the Guildford home.

Nor were any admissions made about any of the guns or ammunition recovered by the task force at any of the Milat family homes. Ivan insisted that he had no knowledge of weapons found in the walls of his home; that he had not bought a Ruger but his brothers could have used one; that he did not own an Anschutz rifle but had sold one to Walter; that Walter owned other weapons; that weapons found by police at his and Walter's homes had been planted there; that ammunition of the type used in the killings had been bought in bulk with his brothers; and that Walter owned silencers.

Ivan's attempt to deny ownership, possession and knowledge of weapons by blaming his brother Wally ran into problems when Wally was called by the prosecution and gave evidence against Ivan. In particular, Wally gave evidence that all of the weapons and equipment found in the alcove under his house at Hill Top, which the prosecution argued belonged to Ivan and incriminated him in the murders, had come from Ivan's house in Eagle Vale in the weeks before his arrest. When called by the prosecution, Richard Milat supported Wally's version of events. He had been involved with Wally and Ivan in moving the weapons and equipment from Eagle Vale to Wally's property.

When he was later called as the first witness for the defence, Ivan was asked why he had moved weapons, ammunition and other property to Wally's place in the weeks before his arrest. He said, 'I had heard the police were making inquiries about some of my guns and that is the main reason and also for better security.'

When it was put to Ivan that his possession of such large quantities of property belonging to the eight backpackers 'are amazing coincidences', Ivan replied, 'Oh, well, yes I suppose so.' He went on to say that he wasn't suggesting the police had planted anything on him, but 'someone' had. One implication was that it was a member of the Milat family, possibly Wally or Richard.

Ballistics expert Detective Sergeant Gerard Dutton swore that of the ten bullets recovered from and under the head of Caroline Clarke, eight were consistent with having been discharged from a Ruger 10/22 rifle (the other two were too damaged to identify positively). All ten cartridge cases found had been discharged from a Ruger 10/22, to which the Ruger bolt assembly found in the wall cavity in the Eagle Vale house had been fitted. The bolt assembly had been fitted to the rifle that was used to shoot Caroline Clarke and Gabor Neugebauer. Two other ballistics experts, Detective Superintendent Ian Prior of the Australian Federal Police and Mr John Barber, a former forensics expert in the New South Wales Police, supported Dutton's findings. (For a summary of the ballistic and other evidence connecting the Ruger rifle parts to the murders and Ivan, see Appendix 2.)

Ivan admitted having bought the Anschutz rifle found in the alcove under Walter Milat's house, and its bolt located in a yellow haversack in the same alcove, but claimed he had sold it to Wally a short time later. Evidence from the three ballistics experts was that 46 cartridge cases found 165 metres from Gabor Neugebauer's body in what searchers labelled Area A of the Belanglo State Forest were consistent with having been fired from the Anschutz rifle and bolt. Detective Superintendent Prior went further, stating that two of the cartridges had been fired from Ivan's Anschutz rifle and bolt. (For a summary of the ballistic and other evidence connecting the Anschutz rifle to the murders and Ivan, see Appendix 3.)

During the trial Ivan was given an alibi for 26 December 1991, the day Anja Habschied and Gabor Neugebauer were last seen. It was said he was at a family gathering at the house in Guildford and could not have been involved in the abduction and murder of the two backpackers. Carolynne Milat, the wife of Ivan's brother William, said that she had arrived at the Guildford house between 1 p.m. and 1.30 p.m. on Boxing Day and had left between 6.30 p.m. and 7 p.m. She said Ivan had been at the house all that time; he could not have left without her knowing because her car blocked the garage where his was parked. William confirmed his wife's version of the gathering and Ivan's attendance.

A photograph, dated Easter 1992, found in an album at Carolynne and William's home in Bargo, showing a Milat family gathering at Wombeyan Caves, appeared to give Ivan an alibi for the period when Caroline Clarke and Joanne Walters were last seen. Police had found the picture when they searched the property in May 1994. An examination of other pictures of the same family gathering revealed they were in fact dated a year earlier. Carolynne claimed to have changed the date on the photo after noticing that she was wearing a pair of shoes she was sure she had bought after Easter 1991. Was the change of date a simple mistake, or was it an attempt to provide an alibi for Ivan for the murders of Clarke and Walters? (The album was seized the day after Ivan's arrest.) The prosecution argued that on both occasions Carolynne's alibi evidence was not credible.

In 1991 and 1992 Ivan was living at the house in Guildford. He supported Carolynne's claims about his attendance at the gathering on Boxing Day 1991. He said that around 9 a.m. he had taken his mother to the Rookwood Cemetery to visit his father's grave. The graves of his sister, his uncle and some other relatives were also at the cemetery. Ivan said they returned to Guildford between ten and eleven o'clock that morning and that he stayed for the rest of the day. He agreed that photographs had been taken of family members that day and these had been presented at the trial, but none showed him being there. After Ivan suggested that the police may have withheld any pictures of him, the prosecution pointed to what it said were lies Ivan had told in various parts of his evidence and argued that his claims to have been at the gathering should not be believed.

Walter gave evidence in support of Ivan's alibi, but the prosecution claimed that he too had been caught out telling lies and argued that his alibi evidence should not be accepted. (When Walter's evidence was detrimental to Ivan, the defence had also accused him of lying.)

Significantly, Ivan's mother was not called to give evidence, despite her name appearing on the notice of alibi prepared by the defence. Ivan's lawyer conceded that, without explanation, one would certainly have been entitled to wonder about her absence.

Nor did the defence call another of Ivan's strongest supporters, his sister Shirley, to back up Ivan's alibi. Shirley had already featured in the trial in connection with the disposal of a gun owned by Ivan, and in connection with a Benetton top owned by Caroline Clarke. Noting Shirley's failure to give alibi evidence, Tedeschi remarked acidly, 'This is the Shirley Soire who has been good enough to bring witnesses to court, like her brother Walter . . . She was good enough to bring them to court, but not good enough to come through those double doors, go to the witness box and take the oath to tell the truth, the whole truth and nothing but the truth.'

Under cross-examination by Tedeschi, Ivan was asked about a .45 calibre pistol that had been retrieved from the backyard of the Eagle Vale house shortly after his arrest and disposed of by Wally and Shirley. Ivan said he'd had the pistol since 1991 and that after moving into the house, 'I made up a little compartment and I used to keep it in the backyard . . . It was weatherproof and I buried it in the backyard near the down-pipe, the drainpipe.' As well as the pistol, Ivan used to keep a pair of ammunition magazines in the bucket. While he was in custody he had spoken to both Shirley and Wally—they were visiting him together—and asked them to get rid of it.

When Tedeschi put it to Ivan that at the time he asked Shirley and Wally to get rid of the gun, he was aware that the police were anxious 'to get their hands on any firearms of yours at all', Ivan replied, 'I imagine they would. I thought they had them all.' Later, he said, 'They never asked me about a pistol.' Shirley later told him, 'It's taken care of.'

Evidence about the recovery and disposal of the pistol had originally been given at the trial by Walter after Justice Hunt directed that Walter could not be charged in relation to any testimony he gave about the pistol that incriminated him. (After the trial Shirley was summonsed on a charge of 'possessing an unlicensed pistol'. On 19 December 1996 she pleaded guilty to the charge and was fined $1000.)

Chalinder Hughes, Ivan's girlfriend at the time of his arrest, gave evidence about the Benetton top Ivan had photographed her wearing. (The two photographs, dated 1992 on the back, had been found by police in an album on the coffee table when they searched the house at Eagle Vale.) Hughes said she had taken the top one day from a bundle of ironing in the house and put it on because the day was cool. Ivan had not yet moved from Guildford to the house in Eagle Vale, and the clear inference from Hughes's evidence was that the top belonged to Shirley. Ivan said he had no memory of Hughes wearing the top, although he agreed that he had photographed her wearing it, using an Olympus Trip S camera given to him by Shirley. Ivan said he had never seen the top around the house and had no idea how Hughes came to be wearing it.

Ivan and his defence team refused to accept that the Benetton top worn by Hughes belonged to Caroline Clarke. Where it came from and what happened to it—the top was never found—are two of the unsolved mysteries of Ivan's trial. Years later, Shirley claimed that the Benetton top was hers and that she didn't know why she hadn't been called to give evidence about it.

The Olympus Trip S camera Ivan claimed to have been given by Shirley, and found in the kitchen of the Eagle Vale house, was a type sold only in the United Kingdom. Though the defence did not formally admit that the camera was Caroline Clarke's, it did not challenge the prosecution's claim that it was Caroline's.

At the trial, Paul Onions reiterated evidence he had given in his 1994 statement: his abductor had told him his name was Bill; he worked for the RTA at Liverpool; he lived at Liverpool; he was going to visit friends in Canberra; he was on four weeks' holiday; his parents were Yugoslav and he was divorced. When arrested, Ivan had denied ever using the name Bill, but he later admitted to having used the name in 1990, the year Onions was abducted. He admitted to having worked for the RTA; to having lived at Guildford, not far from Liverpool; that his parents were Yugoslav; and that he was divorced.

Onions' description of his abductor—6 feet tall, solid build, with a dark complexion, black hair and a moustache like Merv

Hughes, aged in his mid-thirties and wearing sunglasses—generally fitted Ivan, although Ivan was 5 feet 6 inches tall, not 6 feet.

The moustache took up a lot of the court's time, with Ivan denying having a Merv Hughes–type moustache in 1990. The jury was shown a photograph taken in 1990 of Ivan with a moustache and one of Merv Hughes taken in 1989. Ivan's lawyer conceded that Ivan did have a moustache, but argued it could not be described as a 'Merv Hughes' moustache, referring to it instead as a 'drooping Mexican type moustache'. In his final address to the jury, defence barrister Terry Martin conceded that Ivan's evidence that he did not have a moustache in 1990 was a deliberate lie, but maintained the moustache Ivan had was not the one described by Onions.

In opening the prosecution case Tedeschi had told the jury: 'The Crown says it does not have to prove in this case whether or not the accused acted alone in the course of these killings. The Crown says either the accused did it himself, did the acts himself, or alternatively, the acts were done by him with others in a joint enterprise in which he was responsible for the acts of those others.' Fourteen weeks later, in his closing address, Tedeschi suggested the jury may well come to the conclusion that one person alone had committed all eight offences; it did not follow (he went on) that if they acquitted Ivan of the abduction for advantage of Onions, then there was a reasonable possibility that some person other than Ivan had committed the seven murders. Tedeschi also warned the jury against being sidetracked by defence suggestions that 'someone' had planted much of the backpackers' property on Ivan at various homes owned by members of the Milat family and at Eagle Vale, and that Richard and Wally might have been involved in the murders and the abduction of Onions.

As predicted by Tedeschi, Martin told the jury, in what he described as a 'fundamental submission', that: 'There can be absolutely no doubt that whoever committed all eight offences must be within the Milat family or very, very closely associated with it. Blind Freddie can see that. There can be absolutely no doubt . . . the question is, who is it within the Milat family? Who has committed these eight offences?' Martin's argument gelled with Ivan's claim that property belonging to the murdered backpackers had been planted on him by the real murderer, who was either a member of his family (presumably Richard and/or Wally) or a very close associate of the family.

On Thursday 18 July Justice Hunt began his summing up, noting the work both Tedeschi and Martin had put into their final addresses. The next morning proceedings were interrupted when, in the absence of the jury and Ivan, Justice Hunt told both the prosecution and defence that one of the jurors had advised he 'was telephoned this morning just before he left to come to court. A male voice said, "Look out, if you find" and the juror thinks the word "my" was almost half out, "him guilty, you're dead".' After a long discussion, Martin applied for the entire jury to be discharged, saying:

> Of particular concern in this case is the nature of the threat that has been made and the concern that the other members of the jury may have received similar threats, and I realise there is no evidence of that but it would be a very dangerous course to ask them. The threat itself was very serious and immediately causes prejudice against the

> accused. In this case it is compounded because the very nature of the defence argument is that a member of the accused's family has planted evidence against him.

After further discussions, Justice Hunt discharged the juror before he had had contact with other jurors, thereby avoiding the need to abort the trial.

Justice Hunt took five days to complete his summing up. For the first time the jury was told that, because of the intense media attention, they would be locked up at the end of the summing-up to complete their deliberations.

There was plenty for them to consider, including more than 300 exhibits that were delivered to the jury room.

On Saturday morning, 27 July, after deliberating for three days, the jury returned its verdict. Ivan was guilty of the murder of James Harold Gibson; Deborah Phyllis Everist; Simone Loretta Schmidl; Anja Susanne Habschied; Gabor Kurt Neugebauer; Joanne Lesley Walters and Caroline Jane Clarke, and the abduction for advantage of Paul Thomas Onions. Justice Hunt asked Ivan if he had anything to say, to which Ivan replied, 'I'm not guilty of it.' Asked if he wanted to say anything else, Ivan replied, 'No, that's all I can say.'

My friend and colleague Rod Lynch, who had sat through the whole trial, was one of several people who commented that they had rarely, if ever, seen such emotion in a courtroom as when the guilty verdict was read out. To the bereaved parents and relatives of the victims, many of whom had flown from Europe to see this moment, it must have felt as if justice had been a long time coming.

All that remained was for Justice Hunt to sentence Ivan. His Honour observed:

> The case against the prisoner at the conclusion of the evidence and the addresses was, in my view, an overwhelming one. Although his legal representatives displayed tactical ability of a high order, and conducted his defence in a skilful and responsible manner, in my view the jury's verdicts were, in the end, inevitable. I agree entirely with those verdicts. Any other, in my view, would have flown in the face of reality.

He went on to commend the 'police and the associated Government agencies for the extensive and painstaking detection work involved in bringing this case to trial. It was a massive task, and the results of it have been extraordinarily impressive. All involved in that investigation deserve the thanks of the community for their efforts.'

His Honour indicated that he did not propose to list the injuries suffered by any one of the victims, as he did 'not wish to cause further distress to the families of the victims who have had to endure hearing the evidence itself . . . Their understandable distress was evident, and it is unnecessary that it should be repeated. In any event, I frankly do not want to go through that ordeal again myself.' He did, however, observe that each of the victims was between nineteen and 22 years old, and 'at the threshold of their lives, with everything to look forward to—travel, career, happiness, love, family, and even old age'. He continued:

> [I]t is clear that they were subjected to behaviour which, for callous indifference to suffering and complete disregard of humanity, is almost beyond belief. They would

> obviously have been absolutely terrified, and death is unlikely to have been swiftly applied. It is perhaps possible to imagine a worse case, but these murders must unhesitatingly be labelled as falling within the worst class of case . . . [E]ach of the victims was attacked savagely and cruelly, with force which was unusual and vastly more than was necessary to cause death, and for some form of psychological gratification . . . In my view it is inevitable that the prisoner was not alone in that criminal enterprise.

It was not a case, he said, where the prospects of rehabilitation needed to be considered.

> [T]hese truly horrible crimes of murder demand sentences which operate by way of retribution, or (as it is sometimes described) by the taking of vengeance for the injury which was done by the prisoner in committing them. Not only must the community be satisfied that the criminal is given his just deserts, it is important that those whom the victims have left behind also feel that justice has been done.

With these words Justice Hunt sentenced Ivan Milat to penal servitude for the term of his natural life for each of the seven murders, and to six years' penal servitude for the abduction and detaining for advantage of Paul Onions.

13
PAUL GORDON

As we have seen, Detective Paul Gordon was dismissed from the task force after the publication of an article in *The Sun-Herald* under the headline 'Police breakthrough in Belanglo case'. Written by Martin Warneminde, the story appeared on 28 May 1994, after Ivan had been arrested but before he was charged with the murder of the seven backpackers. Gordon's attempts to claim credit for solving the backpacker murder case and his criticisms of the task force and its management went on for several years and received wide media coverage. This book would not be complete without the full story of Paul Gordon's role in the backpacker case.

Warneminde's article came at a critical time in the investigation. Its publication jeopardised both the investigation and the prosecution of Ivan for the backpacker murders and the attempted abduction of Paul Onions. By publicly responding to the story we risked aggravating the damage.

News spread quickly of my decision to remove Gordon from the task force the morning after the story appeared. That day I received phone calls from two journalists, both very supportive of Gordon, pushing for his reinstatement to the task force.

I had to justify dismissing Gordon to the police command, but in giving my reasons I knew that whatever I put in writing could end up in court and might be used by Ivan's lawyers to challenge the integrity of the investigation. I told Police Headquarters:

> Detective Gordon was spoken with Sunday morning and was less than forthcoming about his knowledge of the article . . . This was not the first time Gordon has given cause for concern. He had been previously counselled by Detective Inspector Lynch over management issues . . . Another issue is the extent and nature of the information that flowed back to Ivan Milat following Gordon's inquiries at the RTA, where Milat worked, and the potential loss of evidence this has caused . . . I regard the Gordon issues as being issues of competence. I do not consider he has the level of competence, understanding and communication required of a relatively senior detective on a major investigation.

Warneminde's article had been the last straw. In the days leading up to the raids on Ivan's property, I had seriously considered removing Gordon from any front-line role in the search of Ivan's house and subsequent interviews because of my lack of confidence in him. I decided against it because of the disruption it was likely to create within the task force, and because I was worried Gordon would respond in ways that could severely harm the investigation. Instead, I reminded Steve Leach, an officer in whom I had a lot of confidence, that he had full authority over operational decisions connected with the raid and the interview with Ivan. I trusted Leach's judgement over what role Gordon should play in the operation, but I had not counted on Gordon's leaking of confidential information to *The Sun-Herald*. This was an indiscretion by Gordon that was too great to overlook. He had to go.

After leaving Task Force Air, Gordon worked for just over a year as a detective at Annandale Police Station. In July 1995 he resigned from the police, and moved to Queensland.

By now the case was before the courts, and further comment on the activities of Task Force Air by the media was largely restricted to the reporting of court proceedings. But Gordon was determined to have his say, and three months into Ivan's Supreme Court trial he spoke with Helen Dalley of Channel 9's *Sunday* program. Neither Dalley nor *Sunday* producer Peter Hiscock had been covering the trial. Gordon was interviewed for the program and helped with the research.

The day after Gordon's phone conversation with the detective, Ivan was convicted. The program went to air on Sunday 28 July 1996. It accepted Gordon's version of events and largely followed Warneminde's story from two years earlier. The main difference was in the *Sunday* program's aggressive attack on Task Force Air, and on me in particular.

Sunday claimed that a 'key member of Task Force Air, former Detective Senior Constable Paul Gordon, did most of the investigative work into the Milat family that finally led to Ivan's arrest. He and his partner's leg work cracked the case.' Alongside the story of Paul Gordon's diligent sleuthing, *Sunday* claimed to reveal 'a parallel tale of where the investigation fell short, a story of mistakes made and valuable opportunities lost to nail the killer or killers earlier'. Gordon claimed there were 'flaws in [the investigation], opportunities were lost. We did have some vital leads in the first weeks on the Milat family name that were either overlooked or not acted on, and they should have been acted on . . . it was a long way from being a fine textbook case of a well-executed investigation. In fact it was one of the worst I've ever worked on.'

He cited the case of Alex Milat as an example: 'Within a couple of days [of Alex making his statement] they hypnotised Alex . . . It is usually only used as a last resort. Because having hypnotised him, a potentially good witness was burned and wouldn't have stood up in court.'

Gordon went on: 'The first thing I did when I started in the New Year was [check the] criminal histories on Richard and Alex because of the strange leads we had on them . . . I did, but I have to admit only what was on computer. I didn't check back on microfilm, which held any earlier pre-computer records . . . I was making . . . a report on the Milat brothers to give to Clive Small . . . I thought I just better check Ivan's [criminal history] again, and realised I hadn't checked the microfilm record for him.' It was only when he phoned the Criminal Records Branch, Gordon said, that he learnt of the 1971 rape charge against Ivan, 'So it rang a few bells with me.' On his return to the task force office, Gordon said he 'showed it [Ivan's rape charge record] to Clive Small and in my enthusiasm I named Ivan as our main man'. Gordon claimed that when handing me his report on Ivan, 'Clive said something like go and find out why it couldn't have been him.'

Asked whether 'any greater priority was given to Ivan', Gordon replied, 'Well, he [Clive] did order the dogs, or surveillance people, to watch Ivan's comings and goings, but that was only for about four weeks all up. No other higher priority was given to it.' Asked what should have happened, Gordon said, 'Well, you would think at the least telephone intercepts on his [Ivan's] phone and probably listening devices . . . ordered for his house . . . We definitely would have had enough to convince a judge [to issue an authorising warrant]. And that could have revealed some incriminating evidence, had they been on early enough.'

Noel Newnham, former Queensland Police commissioner and at the time a visiting fellow of the Australian Graduate School of Police Management at Charles Sturt University in Manly, appeared on the *Sunday* program, apparently endorsing Gordon's view of events. He was asked a series of leading questions, including this one: 'As an independent analyst of this case is it fair to say on the strength of the hitchhiker abductions, it could have been solved by Christmas?' Newnham replied, 'I don't think that's an unfair comment.'

The program claimed that 'bad police work allowed the person who attacked Paul Onions to go on and kill another five innocents' and spoke of 'the heavy price paid by a keen detective'. Gordon's own assessment was, 'I can't deny I'm bitter. I think I was treated pretty badly.'

The *Sunday* program made no attempt to challenge Gordon's version of the backpacker investigation, which was frequently at odds with the facts. He told *Sunday*, for example, that hypnotising Alex Milat destroyed 'a potentially good witness' and should have been used only as a last resort. Alex was hypnotised only after close examination of the facts by me and my colleagues on the task force and after consultation with police lawyers. The decision to hypnotise him was made only after he had given and signed a detailed statement. The facts contained in that statement would not be damaged by hypnosis. It was viewed by all of us at the time as a 'last resort' that might, perhaps, yield information that could prove, disprove or add to assertions contained in his statement. As a member of the task force, Gordon should have known this, although his subsequent criticism implied he didn't.

Gordon's account of how he came to check the criminal histories of Richard, Alex, Ivan and other members of the Milat family was simply not true. Gordon researched the criminal histories of the Milats because I told him to. When he failed to check the pre-computer records (causing him to inform me, in the presence of Rod Lynch and others, that none of the Milats had a serious criminal record), I sent him back to examine them. He returned a day or two later and declared, 'Ivan's our man.' Gordon's enthusiasm for Ivan was understandable, but I was concerned by the way he spoke about the 1971 rape charge against Ivan as if it were 'evidence' that could be admitted in court against Ivan in the backpacker case. As even the most junior police officer should have known, it wasn't evidence and it wouldn't be admissible in court. Gordon's only interest was in incriminating Ivan, but such a single-minded presumption of guilt risked overlooking crucial exculpatory evidence, and we could not afford to let this happen; that's why I told Gordon to look for any reasons why Ivan might not be the backpacker killer. The idea that I was arguing against Ivan's guilt, as Gordon implied to the *Sunday* program, is completely false.

The claim that surveillance police were put onto Ivan 'only for about four weeks', as Gordon told *Sunday*, omitted one key fact: that it was cut short because of Gordon's own actions. The unit was assigned to target Ivan on 26 February and surveillance continued until 4 April. It was discontinued because of information received by the task force that Ivan had been tipped off that police were asking questions about him. It was Gordon himself who caused Ivan to be tipped off through his clumsy inquiries at the RTA. This forced us to suspend surveillance in order to minimise operational risks to the investigation. Surveillance was resumed three weeks later and continued until Ivan's arrest.

According to Gordon, phone intercepts and listening devices for Ivan's house should have been sought. 'We definitely would have had enough to convince a judge [to issue an authorising warrant],' Gordon said. 'And that could have revealed some incriminating evidence, had they been on early enough.' This was not true. There were insufficient grounds to justify an application for either a phone intercept or a listening device until Paul Onions made his identification of Ivan on 5 May 1994. Following that identification, an application was made and granted for an intercept on Ivan's phone. The intercept was in operation from 19 May until Ivan's arrest. Surveillance had revealed that Ivan's house had a sophisticated electronic alarm system, which meant it was impracticable to install listening devices. This information, too, was available within the task force and should have been known to Gordon.

Gordon's wider claim of inaction and delays in dealing with critical information received during late 1993 and early 1994 demonstrates his failure to understand the problems the task force was facing during that period. Literally tens of thousands of pieces of information were pouring into the task force and the police did not have an adequate information management system. The first priority for the task force was to ensure that no information received was lost. The second was to create an appropriate information management system. (Both these issues have been discussed earlier in this book.) By the time the task force closed its doors it had more than 1.8 million original documents, files and pieces of information/intelligence, most of which flowed into the task force during the first six months of its operation. While delays did occur, the systems we introduced ensured that no information or opportunities would be overlooked, and that all investigative avenues would be followed up, accounted for and reviewed, increasing the likelihood of an arrest or arrests followed by successful prosecutions. It was not a race to the finish line where mistakes and omissions could be tolerated; finding and then convicting the killer meant covering every possible angle and not making mistakes.

After his appearance on the *Sunday* program, Noel Newnham wrote to me. Among other things, he said:

> I did not know of Paul Gordon, or of any person's removal from the task force or resignation from the Service, until the show went to air.
>
> A great deal of the information they gave me was capable of being portrayed in a negative way, and indeed was put to me in that way, but I put a balanced and a

> more constructive view on their information. Many of those points were matters for judgement and I expressed the view that no criticism could be made on the information available.
>
> A good example of this might be the report to the effect that when Gordon proposed that Ivan Milat was the offender and should be closely targeted you told him to try to show why Milat could not be the offender. I expressed the view that that was sound management and good leadership, and that it indicated you wanted to ensure your people kept an open mind and did a good job. My opinion does not seem to have survived the editing process, and I was disappointed by that.

Newnham went on to say he was supportive of the record of the task force in such matters as 'the hypnotising of a witness, the time of applications for telephone intercept warrants, and the time of the execution of search warrants'.

While sentencing Ivan the day before the *Sunday* program went to air, Justice David Hunt pointedly commended the task force for its 'extensive and painstaking detection work'. Following the *Sunday* program, Acting Police Commissioner Neil Taylor put out a media release, 'Police Service supports senior investigators', which read, in part: 'Chief Superintendent Clive Small and the current commander of Task Force Air, Detective Inspector Rod Lynch, are highly regarded investigators who have been responsible for management of a complex and meticulous investigation conducted in difficult circumstances.' Taylor also drew attention to Justice Hunt's praise of the investigation. Police Headquarters had also endorsed my removal of Gordon from the task force. Years later, during an interview with *Crime Investigation Australia*, Mark Tedeschi QC, by then senior Crown prosecutor, said of the investigation, '[It was] amazing police work. Amazingly painstaking.'

At the time I considered seeking legal advice over the *Sunday* program, but I decided not to pursue the matter in case it was used by Ivan's lawyers as grounds for an appeal.

Gordon's campaign against me and the task force did not end with the *Sunday* program. Three weeks later *The Sun-Herald* ran two stories. One, headlined 'Milat hunting party', reported that 'New information has come to light that a "hunting party" of three or more men may have been involved in some of the Belanglo State Forest backpacker murders.' According to the story, these men, who had supposedly not been interviewed by Task Force Air, had 'boasted about bodies buried in the forest, long before the backpackers' fate was publicly known'. One of the men was said to have been 'a regular drinker at the Blue Boar Inn in Bowral, the scene of one of the last sightings of murdered British backpackers Caroline Clarke and Joanne Walters'. He was said to closely fit 'a profile of the murderer prepared by criminologist Paul Wilson before Milat's arrest'.

This was not new information. The matter had been fully investigated after one of the men was named as a suspect by Tim Bristow, a notorious convicted criminal, private eye, bouncer and standover man who died in 2003. No evidence was found to support Bristow's allegation, or the claim that Clarke and Walters had been seen at the Blue Boar Inn in Bowral. The task force had not obtained, nor was it aware of, any profile of the backpacker murderer by Paul Wilson.

On the same page was a second article headlined, 'Call for review of police probe'. The report stated that the then New South Wales shadow police minister, Andrew Tink, supported a call by Gordon for a review of the backpacker murder investigation: '[I]t was important authorities investigate why a statement by British tourist Paul Onions to Bowral police when Milat shot at him on January 25, 1990, allegedly disappeared.' Gordon himself advocated a much broader review: 'The overall task force investigation should be reviewed to identify any possible mistakes.' The *Sunday* program had claimed that 'bad police work allowed the person who attacked Paul Onions to go on and kill another five innocents'.

As with the Blue Boar Inn claim, there was no need for a 'probe'. It had already been done. Before Ivan's arrest, Task Force Air conducted an extensive search for documents relating to Onions' statement; two months after Ivan's arrest Rod Lynch, then commander of the task force, had submitted a report on Onions' missing statement and other records at Bowral Police to Police Internal Affairs. Following an investigation, disciplinary action was taken against a number of officers and the matter was closed. During an interview with Neil Mercer for his book *Fate: Inside the backpacker murders investigation*, Rod Lynch concluded that failing to follow up Onions' statement was a serious mistake, but probably didn't have a material effect on the outcome: the driver who picked up Onions had been described but not identified, and the connection with Milat had not been established at the time Onions made his report. 'I think it would have been a stretch to get him,' Lynch said.

In an interview for Mark Whittaker and Les Kennedy's book *Sins of the Brother: The definitive story of Ivan Milat and the backpacker murders*, Gordon told how he hadn't been at the task force long when his team leader, Detective Sergeant Royce Gorman, handed him a file and said, 'Have a look at this. I've tried to get Mr Small to have a look and he isn't that interested.' It was a file on the Milats. According to Gordon, Gorman had been keen to have someone look into this family for a while. Unfortunately, Royce Gorman died in 2011 following a series of long illnesses, so he cannot now be asked for his version of events. But again, Gordon's version is misleading.

In January 1994 the task force was divided into teams. Royce Gorman was in charge of the team that included Gordon. Rod Lynch, the deputy commander of the task force, Detective Inspectors Bob Godden and Bob Benson and me—the four most senior officers on the task force, the leadership team if you like—assigned each team one or more tasks. One of the tasks assigned to Gorman was to look into the Milat family. It therefore makes little sense for Gorman to have claimed, 'I've tried to get Mr Small to have a look and he isn't that interested,' when I was part of the team that had specifically assigned him that task. Furthermore, Gorman and Lynch were part of a small circle of close personal friends. If Gorman had been dissatisfied with any aspect of the investigation, he would have had no hesitation in discussing it with Lynch, who would certainly have listened. Gorman raised no such concerns.

As far as I am concerned, the inaccurate and self-serving claims made by Gordon after Ivan's conviction only confirm that I was right to remove him from Task Force Air because he lacked 'the level of competence, understanding and communication required of a relatively senior detective on a major investigation'. As I have demonstrated in the preceding pages, Gordon's view of the backpacker investigation, and his role in it, simply do not stand up to scrutiny.

PART 2

BEYOND BELANGLO

14
HOW MANY MORE?

In the two years between Ivan's arrest and conviction, Task Force Air continued to investigate allegations against Ivan and other members of the Milat family, and to reinvestigate unsolved disappearances and murders. The focus was on people aged between seventeen and 40 who had gone missing in New South Wales between 1970 and 1992, and on unsolved murders, attempted murders and other crimes of violence in which a .22 calibre rifle and/or a knife had been used. The task force paid special attention to victims known to have been backpackers, hitchhikers or travellers. Help was sought from all Australian State and Territory law enforcement agencies.

As a result of information received, the task force identified 43 missing persons and sixteen unsolved murders for investigation. Nine missing persons were found; DNA testing identified a body found in Perth in 1986 as belonging to a woman who, not long before she was reported missing in 1980, had travelled from Darwin to Perth. There was no indication that Ivan had been involved in the disappearance of any of the remaining 33 missing persons.

In thirteen of the sixteen unsolved murders, no evidence was found to implicate Ivan. In three cases there was cause for suspicion, but insufficient evidence to justify the prosecution of Ivan or any other person. I have no doubt, however, that one of these three was Ivan's eighth victim or, to be exact, the first of his eight victims.

Peter David Letcher was only eighteen years old when he left his home in Bathurst to visit his girlfriend in Busby, near Liverpool. He was unemployed and had not been in contact with his family for two years. A week later, on 13 November 1987, with 44 cents in the bank and a borrowed $30 in his pocket, he is thought to have booked a rail ticket from Central station in Sydney to Bathurst. He hitched a lift from Busby to Liverpool with the intention of catching a train to Central. It was the last time he was seen alive. Nine weeks later, on 21 January 1988, Letcher's body was found near a fire trail in the Jenolan Caves State Forest, about 800 metres off the Jenolan Caves Road and 20 kilometres from the caves, by a family visiting the forest. The body was lying face-down in a hollow, next to a log and partly covered by branches and leaf litter. Despite having been in the forest only a short time, the body was badly decomposed. The upper clothing revealed signs of multiple stab wounds to the back. Five bullet wounds were found in the back of the skull. Three .22 calibre bullets were recovered nearby.

In June 1995 a preliminary re-examination of the crime scene was undertaken by the task force, but the weather and the demands of the approaching trial meant that any further efforts had to be put on hold. A week after Ivan was convicted, however, the task force was back at the Letcher crime scene conducting a large-scale search using metal detectors. A fourth .22 calibre bullet was found.

A ballistics examination of the three bullets recovered at the crime scene in 1988 suggested they were fired from the same Ruger 10/22 model rifle that had been used to murder Caroline Clarke and Gabor Neugebauer. The fourth bullet recovered was also identified as a .22 calibre, but it was too badly deteriorated to be able to identify the type of weapon used to fire it.

Several other factors pointed to Ivan's involvement, including the location and circumstances of the attack, the violence associated with it and the 'burial' of the victim. Interestingly, Ivan had worked in the Jenolan Caves area during some of the days Letcher had been at Busby.

Despite all this, there was insufficient evidence to charge Ivan with the murder of Letcher.

As part of the Letcher investigation, the task force conducted a review of all outstanding persons (34 in all) reported missing in the Nepean, Blue Mountains, Central Western, Orana and Southern Highlands police districts between 1 July 1984 and 30 June 1994. Twenty-seven of the 34 had been sighted after being reported missing, meaning they had voluntarily left home for some reason. No connection could be found between Ivan and the other seven.

The second outstanding unsolved murder case involved a twenty-year-old woman we will call 'Mary', whose car was found on Parkes Way, Canberra, on the evening of 20 February

1971. The car had run out of petrol and Mary was last seen walking towards a car with a male driver that had stopped in front of her car. Three months later Mary's body was found 10 kilometres away in the Fairbairn Pine Plantation in the Australian Capital Territory's north-east. She had been raped and her body covered with pine branches. The cause of death could not be conclusively established, although it appeared she had been strangled. One month before the body was found, Ivan was charged with the rape of one of two hitchhikers he had picked up. The location of the attack, its timing and circumstances, and the makeshift 'burial' of the victim all gave rise to suspicions that Ivan might have been involved. Work records also indicated that Ivan was working nearby and had the opportunity.

In the third case, 29-year-old 'Michelle' was last seen leaving the Lake George Hotel at Bungendore on the evening of 6 September 1991 with the aim of hitchhiking home to Queanbeyan. She was not seen alive again. Ten weeks later, two forestry workers found her body in the Tallaganda State Forest near Bungendore, 120 kilometres south of Belanglo. Michelle had been stabbed once in the back. Her underpants and jeans were around her ankles and she had been sexually assaulted. When found, she was lying face-down next to a fallen tree trunk and had been covered with pine tree branches. A number of personal items, including jewellery, were found to be missing, but their value did not suggest the motive for taking them was profit. As with the first case, the location of the attack, its timing and circumstances, the 'burial' of the victim and the apparent taking of 'mementos' all suggested Ivan could have been involved. Work records again indicated that Ivan had the opportunity.

After Ivan's arrest in May 1994, Phillip Polglase approached the task force and claimed that early one morning, possibly during Easter 1992, while he was staying overnight with David Milat, the second youngest of the Milat brothers, at the Milat family home at Guildford, Ivan and Richard arrived home. They were talking about picking up hitchhikers and stabbing and shooting them. Polglase said that they showed him a knife with fresh blood on it, backpacks, passports, a machete and a revolver.

Polglase suffered short-term memory loss as a result of a car accident some years earlier, and during interviews with police his version of events varied significantly. Nonetheless, his claims and the reported statements made by Richard to workmates were investigated. It soon became clear that Polglase's work records did not support all the claims he had made. Further, much of the detail supplied by him had been previously reported in the media. During August 1994 various conversations between Polglase, Richard and David Milat were recorded. Three months later, on 27 November, Polglase was killed in a car crash. During that time, no evidence or information was gained, either electronically or physically, to support Polglase's claims, or otherwise to suggest that either Richard or David were involved in the backpacker murders or any other criminal activity.

In later court proceedings Richard said he couldn't remember saying 'Stabbing a woman is like cutting a loaf of bread'; 'There are two Germans out there, they haven't found them yet'; 'I know who killed the Germans'; or 'There's more bodies out there, they haven't found them all.' At the time Richard was said to have made these claims, there had been a flurry of media reports and speculation about missing backpackers, including 'the Germans', and if they were made it is likely that, tasteless as they were, the comments were not based on any specific knowledge of Ivan's murders, but were perhaps simply a crass attempt by Richard to draw attention to himself, based on things he had read in the media.

Numerous people were nominated as suspects in the backpacker killings, some as lone killers and others as possible partners of Ivan. Suspicions were, generally, based on the violent background of those nominated rather than any specific knowledge of a connection with the backpacker murders. Every piece of information was assessed, after which many were dismissed.

In addition to Ivan and the Milat family, eleven others were the subject of serious investigation by Task Force Air during the six years of its existence. In four cases the suspects had been convicted and gaoled for the sexual assault and murder of hitchhikers in Queensland, New South Wales, Victoria and Northern Territory between the late 1960s and the early 1990s, while others had sexually assaulted and murdered their victims after abducting them. Four of the eleven suspects had buried their victims in forest graves, not dissimilar to the graves of the backpackers, and three were known to have used .22 calibre rifles. Three were investigated because they were said to have either an intimate knowledge of the Belanglo State Forest or an obsession with it. No evidence was found to connect any of these suspects with the murder of any of the backpackers, or to Ivan or his family.

Eight people were charged by the task force with a total of 41 criminal offences. Ivan's charges and convictions relating to the seven backpacker murders and one abduction have been dealt with in detail, but there were other offences. While searching Ivan's home at Eagle Vale police found a .32 calibre Browning pistol hidden in the laundry; the pistol had been stolen during a break-in at the office of the Department of Main Roads at Kenny Hill, west of Campbelltown, in August 1977. Three of the guns found at Walter's home at Hill Top, but known to belong to Ivan, were among property stolen from the home of Shirley's former husband, Gerhard Soire, at Sandy Point in southern Sydney between 31 December 1992 and 4 January 1993. Ivan was charged with 'receiving' the pistols, knowing them to be stolen, but given he was serving several life sentences, there was felt to be little point pursuing the matter. A brief of evidence was also submitted to the Office of the Director of Public Prosecutions over the arson attack on Ivan's former mother-in-law's home at East Lambton in February 1988, but again the prosecution was dropped.

As well as the drug and firearms charges against Walter and Richard Milat, detailed in earlier chapters, Ivan's nephew Christopher Stephan Milat was summonsed over possession of a .44 calibre Ruger Magnum revolver found at the Bargo home of his parents, William and Carolynne Milat, during the police search on 22 May 1994. He was fined $700.

During Ivan's trial, Walter admitted disposing of a .45 calibre pistol given to him by Shirley Soire and owned by Ivan. Walter had given evidence on the basis that it would not be used against him, but as mentioned earlier Shirley was summonsed on a charge of possessing an unlicensed .45 calibre pistol. She pleaded guilty and was fined $1000.

Ivan's nephew, Henry Shipsey, was convicted in the Dubbo Local Court of possessing cannabis and fined $1400.

Anthony Roman Kosorog of Dulwich Hill was charged with 'public mischief' in making an anonymous phone call to police on 3 February 1994, claiming responsibility for the backpacker murders. He was fined $300 and placed on a $1000, eighteen-month good behaviour bond.

Task Force Air was formally disbanded on 30 November 1996. Four months later, on 24 March 1997, Ivan's daughter, Lynise, was charged by local police at Gosford Local Court with possessing a .25 calibre semi-automatic pistol and a prohibited switchblade knife, and with stealing a knife and possessing cannabis. The charges related to a break-in she had committed on her former partner's home at Long Jetty on the New South Wales Central Coast in December 1996. Lynise pleaded guilty, and was fined $400 and placed on a $1000, three-year good behaviour bond.

15
REFORM

On 11 May 1994, eleven days before the arrest of Ivan Milat, the long-serving independent MP for the South Coast, John Hatton, stood up in the New South Wales Parliament and called for a royal commission to investigate corruption and misconduct within the New South Wales Police Service. In particular, Hatton wanted the commission to determine whether corruption and misconduct were 'systemic and entrenched' and, if so, to recommend ways of cleaning up the police. The Liberal–National government resisted Hatton's demands for many months, but eventually caved in. The commission opened on 15 June 1995 and ran until March 1997.

I had been commander at the St George–Sutherland police district for a year when the Wood Royal Commission began. One month later I was assigned to a major corruption inquiry centred on Fairfield and Cabramatta. Designated Task Force

Medlar, the inquiry spanned more than a decade from the early 1980s, and was widened to include much of Sydney's west. While the royal commission never took evidence from Medlar, it was provided with periodic briefings and received copies of the task force's final reports.

Crime in Cabramatta had been policed from Fairfield until the early 1990s, when Cabramatta was given its own detective force. Between 1984 and 1994 the area had been largely controlled by a group of detectives known as the 'Rat Pack', led by a junior detective who gave directions to both junior and some senior police. The Rat Pack was involved in drugs and money rip-offs (at least $20,000 cash on one occasion), the theft of money from illegal card games ($40,000 on one occasion and $30,000 on another), the fabrication of evidence and a range of other corrupt practices. Double- and triple-crossing were routine. One informant told Medlar he had set up around 60 drug dealers for the head Rat to rip off. The Wood Royal Commission rollover witness WS14, who admitted widespread corruption, offered the following description of the way the Fairfield detective office was run: 'If you're supervising a crime wave, it was run pretty good.'

In mid-1996 I was appointed acting assistant commissioner in charge of the North Region police command, based at Gosford. In September, as the royal commission was winding down, Englishman Peter Ryan was appointed New South Wales police commissioner, and in February 1997 I was made head of Crime Agencies (now called State Crime Command), which was to replace the existing system of centralised crime commands and regional crime squads.

By the time it closed its doors, the commission had held 451 hearing days and heard from 902 public witnesses, at an estimated cost of $64 million. Two months later, in May 1997, the commission released its final report. Almost immediately, Ryan announced plans to sack up to 200 police who had been adversely named by the commission, the overwhelming majority of whom were detectives or former detectives.

I found myself in charge of an 'empty agency': there were to be no automatic transfers or appointments, and positions had to be applied for and approved through Police Internal Affairs. Crime, however, had not stopped, so my first task was to find out where all the previously centralised detectives were and what they were doing.

A handful of clearances went through quickly. Among them were Rod Lynch, who had recently been promoted to detective chief superintendent, and Detective Chief Superintendent Rod Harvey. Lynch's job was to bring a strategic focus to major investigations and resource deployment, while Harvey would handle the day-to-day management of operations.

In our search for detectives we identified around 760 positions in the now-disbanded centralised investigative commands. In addition, we found around 250 on long-term secondment to the centralised commands, including task forces. There was no comprehensive record of these secondments, details of which had to be obtained separately from each command.

Five hundred and eighty-three positions were allocated to Crime Agencies. As a result of sackings, resignations and reassignments following the royal commission, Crime Agencies was never assigned its full complement of staff. The shortages had to be shared by all the individual agencies within the command, including the Homicide and Serial Violent Crime Agency. At the 1999 election, the government pledged to appoint another 150 police to Crime Agencies, but two years later not a single extra detective had been recruited, and the command was almost 300 detectives below its authorised strength for the investigation of major and organised crime.

Task Force Air offered a valuable template for the reform of criminal investigation that followed the Wood Royal Commission, especially in its improved management, information and record-keeping systems. Detective Sergeant (later Detective Inspector) Scott Whyte led the development of a new information management system, based on feedback from practitioners in the field, that came to be known as E@gle.i. The system was designed to record, track, analyse and report on information gathered during any type of investigation. Built by an external contractor in the latter half of 1999, it has been continuously refined and upgraded ever since.

In 2001 E@gle.i was described by Commissioner Ryan as 'an innovative computer system that will assist the Service to conduct major investigations, improve productivity, make better use of scarce resources and establish a "best practice" model of investigation'. In 2000 the project won the 'Implementation Australian Government' category of the national IT industry awards—a category that recognises the best use of technology to improve operations and services to benefit government and taxpayers. Today it holds the records of sixteen years of major investigations conducted by the New South Wales Police, together with unsolved homicide reviews going back to 1970.

In the aftermath of the Wood Royal Commission, one of the first tasks of the newly formed Homicide and Serial Violent Crime Agency was an informal review of pre-1997 unsolved homicides. During the first twelve months, reviews of six unsolved cases resulted in the arrest of eight people for murder, and one person for conspiracy to murder. (These figures do not include eleven murder charges laid by Strike Force Yandee, working with the New South Wales Crime Commission, against four offenders for seven murders committed between 1984 and 1994.)

In 1998 the review of unsolved homicides was formalised with the appointment of a team of seven detectives headed by Detective Superintendent Ron Smith and Detective Inspector (now Deputy Commissioner) Nick Kaldas. In practice, it was rare for more than a couple of those detectives to be looking at unsolved homicides; the rest were usually 'borrowed' to work on current cases. Nevertheless, by 1999 the team had conducted preliminary reviews of 266 unsolved cases between 1970 and 1996. (Around 2350 murders were recorded as having been reported during the period.)

By the mid-2000s, the number of unsolved cases since 1970 had grown to around 400.

A sign at the entrance to the Belanglo State Forest gives an ominous, if unintended, reminder of the murders to visitors.

Superintendent Clive Small, Task Force Air Commander, inspects a murder crime scene in Belanglo State Forest in November 1993. *Courtesy of News Limited and News Pix*

Police guard the crime scene of the murdered backpackers Gabor Neugebauer and Anja Habschied in the Belanglo State Forest.

Above: Terrain typical of the area where the murders occurred and the police search was conducted.

Right: Missing person poster for Debbie Everist, posted by her mother, Peggy, and brothers, at various stops along the Hume Highway between Melbourne and Sydney.

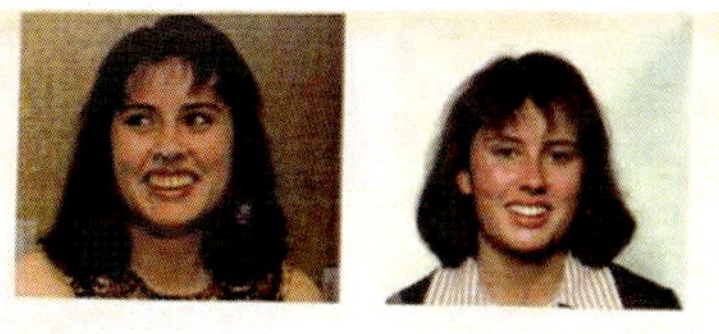

MISSING

Debbie Everist

Have you seen her?

Went missing Dec '89 in Sydney with James Gibson.

WITH ANY INFORMATION PLEASE RING –

MISSING PERSONS INVESTIGATIONS

03 – 865 2821

The Neugebauers visiting the O'Malleys in Easter 1992: (left to right) Angela Klaassen, Anke and Manfred Neugebauer, Peter and Rita O'Malley and Frank Klaassen.

Deborah Everist and James Gibson, both of Victoria, last seen on 30 December 1989 when they left Surry Hills to hitchhike to Confest near Albury. Their bodies were recovered in the Belanglo State Forest on 5 October 1993.

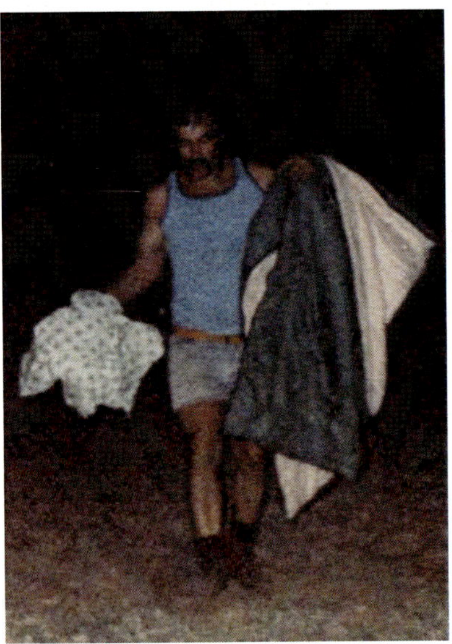

Photograph, dated 29 March 1991, located by police at William Milat's house at Bargo showing Ivan carrying Everist's green sleeping bag.

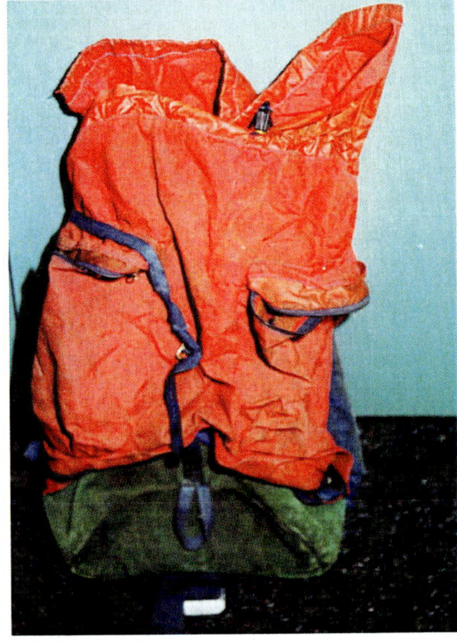

Gibson's Berghaus 'Cyclops Echo' backpack, found on the side of Galston Road, Galston.

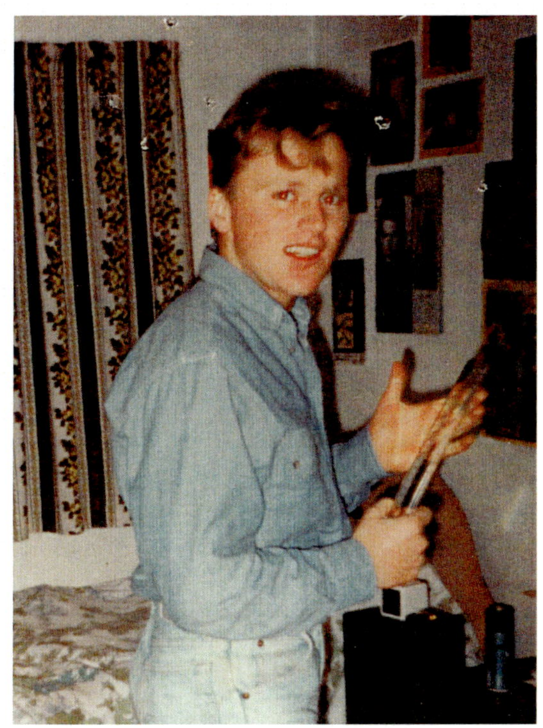

Paul Onions, an English backpacker, was given a lift near Liverpool on 25 January 1990 and escaped when a person later identified as Ivan Milat attempted to abduct him and fired at him as he escaped.

Onions indicating to Detective Stuart Wilkins where he escaped from Ivan Milat. He was picked up by a passing motorist and driven to Bowral Police Station.

Next denim shirt owned by Onions and found in the garage of the Milat family home at Guildford.

A close-up of the shirt label.

Ivan's 4WD, as described by Onions.

Simone Schmidl, a German backpacker, last seen on 20 January 1991 when she left Guildford to hitchhike to Melbourne. Her remains were found in Belanglo State Forest on 1 November 1993.

Schmidl's High Sierra backpack, found in an alcove at Walter Milat's house at Hilltop.

Schmidl's water bottle, found in a bedroom of Ivan's Eagle Vale house.

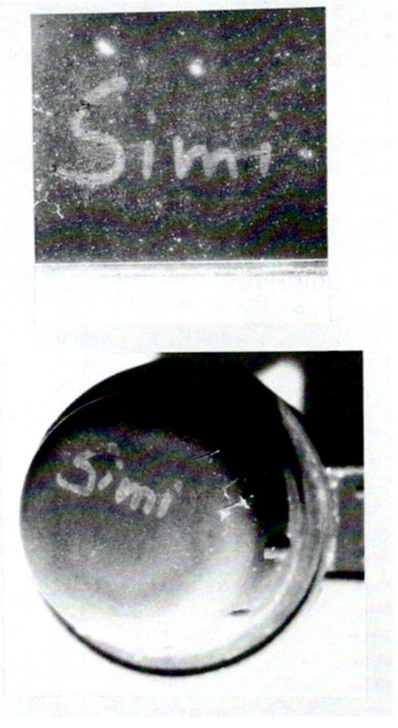

Infra-red photograph identifies Schmidl's nickname scratched from the bottle lid.

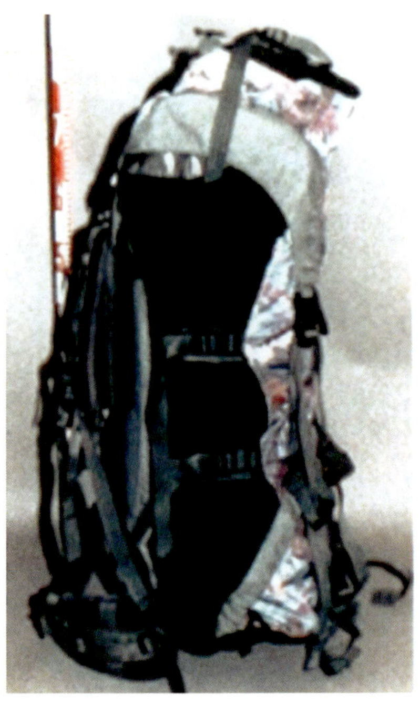

Schmidl's Salewa 'Canyon' backpack, given by Ivan to Alex and Elizabeth Milat.

Schmidl's Salewa blue sleeping bag cover, containing her green Vaude Hogan tent, found in garage at Ivan's house.

Police search Walter Milat's property at Hilltop using a metal detector.

Anja Habschied and Gabor Neugebauer, German backpackers, last seen leaving Kings Cross on 26 December 1991 to hitchhike to Adelaide. Their remains were found in the Belanglo State Forest on 4 November 1993.

Black electrical tape with brown leather strap, a white sash cord and black cable tie discovered near the body of Neugebauer. Similar materials were found at Ivan's Eagle Vale house.

Indonesian and other currency found in bedside table of bedroom at Ivan's house. Habschied and Neugebauer arrived in Darwin from Indonesia.

Caroline Clarke and Joanne Walters, British backpackers, last seen at Kings Cross on 18 April 1992 when they left to hitchhike to Mildura. Their bodies were found in the Belanglo State Forest on 19 and 20 September 1992 respectively.

Left: Ivan's photograph, dated 1992, of his then girlfriend, Chalinder Hughes, wearing Clarke's Benetton top.
Inset: Caroline Clarke wearing her Benetton top.

Below: Walters' Caribee sleeping bag, found at Richard Milat's Hilltop house.

Close up of a .22 bullet fired into a tree near where Neugebauer was found.

One of thirty-eight packets of Winchester Winner .22 calibre bullets, batch ACD1CF2, found in an alcove at Walter's house at Hilltop. The bullets were of the same batch number found at the Neugebauer murder scene.

Left: The shooting range at the former home of Alex Milat at Buxton.
Below: Police sifting the shooting range. Thousands of fired .22 calibre bullets and cartridges were found, including some fired by the same .22 calibre rifles used at the murder scenes.

Ivan holding a rifle, with a revolver in holster. He called himself 'Tex'.

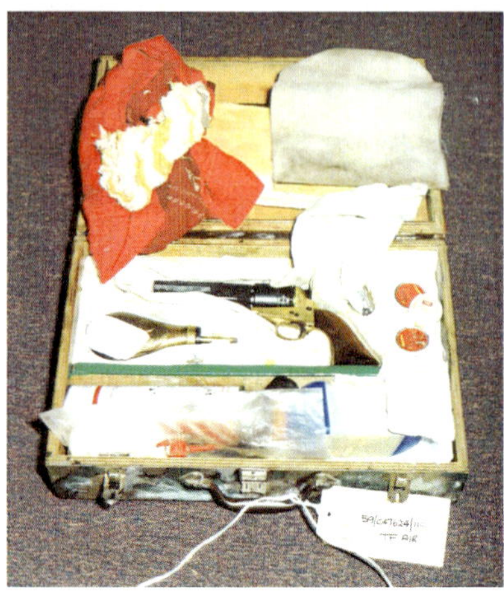

Six shot .44 calibre revolver with the word 'Texas' scratched into side. Found in an alcove at Walter Milat's Hilltop house.

Ivan's house at Eagle Vale.

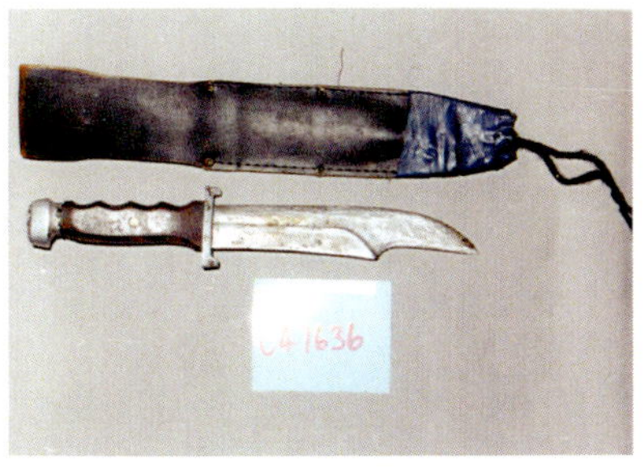

Knife carried by Ivan in his car.

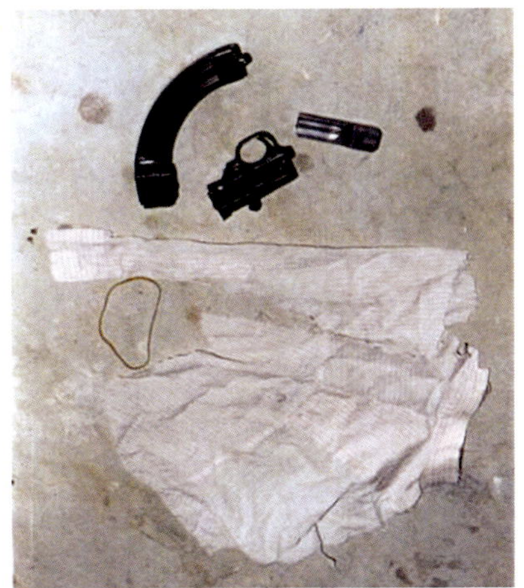

Plastic bag and Ruger bolt assembly, trigger mechanism and magazine recovered from a wall cavity in Ivan's Eagle Vale house.

Close-up of the hole in the wall near the north-eastern corner of the loungeroom in Milat's house made by police to retrieve the hidden Ruger bolt assembly.

Photograph of prosecution legal team and several police involved in the trial of Ivan Milat. The picture was taken following Ivan's conviction and gaoling for life. Front row (left to right): Instructing Solicitor Sarah Huggett, Senior Crown Prosecutor Mark Tedeschi, Crown Prosecutor Dan Howard. Back row (left to right): Task Force Air detectives Bob Benson, Gary Miller, Louise Donald, Andy Waterman, Rod Lynch, Steve McLennan, Shaun Gagan, Steve Leach and Bret Coman.

An older looking Ivan Milat in January 2009 being led from Goulburn Hospital after treatment for cutting his finger off and attempting to post it to the High Court. *Courtesy of Gary Ramages and News Pix*

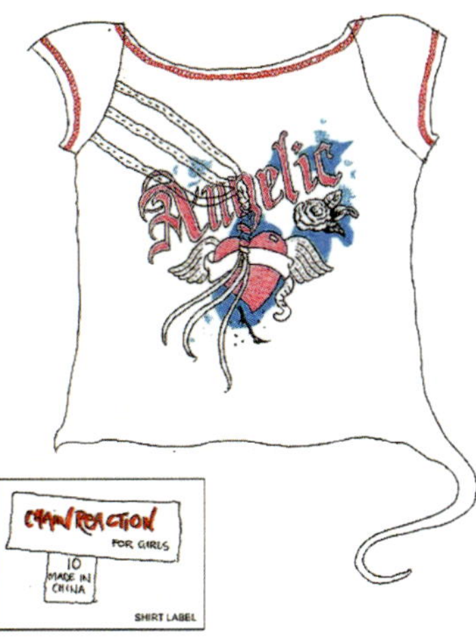

Police sketch of an unidentified female murder victim found in the Belanglo State Forest in 2010 who became known as Angel because of the T-shirt she was wearing when murdered (above right). *Courtesy NSW Police*

Matthew Milat, Ivan's great nephew, being led from the New South Wales Supreme Court after he is sentenced to 43 years' gaol for murder. *Courtesy Stephen Cooper and News Pix*

Clive Small visits the memorial to Ivan Milat's victims in the Belanglo State Forest.

The plaque reads:

This plaque commemorates the memory of the following persons whose remains were found in the Belanglo Forest during 1992 and 1993

Caroline Jane Clarke	United Kingdom
Deborah Phyllis Everist	Australia
James Harold Gibson	Australia
Anja Habschied	Germany
Gabor Kurt Neugebauer	Germany
Simone Loretta Schmidl	Germany
Joanne Lesley Walters	United Kingdom

Acknowledgement is made of the efforts of members of the New South Wales Police Service and State Emergency Service in extensive investigations and in searches undertaken in the adjacent areas

'Nothing can separate us from the love of God in Christ Jesus our Lord'
Romans 8:39

Unveiled by
The Honorable John Fahey, M.P.
Premier of New South Wales
and member for Southern Highlands
5th February 1994

16 NEWCASTLE

In early 1998 the Newcastle Legal Centre, on behalf of the families and relatives of missing persons in the Hunter Region, wrote to the police minister, Paul Whelan, seeking a review of several unsolved disappearances over the past twenty years. As commander of the newly established Crime Agencies, I was asked to meet representatives of the legal centre to hear what they had to say. Their case was persuasive and I agreed to an investigation.

Led by Detective Superintendent Ron Smith, Commander of the Homicide and Serial Violent Crime Agency, Crime Agencies, and Detective Inspector Wayne Gordon as his deputy, Strike Force Fenwick comprised detectives drawn from Crime Agencies and from around Newcastle. Gordon was familiar with some of the cases, having played a key role in an investigation, begun a year earlier by Crime Agencies, into a number of missing persons from the Newcastle area and elsewhere. Based at Newcastle Police Station, Fenwick began work on 23 March with 38 investigators and analysts.

The legal centre had referred specifically to the disappearance of ten young people, and these ten cases, occurring between 1978 and 1993, became the focus of Strike Force Fenwick.

As with the backpacker inquiry, existing police records on the cases under investigation had to be re-entered and original documents scanned into a new information management system. Some exhibits were found to be missing, while others had been destroyed because of the age of the case.

News of the strike force aroused intense community interest, especially in the Newcastle area, and over the next few months information poured in. Reports of unpleasant odours, grave-like disturbances of the ground and suspicious activities by unidentified persons on or around the dates when people disappeared suggested the existence of as many as 200 different clandestine grave sites around the Hunter Region. One hundred and thirty locations were visited by detectives, and 51 sites were investigated by a range of specialists including forensic anthropologists, forensic pathologists, botanists, geologists, dog handlers, divers and sub-surface search experts equipped with ground-penetrating radar.

Blood samples were taken from the families of the missing persons for DNA profiling, and inquiries were made with social security, Medicare, immigration, banks, law enforcement and any other state and commonwealth agencies likely to have had dealings with the missing persons if they were still alive.

Original witnesses were reinterviewed, new witnesses found, and other people of interest interviewed.

Eventually the strike force was able to draw up a list of 40 potential suspects. Some were identified from a review of police records. Many had criminal records for violent crimes such as murder and sexual assault, or had been investigated for these crimes and had links to the Hunter Region. Others were considered to have shown an 'obsession' with the missing persons, or to have made comments implying an intimate knowledge of the disappearances, while others attracted attention simply because of their 'suspicious behaviour'. Among the list of potential suspects was Ivan Milat.

Over four months from late 1978 to early 1979, Leanne Beth Goodall, Robyn Elizabeth Hickie and Amanda Therese Robinson all went missing from the Newcastle area. Ivan was a person of interest in the disappearances of all three.

By the time the strike force began its reinvestigation, there was already widespread media speculation linking Ivan Milat to the disappearances of hitchhikers in the Hunter during the 1970s and 1980s. From time to time people had reported sightings of Ivan in the area. In June 2001, after reviewing the holdings of Task Force Air, Fenwick investigators interviewed Ivan at the Supermax in Goulburn gaol. He denied any knowledge of or involvement in the disappearances of Goodall, Hickie or Robinson.

In 2002, having taken its inquiries into the three disappearances as far as it could, Fenwick presented its findings to the New South Wales state coroner, John Abernethy. Because of the similarities between the cases, Abernethy conducted a joint inquest into the disappearances. Around 160 witnesses were called.

Leanne Goodall was twenty years old and living at North Lambton when she disappeared on 30 December 1978. An investigation at the time of her disappearance established that she was last seen by her brother Warren and a family friend, boarding a Newcastle train at Muswellbrook railway station on the afternoon of Saturday, 30 December 1978. However, Fenwick discovered that Leanne arrived in Newcastle late that afternoon and that she was seen at about 4 p.m. by a former school friend, Kathryn Pearson, who spoke to her outside the Star Hotel in King Street. Leanne had left some belongings behind the counter of the hotel. The hotel had been quite crowded that afternoon and among the patrons who would have seen Leanne were Pearson's partner at the time and his mate, both of whom had died before the coroner's inquiry. A recreational drinker and smoker of cannabis, Leanne was known to hitchhike alone. 'She came and went like a bird,' was how her mother described her, but the evidence was that 'Goodall would go to great lengths to contact her family when she was away.'

Robyn Hickie was eighteen years old when, on 7 April 1979, she left her home in Belmont to meet some friends at the Belmont Hotel. She did not arrive at the hotel and has not been seen since.

Amanda Robinson was just fourteen and lived in Swansea. On 20 April 1979—thirteen days after Robyn Hickie disappeared—Amanda went to a school dance with friends. Around midnight, she phoned her stepfather and told him she was about to catch a bus home. Amanda caught her bus and was later seen walking along a road in Swansea towards her home. She did not arrive.

The coroner found that his inquiry had been significantly hampered by the passage of time since the three went missing, and by the fact that several witnesses were now dead or otherwise unable to give evidence. He was also scathing of the original investigations, particularly those into the disappearances of Robyn and Amanda, noting a lack of adequate record-keeping; the failure to locate original documents, including statements, running sheets, notebooks, exhibits and other records; the failure to obtain written and/or signed statements, particularly from persons of interest and people who purported to provide alibi evidence for persons of interest; the failure to follow up important leads; and the failure of police to comply with their obligation to report these matters to the coroner. Abernethy observed that after Leanne's disappearance was reported to Newcastle Police on 7 September 1979:

> Amazingly, no formal, detailed investigation was undertaken by the New South Wales Police Force into the disappearance of Leanne Beth Goodall. Leanne was merely listed as a 'missing person' and only the most cursory inquiries into her disappearance were made by police . . . no Newcastle police officer appears to have made any attempt to link Leanne's disappearance with the disappearance of Robyn Hickie and Amanda Robinson a matter of four months later . . . The overall failure of the NSW Police Force and its personnel to investigate the disappearance of Leanne Beth Goodall as a likely homicide must also be heavily criticised. This criticism is aimed at all relevant Newcastle police officers, together with personnel of the Missing Persons Bureau over the years.

It was, the coroner concluded, a 'parlous initial investigation'.

Ivan was interviewed by police and called as a witness at the Robinson, Hickie and Goodall inquest. Fenwick had been unable to account for Ivan's movements on the days each of the three disappeared, although this was not surprising given the disappearances had occurred around twenty years earlier. At the inquest Ivan again denied any knowledge of or involvement in the disappearance of the girls. He did concede that he had worked and stayed in and around the Hunter Region at or about the time the three disappeared, and that in the 1980s he had owned numerous weapons. Other evidence given by Ivan was contradicted by various witnesses, causing the coroner to observe:

> Given the past history of Ivan Milat, his known propensity for violence, his picking up of hitchhikers going back to . . . at least 1971, his possession of a large number of firearms, and other weapons, and his connection with the Hunter Region both in a work and social setting make Ivan Milat a major person of interest in relation to the missing girls, perhaps more so Leanne Goodall than Robyn Hickie or Amanda Robinson.

On 5 July 2002, after a lengthy inquest, Abernethy handed down identical findings for Robyn Hickie, Amanda Robinson and Leanne Goodall, stating that each was 'deceased despite the fact that her body has never been located'.

A fourth disappearance in the Hunter Region investigated by Strike Force Fenwick was that of 24-year-old Debbie Rae Pritchard, who was living at Merewether, a suburb of Newcastle, when she was reported missing in the early hours of

7 March 1982. The previous evening, Debbie had completed her shift as a barmaid at the Federal Hotel in Hamilton, returned home, drunk some wine and then gone to a party in Merewether with her female housemates. After leaving the party she visited a number of nightclubs in the Newcastle CBD. Sometime after midnight Debbie spoke to the doorman at the Palais Royale dance hall in Hunter Street, telling him she had argued with her boyfriend, and asking him about the cost of a taxi fare to the boyfriend's home in Whitebridge. Soon afterwards Debbie was seen crossing Hunter Street in the company of a 'dark-skinned, well-built man'. Both got into a taxi. She was not seen again.

An investigation into Debbie's disappearance—which was regarded as suspicious—began the next day at Newcastle Police Station. A pair of men's Wrangler trousers, a pair of brown Windsor Smith shoes and a denim skirt were quickly found underneath the Stockton Bridge, Kooragang Island. The skirt belonged to Debbie. A search of the area failed to find any more clothing or anything else that could be linked to Debbie's disappearance. While Newcastle Police soon concluded that Debbie had been murdered, for the next ten years she was recorded only as a missing person.

On 11 May 1992, a road crew widening and excavating Coxs Lane, Fullerton Cove, for the construction of a small bridge, found skeletal remains, including an upper and lower jaw. Dental records identified the remains as being those of Debbie. The discovery sparked a murder investigation. The condition of the remains made it impossible to determine the exact cause of death, but underwear found with the remains had been slashed. Four years earlier, a bone found nearby had been handed in to police. An inquest held into Debbie's death by the Newcastle coroner in April 1993 resulted in an open finding. It found the last confirmed sighting of Debbie was by a taxidriver named Garry John Renshaw.

Five years later, Strike Force Fenwick reopened the murder investigation. Again, it uncovered serious flaws and omissions in the initial investigation, and the loss or disposal of crucial evidence. The bone handed in to Stockton Police in 1989 and later disposed of as a cow's bone was now believed to have been Debbie's right femur. Fenwick also identified significant avenues of inquiry that had not been pursued during any previous investigation.

In 2003 Fenwick's findings convinced the state coroner, John Abernethy, to conduct a second inquest into Debbie's disappearance. The findings of the coronial inquest a decade earlier were quashed. Once again, the coroner was scathing of the original police investigations:

> [M]y heart goes out to this family [the Pritchard family] who have remained so dignified in the face of a somewhat insensitive bureaucracy [the New South Wales Police] which has not handled the most serious case of homicide of its daughter particularly well, but even in my witness box has not been prepared to admit its failings . . . At the time in Newcastle [the 1970s through to the 1990s] there appears to have been a criminal investigation system which was below acceptable standards inherent in the investigation of homicides.

Even the Newcastle Coroner's Court could not escape Abernethy's wrath. Searches by both Fenwick and the coroner had been unable to find either taped recordings or typed transcripts of the 1993 inquest into Debbie's murder. The tapes had apparently been recorded over, causing Abernethy to order that in future, 'transcripts must be obtained and placed with the papers on all "open finding" cases, and a range of other cases'.

The taxidriver, Garry Renshaw, told the 2003 inquest that on 7 March 1984 he had driven Debbie and a male passenger to a cul-de-sac in Whitebridge where Pritchard's boyfriend lived. After Debbie and her companion left the taxi, Renshaw drove off but, based on what he called 'a hunch that something was wrong, that something wasn't right', he returned to the cul-de-sac, but saw no one.

Twenty-two-year-old Maurice Joseph Marsland, a sex offender serving a prison sentence of three and a half years for burglary, had escaped from Cessnock gaol about fifteen hours before Debbie disappeared, and matched the description of the man who had shared a taxi with her to Lonus Avenue. Seven weeks after his escape, Marsland was arrested in Cairns, Queensland, for robbery and assaulting a police officer. Newcastle detectives travelled to Cairns and interviewed Marsland, who claimed to have an alibi for the night Debbie vanished: he was in Sydney. At the same time Marsland admitted to stealing a yellow station wagon after his escape. The station wagon had been found on 21 March by police in Tamworth. When the owner picked up his car he found two ticket stubs for a concert at Newcastle's Civic Theatre on 6 March in the glove box, and a blood stain on the front seat. No forensic tests were done on the car. A pair of men's Wrangler trousers and a pair of brown Windsor Smith shoes that had been in the car were missing.

Despite Marsland's admission that he had stolen the wagon, its link to Debbie (the owner's missing shoes and jeans were found with Debbie's skirt the day after her disappearance), Marsland's resemblance to the man who had shared a taxi with her (Marsland, a Torres Strait Islander, was dark-skinned and powerfully built), and the stubs for the Newcastle concert on the night Debbie disappeared, the police accepted Marsland's alibi. The second investigation, which was launched after the discovery of Debbie's remains in 1992, ignored Marsland and went down a 'tunnel' by chasing the taxidriver Garry Renshaw as the killer. Renshaw remained a suspect after the 1993 inquest.

Evidence was given to the 2003 inquest that Marsland's alibi had never been adequately tested. After his arrest in Cairns, Marsland spent a little time in gaol before emerging in Sydney in the mid-1980s, where he robbed and raped women in the city's eastern and inner western suburbs. In 1986 Marsland was arrested and charged with raping four women in the eastern suburbs. Inexplicably, he was given bail, which was continued even after he was committed for trial.

In late October 1987, Marsland, then unemployed and living at Summer Hill, was again arrested and charged with two counts of sexual assault, two of assault and robbery, two of breaking and entering with intent, and one of entering a building with intent to commit a crime. This time bail was refused. Two weeks before his arrest Marsland, wearing a mask, had broken into a house at Summer Hill, threatened the two inhabitants with a knife, assaulted and robbed the man of $5000 and then raped the man's partner several times. A week later he had broken into another Summer Hill house and raped a woman after robbing her of $30.

In May 1990 Marsland was gaoled for twelve years. Six years later Marsland, aged 35, was stabbed to death in Goulburn gaol, apparently as part of a gaol-yard dispute. Three days later, convicted murderers Mark Morris and Jason Richards and armed robber Raymond Carrion were charged with his murder. On 24 February 1998, Morris pleaded guilty in the Supreme Court to attempting to persuade a witness to give false evidence and was sentenced to 21 months' gaol. The murder charges against all three were dropped, due to a lack of evidence.

Five months later Carrion was stabbed several times in the chest and head with a 'shiv' (a gaol-fashioned knife) while in the shower block of Wing 12 at Long Bay gaol. Long-term inmates Peter Buchanan, Trevor Thomas and Justin Smith were charged with the murder. Again, it was believed to be the result of a gaol dispute. All three were committed for trial for murdering Carrion; in 2004 all charges were dropped because of difficulties with the evidence.

Fenwick presented a compelling case against Marsland to the 2003 inquest. It included his long criminal record for sexual assaults and other serious crimes; the timing of his escape from gaol; the fact that he had given a false alibi (Marsland had been seen in the Newcastle area on the night of the disappearance); his habit of going to local nightclubs, including the Palais Royale; statements by several witnesses who had seen Debbie near the Palais Royale with a man closely fitting Marsland's description; evidence linking soil samples taken from Pritchard's skirt with Whitebridge, where she left the taxi with a man resembling Marsland; the fact that Debbie's underwear had been cut with a knife, Marsland's weapon of choice; and the fact that fifteen months before Debbie's abduction Marsland had been charged but acquitted of raping a woman he had met at the Palais Royale.

The coroner, John Abernethy, agreed with the strike force, finding that 'Debbie Rae Pritchard on 7 March 1982 at or near Newcastle, was murdered by a person since deceased'—that person being Maurice Joseph Marsland. He formally cleared Garry Renshaw of any connection with Debbie's murder.

Debbie's sister-in-law, Val Pritchard, described the findings as an 'opportunity of bringing this to a closure . . . We firmly believe that Debbie's murder should have been concluded in 1982 when it was committed. We've waited 21 years.'

Commenting on the series of inquests into the deaths of Robyn Hickie, Amanda Robinson, Leanne Goodall and Debbie Rae Pritchard, the coroner observed: 'The strike force [Fenwick] is in my view something of a showpiece. It shows what can be done where the resources are provided. My hope is that from it, many of the innovations of the strike force will be utilised in other major investigations, particularly of homicides and other critical incidents.' In his correspondence to the police commissioner, Ken Moroney, Abernethy recommended:

> That this case and my comments be analysed by those responsible for the training of criminal investigators and of leaders of teams of criminal investigators, with a view to ascertaining whether it is appropriate to utilise it as a teaching tool.
>
> That NSW Police implements the recommendations made in the Hickie, Robinson and Goodall Inquests to the extent that they have not been implemented.

> That the NSW Police Homicide Squad be adequately resourced on a 'teams' basis with each team to be led by an experienced investigator, preferably a Commissioned Officer with proven Homicide experience; that the Squad contains a team deployed to deal solely with unsolved Homicides; that the State Coroner's Support Section contain Homicide Squad members in order to ensure the proper presentation of unsolved Homicides to the State Coroner.

The coroner also recommended that 'the NSW Police formally commends the leadership and membership of Strike Force Fenwick for the exemplary manner in which it conducted a re-investigation into all relevant matters'.

In February 2004 Moroney announced the creation of a unit dedicated solely to the investigation of unsolved historical homicides—four years after the Police Executive had argued against the establishment of such a unit. In 2006 *The Sun-Herald* reported that, contrary to promises Moroney had given to the families of victims, detectives were still being diverted from unsolved historical homicides to current cases. It took another two years for the 'teams' recommended by the coroner to be established within the Homicide Squad to pursue cold case reviews.

Suspicions that Ivan Milat was involved with at least three of the Newcastle disappearances did not end with Ivan's denials. Yet for all its efforts, Strike Force Fenwick could find no evidence linking Ivan to the disappearances of Robyn Hickie, Amanda Robinson or Leanne Goodall. At the time the three went missing, Ivan was living with his then partner and future wife, Karen. Ivan's abductions and attempted abductions appear to have occurred when he was not in what he considered to be a stable and controlling situation with a woman. Ivan's violent history will always make him a person of interest but, unless new evidence comes to light, it is not possible to implicate him in the Newcastle disappearances.

17
COLD CASES REOPENED

The achievements of Task Force Air and Strike Force Fenwick were catalysts for the reinvestigation of unsolved murders in New South Wales. Of the 400 unsolved homicides identified by the cold case unit, around 100 were eventually given priority. As the years passed, reopening or even reviewing these cases had become increasingly difficult due to the loss or destruction of operational records and other irreplaceable documents and exhibits. The loss of this material denied investigators the opportunity to take advantage of new technologies and investigative methods in areas such as blood and DNA analysis, fingerprint comparison and ballistics. But, as the following chapter shows, where exhibits had survived, modern technology could sometimes be used to extract vital new information that could both transform and energise an investigation.

Around 1 a.m. on Saturday, 18 February 1984, 24-year-old Johanne Coral Hatty from Victoria finished her shift in the restaurant at Sydney's Regent Hotel, where she worked as the assistant manager. It was the last time Johanne was seen alive. The next morning police received a call from two people who had found the body of a woman at Spains Lookout at Neutral Bay, on the harbour's north shore. Hearing the police car arrive, Johanne's partner went to the lookout across the road from the flat they shared and identified her body. She was lying face-up on a narrow rock ledge. Her car was parked nearby. The evidence suggested that Johanne had been attacked after leaving her car and taken to Spains Lookout, where she was bashed, sexually abused and strangled. It appeared her clothes had been removed during the attack, and put back on after her death.

Swabs taken from Johanne's body showed the presence of semen, but at that time DNA testing did not exist and the police inquiry came to a halt. Five years later police asked the Division of Analytical Laboratories to re-examine the exhibits, but the technology available did not allow extraction of sufficient material for DNA testing. In May 2004 the police again asked for the exhibits to be re-examined. This time the examiners were able to produce 'a very clear complete profile'.

David Graham Fleming, 31 years old at the time of Johanne's murder, had been one of a number of suspects in the original 1984 police investigation. Fleming had recently moved to Sydney and was living in a boarding house about 700 metres from the reserve where Johanne's body was found. Three months after Johanne's murder, Fleming was charged over the alleged bashing and robbery of a 26-year-old woman.

He had taken the Waterloo woman back to the boarding house where he lived, attacked her with a hockey stick and robbed her of $100, threatening to kill her if she told police. Released on bail, Fleming absconded. A warrant was issued for his arrest.

Fleming was born in Mackay, Queensland, and grew up in Cairns. He had two daughters and one son from various relationships in Queensland. In 1971 he was diagnosed as having a personality disorder and reactive depression following a car accident. A year later he was rediagnosed as having a personality disorder and suffering a depressive illness. In 1974 he was admitted to Cairns Hospital after being shot in the left leg. The same year Fleming's parents expressed concerns about his violent behaviour at home and he was admitted to hospital for a drug overdose. In 1975 he was admitted to Cairns Hospital for the amputation of a finger on his right hand. The next year he was convicted and sentenced to eight years' gaol for rape. After his release from gaol, Fleming moved to Sydney.

Having fled Sydney in 1984, where he was still wanted for skipping bail, Fleming returned to Queensland. Again he was in and out of hospital, having his left leg removed at the knee and being treated after an overdose of barbiturates and narcotics. About eight months after Johanne Hatty's murder, Fleming met the woman who became his wife.

In 2004 Fleming, by then a wheelchair-bound invalid pensioner, was living at Willatook in south-west Victoria. The New South Wales Unsolved Homicide Unit discussed with the Victoria Police the possible surveillance of Fleming, but the remoteness of the house made it impracticable. Another strategy was needed. Sergeant Vick of the Victoria Police knew Fleming as the result of a complaint, twelve months earlier, about a drover and Fleming's subsequent allegation that the police had been rude to him. Sergeant Vick visited Fleming at home and asked him to sketch the location where he had seen the drover. While making the sketch, Fleming dribbled onto the paper. The sketch was sent to the Division of Analytical Laboratories, which recovered a DNA profile that matched a partial profile developed from swabs taken from Johanne's body. The partial profile could be expected to occur in one in 52,000 people in the general population. On 19 January 2005 Fleming was arrested and extradited to New South Wales.

In Sydney police took a cheek swab from Fleming, which matched the DNA profile from the sketch and the DNA profile obtained from swabs taken from Johanne's body in 1984. There was a one in 8.6 billion probability that anyone else in the general population shared that profile. Fleming insisted he had been in Queensland on the day of Johanne's murder, and claimed that two soiled condoms had disappeared from his room in 1984. The police might have taken them, he suggested, in order to plant his DNA.

On 26 April 2007 it took the Supreme Court jury only two hours to find 54-year-old Fleming guilty of Johanne's murder 23 years earlier. DNA evidence was central to the prosecution case. Sentencing Fleming to 21 years' gaol, Justice Studdert said of the murder: 'It is the crime of a predator who took advantage, under cover of darkness, of a vulnerable and unsuspecting young woman . . . A high degree of violence was employed and the crime was motivated by the desire for sexual gratification.'

In June 1998 I established Strike Force Lincoln to draw together several strike forces investigating the unsolved killings of three gay men in Sydney and Wollongong. The strike force, led by Detective Inspector Paul Mayger, was also to identify and investigate any similar unsolved murders. On 29 December 1997, 36-year-old Trevor John Parkin, a known sex offender, was murdered in his inner Sydney Glebe unit. He had been bashed to death and his body mutilated. Seven months later, on the afternoon of 12 June 1998, 59-year-old David John O'Hearn, a shopkeeper of Albion Park in the Wollongong metropolitan area, was murdered in his home. His head had been smashed in with a wine decanter and severed from his body, and he had been partially disembowelled. One of his hands had been cut off and used to draw satanic pictures on the living room walls. Knives used to dismember the body were found on the floor. Fourteen days later, on 26 June, the body of 63-year-old Francis Neville 'Frank' Arkell, a former member of the New South Wales Parliament and former Lord Mayor of Wollongong, was found dead at his Wollongong home. His head had been smashed in with a bedside lamp and the lamp cord had been wrapped around his neck. Tie pins had been stuck in Arkell's eyes and cheeks. Both O'Hearn and Arkell were gay and there were rumours they had been involved in paedophile activities.

Nineteen-year-old Mark Mala Valera, also known as Van Krevel, surrendered himself to the Wollongong Police three months after Arkell's murder. He admitted to killing both O'Hearn and Arkell. Valera told police he did not know O'Hearn, but on the day of the killing he just wanted to kill someone and the choice of O'Hearn's house was 'just random'. He described Arkell as 'a very, very horrible man' because of 'all the nasty things he has done to kids'. He had made up his mind to kill Arkell and had gone to his home on the pretext of being gay and needing somewhere to live. Valera pleaded not guilty to murder but guilty to manslaughter. His pleas were not accepted and the murder trial proceeded in mid-2000. After being found guilty of both murders, Valera was gaoled for life for each one.

On 22 January 1999, while Valera was awaiting his committal hearing, Christopher Andrew Robinson was arrested and charged with murdering Parkin. Robinson, who had been seventeen years old when he killed Parkin, pleaded guilty to the murder. In the Supreme Court on 19 October 2000, Justice Adams sentenced him to 45 years' gaol. Robinson claimed to have killed Parkin because of unwanted homosexual advances, but Justice Adams rejected this explanation. Robinson, who had previously mutilated a cat and burnt another, had calmly confessed to a friend, saying 'killing someone is liberating'.

In the course of solving the murders of O'Hearn, Arkell and Parkin, Strike Force Lincoln identified several characteristics reminiscent of the ten-year-old unsolved murder of Leo Press. Within Strike Force Lincoln, the Press investigation was led by Detective Sergeant Stuart Wilkins, with whom I had worked years earlier on Task Force Air, and who had played a significant role in the investigation of the attempted abduction of Paul Onions by Ivan Milat.

In the early hours of Saturday, 13 February 1988, Kenneth Press arrived at the home he jointly owned with his brother Leo at Harbord in Sydney's northern beaches, after completing a shift at their Chatswood bakery. He opened the front door to find 62-year-old Leo lying in the hallway in a pool of blood, the result of multiple head wounds—a post-mortem examination found massive fractures to the skull caused by seven separate blows. A stonemason's mallet, which belonged to Leo and was usually kept in his toolbox, was lying beside the body. There were more blood stains in his upstairs bedroom. Leo was taken by ambulance to Royal North Shore Hospital, where he died at 9 a.m. that morning.

A forensic examination of the crime scene revealed only two clues to the identity of the killer: two unidentified fingerprints on two of four empty or partially drunk beer cans in the upstairs office of the house, and several cigarette butts. Neither Leo nor Kenneth drank alcohol or smoked. A check of police records failed to find a match for the fingerprints.

Detectives soon established that Leo was an active homosexual who had casual relationships with numerous young men in the Manly, Chatswood, Ryde and Kings Cross areas where the brothers' bakery business operated. A former employee told police that Leo would bring young men to the bakery and take them to the basement, where he had sex with them and gave them 'gifts' of money. Leo was also in the habit of going out around midnight and driving around in an attempt to pick up young male hitchhikers. On occasions he would bring a man home for sex before giving him cash. Leo was widely known to keep large amounts of cash and had been the victim of several armed robberies in the few years before his murder. His homosexual activities also made him a target for extortion. Police investigating his murder believed it was either a result of his homosexual activities, or the result of a robbery gone wrong, but without new leads the investigation came to a halt, and by the end of 1988 it was officially wound up.

In the Press case it was not new technology that provided a lead, but the re-examination of existing evidence and a bit of luck. Analysis of the fingerprints found on beer cans at the scene of Leo Press's murder identified these as belonging to Barrie Alan Hodge, who was eighteen years old at the time of the murder and had only minor convictions as a juvenile. Juvenile records had not been checked when the fingerprints on the beer cans were originally compared with those on the police database. However, in the ten years since the killing, Hodge had been convicted of several minor offences, including being in a stolen vehicle and drink driving, as a result of which his fingerprints were now on record. This was the breakthrough the investigators needed.

On 9 October 1998, based on the fingerprint identification, Hodge was charged with the murder of Leo Press. Two months later, following committal proceedings in the Manly Local Court, the magistrate dismissed the charge, essentially on the basis that, by themselves, the fingerprints were not sufficient to connect Hodge to the murder. Police immediately resumed their investigation. A flurry of newspaper coverage followed, which was seen by Hodge's former girlfriend, who was then living in England. She contacted New South Wales Police and, when spoken to by the Homicide Squad, said that on the night of 12 February 1988 she and Hodge had gone to a party at a friend's house in Chatswood, and that afterwards Hodge had dropped her at her home at Manly. A few hours later, in the early hours of the morning of 13 February, Hodge had returned to her house shaking and crying, with blood on his clothes. He told her he thought he had killed someone.

During several lengthy phone calls to England, a detailed statement was obtained by police.

The information provided by the former girlfriend led detectives to another friend, who said that on leaving his girlfriend's residence, Hodge had caught a taxi to his home at Beacon Hill, where he changed his clothes before returning to the friend's house in Chatswood where the party had been held. Hodge told his friend that while hitchhiking home from his girlfriend's place, he had met a man who invited him to his house for a few beers. Hodge drank a few beers and fell asleep, but woke suddenly to find the man grabbing him 'in a sexual sort of way'. Hodge told his friend he had hit the man and was worried that he had killed him.

Inquiries led to a third friend who said that a few weeks after the murder of Leo Press, he had seen Hodge distressed and crying at a party. When asked what the matter was, Hodge said that he had gone to a man's place to have a couple of beers and had then 'crashed out'. The man had fondled him while he was asleep and Hodge had hit him and left the house. Hodge claimed not to know whether he had hurt the man badly or not.

On 22 January 1999, just five weeks after the dismissal of the charge at Manly Court, Hodge was rearrested. When interviewed by police, he confirmed the stories told by his friends: he had gone to a party at Chatswood on the night of Friday, 12 February, where he had drunk some beer and inhaled a line of what he believed to be speed or amphetamines. After getting a lift with a friend to Manly, he dropped off his then girlfriend at her home, intending to hitch a ride to his home in Beacon Hill. As he walked along the road trying to thumb a lift, a male driver stopped and offered him a lift, which Hodge accepted. The man then invited Hodge back to his house at Harbord. Hodge said he couldn't remember arriving at Leo's house or getting out of the car, but remembered being in the house, drinking beer and smoking cigarettes. Hodge said he was drunk, 'crashed out' on a bed and awoke to find Leo groping him. He lashed out and went downstairs. When Leo approached him again, Hodge picked up the mallet and hit him. According to Hodge, the next thing he remembered was being outside the house, disposing of the keys, hailing a taxi and going to his girlfriend's place, where he told her he thought he had killed somebody. Following the interview Hodge was, for the second time, charged with the murder of Press.

Hodge's trial for murder began in the Supreme Court on 4 July 2000. He pleaded not guilty to murder, but guilty to manslaughter. While not disputing the substance of the Crown case, he relied on the defence that he was provoked into his actions by an unwanted homosexual approach by Press. Hodge's defence was rejected by the jury, which found him guilty of murder. While agreeing with the verdict, Justice John Dunford said the case was also 'a tragedy for the prisoner and for his family'.

Acknowledging what he called 'the well-known trait of the Australian character not to "dob" on another person', Justice Dunford said he was 'shocked and amazed that none of the persons to whom the accused confided that he believed he had killed someone reported such matters to the police'.

Dunford noted that at the time of the killing Hodge was eighteen years old, but that he was now almost 31 years old, and that he had generally been in regular employment, was married and running two businesses with his wife, and had a two-year-old son, with another child on the way. All the referees spoke of Hodge's non-aggressive nature, trustworthiness and devotion to his wife and child. Dunford said that he considered the killing to have been unpremeditated and out of character. He also considered what he called the 'staleness' of the case. Given all the circumstances, he considered 'rehabilitation is hardly an issue'. What he did consider relevant was that Hodge 'was a young man when the offence was committed and since then has built a life for himself which must now be disrupted many years later whilst he serves his sentence'. Taking all these factors into account, Dunford sentenced Hodge to fifteen years' gaol with a non-parole period of seven years for the murder of Press.

For Strike Force Lincoln it was a success rate of four out of four, one of which had resulted from a cold case review. It was a great result for Detective Inspector Paul Mayger, leader of the strike force, and his team.

■ ■ ■

Stacey Lee Kirk was a sixteen-year-old schoolgirl when she was last seen, around 9.30 p.m. on 16 February 1984, walking away from the shooting gallery in Side Show Alley towards the toilets at the Maitland Show. Two days later her body was found under a tarpaulin behind the toilet block. Stacey's jeans were around her knees, her black T-shirt was pulled up and a pair of men's floral underpants were tied around her neck. She had been sexually assaulted before being strangled. There were numerous traces of another person's blood on her body. Swabs were also obtained as a result of the sexual assault.

The investigation had been conducted by local detectives. From the outset the case was difficult because of the nomadic lifestyle of show workers, but within weeks four were identified as suspects. All four were known as 'sniffers' and 'prodders', show people who sought 'sexual favours [from young girls] for free rides on the amusement machines'. One of the four was 25-year-old Richard Stevens. Interviewed by police, Stevens denied any involvement in or knowledge of the murder, and gave an alibi for the night it occurred. While it was true that Stevens had been treated for a lacerated wrist at the Mater Hospital in Newcastle earlier that day, his claim not to have been at the show in the evening did not hold up: there were several 'possible sightings' of him at the showground around the time Stacey disappeared.

To the police, Stevens was a prime suspect, but they had no evidence to charge him with any criminal offence. Blood tests were carried out on a number of suspects, including Stevens, but they failed to detect any link with the blood found on Stacey's body.

In April 1988 a three-day inquest was held into Stacey's death at Maitland Coroners Court. Assisting the Coroner, Mr Stent, was Sergeant Bell, who told the hearing: 'It has become patently obvious . . . that there is a great amount of information that witnesses who have been called to this hearing are aware of and has not been disclosed to this Court . . . There is little doubt . . . that there are witnesses who have given evidence in this Court who have either been involved or are aware of persons who have committed this crime, but are not prepared to disclose it to Your Worship.' The coroner agreed, finding that the evidence contained a number of inconsistencies, particularly:

> in relation to evidence given throughout the hearing by members of whom I shall call showmen. I am left with a distinct impression that not all witnesses have been entirely truthful. My inescapable conclusion would be that not everyone has co-operated fully and in some cases not at all with the police in their investigations . . . I am quite satisfied on the evidence before me and the conclusions one can draw from it that more than one person knows of the perpetration of this offence.

The coroner found that Stacey died of strangulation, but that there was no evidence to establish a prima facie case against any person.

Inquiries into the murder continued for another two years. In May 1990 Crime Stoppers sought information from the public about the murder, and a week later *The Daily Telegraph* published an article under the headline 'Murder at the local showground'. As a result of this publicity, police received information from someone who claimed to have heard Richard Stevens admit to his involvement in the murder. Police flew to Queensland, where they interviewed and obtained signed statements from brothers Tony and Mark Midgley, and from Mere Faith Marshall. Tony claimed that Stevens had told him about Stacey's murder the day before her body was found. According to Tony, Stevens had said Stacey 'was raped and thrown out of a caravan, thought to be unconscious and found there the next morning deceased, when she was moved behind the toilet block'. Mere, who said she was present during the conversation, corroborated Tony's version of events. Mark told police of a conversation he had with Stevens in a hotel five months after the murder, during which Stevens admitted to killing Stacey.

A year later, on 1 May 1991, after police had done everything they could to corroborate the information provided by the Midgleys and Marshall, Stevens was arrested in Dubbo and charged with Stacey's murder. Six months later, Stevens' committal hearing began at the Glebe Coroners Court before the state coroner, Mr Waller. By this time, however, Tony and Mark Midgley and Mere Marshall had changed their stories, either refusing to give evidence or retracting the information they had previously given. Each claimed that giving their evidence might make them liable to criminal charges themselves. As a result, the charge against Stevens was dismissed. In his findings, the coroner was scathing of the witnesses' 'memory lapses', and voiced his suspicion that there had been gross tampering with the witnesses by people connected with the defendant.

Throughout the 1990s, Stacey Kirk's murder remained a controversial case, with various individuals accused of the murder, and police accused of corruption and of having botched the investigation. Among other things, it was alleged that the tarpaulin that covered Stacey's body had not been forensically examined, and that samples that could have been subjected to DNA profiling, when that technology became available, had been tampered with.

In 1995 the investigation was reviewed, together with the evidence given by witnesses to the 1991 coroner's inquest. The review found no evidence of corruption by police and no evidence that the investigation had been botched. A prisoner who admitted to another prisoner that he had murdered Stacey was found to have fabricated the story and was eliminated as a suspect. No new leads were uncovered. In 1997 the Homicide and Serial Violent Crime Agency undertook another review of the investigation, with the same results. It found that the investigation had been thorough and that all complaints and allegations had been properly examined.

In 1998 the results of the review were returned to Newcastle. After some time the case was once again reopened when Strike Force Shylock was established under Detective Senior Sergeant Alex Pollock. Traditional testing in the 1980s to produce blood type had failed. This time the focus would be on newer technology: DNA analysis and comparison. DNA was extracted from seminal fluid found in Stacey's body. Traces of DNA were also found on the men's floral underpants that had been used to strangle Stacy. Samples were covertly obtained from several suspects, some of whom had previously been subjected to blood testing. DNA samples once again eliminated them, but one person who hadn't been tested was Ian Raymond Sargent, one of the original suspects, by now a married interstate truck driver living near Picton, 80 kilometres south-west of Sydney. On 21 February 2002, as the police looked for him, Sargent was killed when his vehicle left the Pacific Highway near Grafton, about 630 kilometres north of Sydney, and hit a tree. Police requested DNA tests of blood samples taken during his post-mortem. They matched.

In August 2003 the coroner, Mr Abernethy, held the third inquest into the death of Stacey Kirk. He found that DNA obtained from Sargent's body after his death conclusively linked him to Stacey's rape and strangulation. 'The prospects of the DNA [found in Kirk's body] belonging to a person other than Sargent are fewer than one in 10 billion,' he said. Traces of Sargent's DNA were also found on the men's floral underpants that had been used to strangle Kirk. Police told the coroner that several witnesses had named Sargent, at that time a nineteen-year-old sideshow worker, as trying 'to get onto' Kirk. The pair had been seen walking together before she disappeared. Sargent himself had given evidence at the 1988 inquest and had been reinterviewed by police conducting the 1995 review. On each occasion he told the same story: he was working at the Maitland Show with his girlfriend and saw Stacey Kirk, but knew nothing about her murder.

Mr Abernethy said the investigation had been hampered by the 'clannish' culture of showmen and show workers, who were 'a difficult breed of suspects'. Despite rumour and innuendo, there was no evidence linking anyone other than Sargent to Stacey's murder, nor was there any evidence of police corruption at any stage of the inquiry. Mr Abernethy said he hoped the inquest would finalise the matter for Stacey's parents, her extended family and their community.

■ ■ ■

Nine-year-old Samantha Therese Knight's mother, Tess, arrived at the family home in Bondi about 7 p.m. on 19 August 1986 after a day at work to discover her daughter missing. There was evidence that Samantha had come home after school, changed her clothes and left. Tess reported the disappearance to local police, who quickly established that Samantha had been seen by a number of people between 4.30 p.m. and 6.45 p.m. wandering along Bondi Road, accompanied by a man. Samantha was never seen again.

From time to time fragments of information about Samantha were followed up by police, and each year, on the anniversary of Samantha's disappearance, a story was printed in the local newspaper, but essentially the case lay dormant until the arrest, ten years later, of convicted paedophile 46-year-old Michael Anthony Guider. Early in 1996 two seven-year-old girls complained that Guider had indecently assaulted them and taken nude photographs of them. Guider, who was then working as a gardener at the Royal North Shore Hospital, was arrested on 6 February. His workshed and later his house on Eastern Valley Way were searched, and thousands of 35 mm slides and indecent photographs of children were found and seized. Interviewed by police at Manly Police Station, Guider admitted to being a paedophile and spoke of his desire to photograph and fondle children. He was charged with several counts of indecent assault and related offences. As a result, Strike Force Jadite was formed to investigate Guider's paedophile activities dating back to the early 1980s.

Two months later Guider was again interviewed about the slides and photographs. He admitted to sexually assaulting many of the children in the pictures and identified some of them by name. He admitted having given many of them the drug Normison—which heroin users sometimes used to increase the effects of the narcotic—before assaulting them. Questioned about a scrapbook he owned of pictures and newspaper reports relating to the disappearance of Samantha Knight, Guider said he had met both Samantha and her mother, Tess, in the mid-1980s at the Manly home of a common friend whose child he sometimes babysat. The young girl was a schoolfriend of Samantha. He also claimed to have met Samantha's father. Guider said he had only met Samantha 'once or twice' and denied any knowledge of her disappearance, except for the information he had gathered from newspaper articles. He suggested Samantha might have been 'kidnapped by white slavers'.

Guider was then charged with 60 offences including indecent assault, administering a stupefying drug (Normison), and sexual intercourse without consent against eleven victims ranging in age from two to sixteen years between 1976 and 1995. In September 1996 Guider pleaded guilty to these charges. Before he was sentenced, Guider was again interviewed about Samantha Knight's disappearance at the Junee Correctional Centre by officers from Strike Force Jadite. He repeated his earlier story: he had first met Samantha and her mother at a picnic at Fairlight Beach and he had seen Samantha 'no more than three times', once at the picnic and a couple of times at the Manly house of a common friend, where he might have 'photographed Samantha'.

Guider said he could not remember talking much to Samantha, but recalled taking pictures of her in a 'green' top when they were 'laying down' and were 'playing dead', and that he had 'some older slides' of Samantha with a 'painted face' but that they weren't his; he had 'filtered' [stolen] them. Explaining his relationship with the Knight family, he said, 'I've never ever had Samantha Knight in a car for instance, she never ever entered a vehicle that I owned.'

Guider told police, 'They call me a paedophile now and I guess that's a paedophile in a truer sense as a lover of children; I have loved children as children, not as a sexual thing.' Guider was sentenced to a total of sixteen years' gaol.

The investigation into Samantha Knight's 'disappearance' went quiet for about eighteen months until May 1998, when Detective Sergeant Tuckerman of the Homicide and Serial Violent Crime Agency was told by an informant that Guider had pornographic pictures of young children hidden in a previously unknown storage facility. Strike Force Harrisville was formed to investigate these claims and Guider's activities between 1982 and 1986. Detective Sergeant Steve Leach of the Homicide and Serial Violent Crime Agency was put in charge. It was Leach who, as a member of Task Force Air, had physically arrested and interviewed Ivan Milat in 1994.

On 16 June police executed a search warrant on Guider's self-storage unit at Girraween, in Sydney's western suburbs. They discovered pictures and transparencies of children, including pictures of Samantha Knight with another young girl. The second girl was soon identified; she had been living at Manly at the time the picture was taken. Samantha and the other young girl were in the home of a third young girl who had also been abused.

Potential witnesses interviewed during earlier investigations were reinterviewed, as were prisoners who had spent time in gaol with Guider. Several confirmed that Guider had spoken frequently about his exploits with young children and had mentioned Samantha several times. His association with Samantha was much greater than he had admitted to police. Guider told one gaol inmate that the police had interviewed him over the murder, then said, 'I must have put too much Normison in her Coke and she wouldn't wake up.' Another inmate, with whom Guider had several conversations about the abuse of children, said that on one occasion he had been in his cell talking with Guider when something came up about Samantha Knight and Guider said, 'You know they'll never find her body . . . They'll never find her, I know they won't.' Later, Guider told the inmate that he had picked Samantha up about a block away from her house and bought her a soft drink and some lollies. He then drove her to an area and carried her to a cave where he left her. Guider said, 'I didn't do anything to her she just died, I didn't want her to die not then.' Guider said he took naked photographs of her in the cave. Talking about the police, Guider laughed and said, 'The police can't get me they don't know where to look, they can't touch me.' Guider had spoken with other inmates and with Corrective Services staff about Samantha, making claims that implicated him in Samantha's disappearance.

On 19 July 1999 officers from Strike Force Harrisville interviewed Guider. As before, he admitted having met Samantha a few times and having taken pictures of her when she and her family lived at Manly, but denied any knowledge of or involvement in her disappearance. As a result of the evidence found in the Girraween storage unit and information from witnesses, Guider was charged with three counts of indecent assault, five counts of sexual intercourse with a victim under the age of sixteen years and nine other offences involving acts of indecency or incitement to commit such acts. Guider was convicted of the charges and, on 11 February 2000, Justice O'Reilly sentenced Guider, describing him as a 'compulsive paedophile' and the attacks as 'appalling'. Justice O'Reilly noted that these further offences could have been dealt with when Guider was sentenced in 1996, and considered there was little point in increasing the original term.

With no solid case against Guider for Samantha's disappearance, the strike force sought the help of the New South Wales Crime Commission and Corrective Services, interviewing new witnesses and reinterviewing old ones, executing search warrants, examining photographs, undertaking electronic and physical surveillance and searching various locations where it was thought Samantha might be buried.

A year after Guider was sentenced in 1996, the strike force had sent the accumulated evidence to the deputy director of public prosecutions for advice. The strike force wanted Guider charged with murder. After lengthy consultations and further investigations, the advice came back: charge him. On 22 February 2001 Guider was charged with the murder of Samantha Knight on 19 August 1986. Fourteen months later he was committed for trial. On 23 August 2002 Guider pleaded guilty to the manslaughter of Samantha. Justice Woods noted that Guider claimed to be 'heavily into drugs' at the time Samantha was killed. Explaining her death, Guider said, 'I never physically harmed the girl, I intended to take her home, it's a very sad thing. It caught me by surprise that the drug [Normison] had any effect like that. Naturally I panicked, I went into a, I knew I was in trouble and the other side of me took over, the protective side which tried to find some way out of the problem, disposing of the evidence I guess.'

Guider claimed to have been involved in incestuous behaviour with his mother, who was by then deceased and who had suffered from paranoid schizophrenia, and to have been sexually abused while in primary school, in boys' homes and custodial institutions. He also said that he was involved in the sexual abuse of other boys and inmates while in homes and institutions. He didn't know his biological father, but the person he referred to as his father was an alcoholic with a gambling addiction who had been physically abusive towards him. Guider also claimed to have developed an alcohol and drug habit, using Normison, cough medicines, prescription pills, cannabis and LSD. Justice Wood gaoled Guider for seventeen years. He will be eligible for parole in June 2014.

One critical question remains unanswered. What did Guider do with Samantha's body? Guider refuses to say, offering a variety of stories and excuses, but not the truth. Guider has already been convicted and is doing time for manslaughter, so what has he got to lose by telling police where to find the body? Perhaps the answer is this: if Samantha's body revealed a violent death rather than the accidental death Guider has always claimed it was, the additional evidence might justify a murder charge against him. If convicted, he would die in gaol.

■ ■ ■

On Tuesday, 6 May 1997, 39-year-old Kerry Whelan left her home at Kurrajong, an hour's drive north-west of Sydney, telling her husband, Bernie, that she had a 9.30 a.m. appointment 'at the beautician at Parramatta'. Bernie never saw her again. She planned to meet Bernie at 3.45 p.m. that afternoon at his Smithfield office in Sydney's outer western suburbs before the couple flew to Adelaide. Bernie had business there, but they also intended to visit a few of the local wineries. At about 9.40 a.m., security cameras caught Kerry walking out of the car park at Parramatta's Parkroyal Hotel and onto the street.

When Kerry didn't turn up to meet Bernie, he rang family and friends and tried without success to contact her on her mobile. Knowing she would park at the Parkroyal Hotel, he went there and found her car locked in the car park. When she left the house, Kerry had been wearing more than $50,000 worth of jewellery.

Bernie reported his wife's disappearance to Parramatta Police, and detectives were in touch with him the next morning. Bernie did not open the mail until about seven o'clock that evening. When he did, one letter grabbed his attention. He opened it. The letter was typed in capital letters and began, 'THERE WILL BE NO SECOND CHANCES. FOLLOW ALL INSTRUCTIONS OR YOUR WIFE WILL DIE.' It went on:

> TO ENSURE HER SAFE RETURN YOU MUST AT NO TIME BRING IN THE POLICE THE PRESS ANY AUTHORITIES OR OUTSIDE ASSISTANCE. WE WILL KNOW IF YOU DO SO . . . YOU ARE NOT OUR FIRST AUSTRALIAN TARGET THERE HAVE BEEN OTHERS . . . DO NOT UNDERESTIMATE OUR CAPABILITIES . . . THE RANSOM FOR HER RETURN IS ONE MILLION U.S. DOLLARS. THE RATE OF EXCHANGE MEANS YOU WILL PAY ONE MILLION TWO HUNDRED FIFTY THOUSAND AUSTRALIA DOLLARS TO BE PAID IN ONE HUNDRED DOLLAR NOTES.

The extortionist gave detailed instructions about the make-up of the ransom cash and how it was to be paid. In seven days a notice was to be placed in *The Daily Telegraph*: 'ANYONE WHO WITNESSED A WHITE VOLKSWAGEN BEETLE PARKED BESIDE THE EASTERN GATES OF THE SYDNEY OLYMPIC SITE AT 10.30 PM ON TUESDAY 5.4.97 PLEASE CALL . . . THEN PUT YOUR HOME

TELEPHONE NUMBER AT THE END OF THE ADVERTISEMENT.' Within three days the extortionist would contact with further instructions. A distraught Bernie contacted police, and Strike Force Bellaire was formed under the command of Detective Inspector Mike Howe and Detective Sergeant Dennis Bray.

The police began by asking questions about the Whelans' marriage. Was either of them having an affair? Had Kerry run off? They were obvious questions, but Bernie's answers convinced them that the kidnapping and demands were genuine and that Kerry's life was at risk. Her safe return would depend on the police operation remaining covert for as long as possible.

Through interviews with family friends, detectives found that two weeks earlier Kerry had been visited at their 30-acre Kurrajong property by a man and that she had been upset after he left. Amanda Minton-Taylor, a friend who was employed by the Whelans as a horse trainer and nanny, told police that Kerry had asked her not to mention the incident to anyone, but Amanda suspected that the man's visit might have something to do with Kerry's disappearance. She thought she remembered Kerry saying the man's name was 'Bruce' and that he was 'an old family friend'. Shown some family pictures, Amanda identified Bruce Burrell as the visitor. The Whelans' eleven-year-old son, James, also identified Burrell as the person who had visited his mother.

Bernie told police that he had met Burrell, then an advertising manager, in 1985 when Bernie's company, the Australian and Asian arm of Crown Equipment, employed Bruce's agency to handle its account. From that time Bernie liaised regularly with Burrell and they became friends. Bernie sacked Burrell in 1990, but the pair continued to socialise, at times going on shooting expeditions together. Two years later, Bernie mentioned to Burrell that the drought had made it difficult for his cattle to graze. Burrell said that his property, a 500-acre farm next to a national park at Bungonia in the Southern Tablelands, had plenty of feed and the cattle could stay there. Bernie accepted the offer and shipped his pedigree cattle to the property. A few weeks later, Bernie received a call from Burrell who said that the cattle had wandered off the land and couldn't be found. The following year, 1993, Burrell rang Bernie and asked if he wanted to sell his Ruger .223 semi-automatic rifle as Bruce said he had a neighbour who was interested in buying it. Burrell picked up the rifle, then two weeks later rang Bernie to say it had been stolen from the boot of his car when the car was parked at Redfern in Sydney.

Bernie remembered receiving a phone call from Burrell a month before Kerry disappeared. It was four years since the two had spoken and Bernie described the call as 'bizarre', with Burrell talking about his separation from his wife, Dallas, and rambling incoherently from topic to topic.

Despite the lack of firm evidence, Burrell was now a person of interest, and the strike force began building a profile. He was born in 1953. At the age of 32 he married Dallas Bromley and in 1988, together with Dallas's parents, Bruce and Dallas bought the Bungonia property. In January 1994 Dallas was diagnosed with cancer and began treatment, including chemotherapy. The Burrells separated and divorced in 1996.

The strike force and Bernie prepared for the ransom exchange. Bernie had raised the cash through Crown Equipment. A few days before the exchange was due, the heavily armed State Protection Group, trained in hostage negotiation and high-risk operations, took up positions both inside and outside the house. On 13 May, Bernie did as he was told and placed a notice to the kidnapper in *The Daily Telegraph*, but there was no response.

Three days later, by arrangement with the strike force, Burrell was pulled up in Goulburn by the highway patrol. The number plates on the Pajero he was driving did not match the car, and the car itself was found to be unregistered. Burrell was arrested and taken to the local police station, where he was charged with stealing the Pajero and related offences. The charges created an opportunity for the strike force to search his property, which it did. In the house police found (but did not confiscate) an empty chloroform bottle, a number of guns and various types of ammunition, as well as a typewriter, from which they took a sample of typing. Burrell was charged with receiving a stolen car, driving an unregistered and uninsured vehicle, and using number plates calculated to deceive. He was released on bail.

Another three days went by and there was still no contact from the kidnappers. By this time the media had begun to hear stories of a kidnapping and were asking questions. A media release was prepared and the media were asked to broadcast a plea to the community for help. On 19 May the strike force began a major search of Burrell's property, organised and led by Detective Inspector Bruce Couch, who had played a major role in the search for bodies in the Belanglo State Forest. It was the first Burrell knew that the police regarded him as a suspect.

This time investigators seized a crossbow, Bernie Whelan's .223 Ruger rifle, the typewriter, the empty chloroform bottle and a dozen other items, including two notes with 'numbered points', which were later identified as having been written by

Burrell and interpreted by police as an early outline of the planned kidnapping. The first note consisted of six points (the words in brackets represent the strike force's interpretation of each point):

1. Collection [a reference to the 'collection' of Kerry Whelan]
2. Advisement [a reference to 'advisement' of kidnapping in a ransom note to her family]
3. Waiting [a reference to 'waiting' until further instructions on how to proceed]
4. How to proceed [a reference to 'how to proceed' in delivery of the ransom]
5. Pick up [a reference to 'pick-up' of the ransom], and
6. Cover all [a reference to cover-up of the crime].

The second note consisted of five points and has been interpreted as being the outline of the ransom note (again, the words in brackets represent interpretations by the police):

Has been K[idnapped]
No P[olice to be involved]
Letter within 2 days [to be received with further instructions]
Nothing until received [do nothing until second letter received]
Stress 2 [no police]

Police also seized a Yamaha quad bike that had been stolen from Burrell's neighbour's property about seven weeks earlier, and a 1995 silver Jaguar Sovereign, which had been stolen from a car sales dealer in November 1995. Under the front seat of the Jaguar they found a UBD street directory marked with the location of the Parkroyal Hotel in Parramatta, with the hotel's address written in highlighter pen. The route from the Parkroyal Hotel to the headquarters of Crown Equipment in Smithfield was also highlighted.

A guard was placed on the house overnight and the search continued for several more days, with divers searching the property's six dams. Burrell admitted to police that he had visited Kerry at the Whelans' property about a month earlier. It had been a social visit, he said, and he had intended to ask Bernie if he had any work for him. Burrell denied meeting Kerry three weeks later at Parramatta. As the search continued, the receptionist at Crown Equipment received a phone call: 'Mrs Whelan is okay. Whelan must call off the police and media today. Tell him it's the man with the white Volkswagen . . . He must call off the police and media today . . . will be in touch in two weeks.'

By now Kerry's disappearance was front-page news. Burrell was arrested and charged at Goulburn with stealing the Jaguar and firearms offences and bailed. A photograph of a Suzuki vehicle was found in Burrell's house. The vehicle was traced and found to have been stolen and sold. Burrell was later charged with receiving the vehicle.

After five days the search of Burrell's property was called off. The searchers had found no trace of Kerry. The next night, Monday 26 May, the strike force received some extraordinary news. News reports of Kerry Whelan's disappearance had reminded Maroubra Detective Sue Whitfield of her own investigation, two years earlier, into the disappearance of 74-year-old Dorothy Davis from Lurline Bay in Sydney's eastern suburbs. Just after 1 p.m. on 30 May 1995 Dorothy Davis had left her home to visit a friend. She was never seen again. Bruce Burrell had been questioned over the disappearance and remained a person of interest.

Whitfield was seconded to the Whelan strike force and the Davis case was reopened. There were striking parallels between the cases. Around 1 p.m. on 30 May 1995 Dorothy told a builder who was attaching an awning to her home that she was going to walk to the home of a friend who had cancer. The friend was Dallas Burrell but she was not at home; she was at work that day. The only other person who lived in the house was Burrell.

Twelve months later the marriage failed and Dallas left Burrell. Their financial settlement required each of them to borrow $125,000 in order to buy out Dallas's parents' interest in the Bungonia property. While Burrell ended up as the sole owner, he was unable to meet the mortgage payments.

When police first interviewed him over the disappearance of Davis, Burrell had an alibi: he was at lunch at Crows Nest on Sydney's north shore with two business colleagues. After the Davis case was reopened, the strike force interviewed the colleagues. One remembered the lunch being on his birthday, 30 May, the day Davis disappeared. But credit card and restaurant records established that the lunch had in fact taken place two days earlier. Burrell's mobile phone records confirmed that he had been in Sydney on the morning Davis disappeared and in Moss Vale a few hours after she was last seen, and that he had returned to Sydney later that afternoon.

While the strike force continued investigating the Whelan and Davis disappearances, Burrell was making his way through the courts on motor vehicle theft, firearms and related charges. On 3 August 1998 he pleaded guilty in the District Court to larceny as a bailee, three charges of receiving stolen motor vehicles (a Suzuki, a Pajero and a Jaguar), disposing of a stolen motor vehicle (the Suzuki), and possessing a prohibited weapon. Burrell was convicted of four more offences: having registration plates calculated to deceive, driving an unregistered motor vehicle, driving an uninsured motor vehicle and using a firearm without a licence or permit. All offences were committed between 1992 and 1997. He was gaoled for a total of three and a half years.

By now the strike force had checked the security cameras in Parramatta where Kerry had parked her car. These recorded her entering the hotel car park at 9.35 a.m., talking with the parking attendant and walking up the ramp leading from the car park onto Phillip Street. Forty-four seconds later Kerry was seen on the parking station security camera. Another security camera recorded a reflected image of a two-tone, two-door Mitsubishi Pajero pulling away from the kerbside in Phillip Street outside the hotel. It was the same model of Pajero that Burrell was driving at the time. Other features—a bull-bar, a running board and heavy dirt stains on the rear window—matched Burrell's Pajero. Kerry was believed to have entered the vehicle, although it was not known why. In the following months police tracked down most of the people who owned similar Pajeros and excluded them from their inquiries.

On 1 April 1999, as he neared the end of his gaol sentence, Burrell was charged with kidnapping and murdering Kerry

Whelan. Three years later, following legal argument at trial, the charges were dropped, but the police were not finished with Burrell.

Dallas and her parents had been close friends of Dorothy 'Dottie' Davis since Dallas was a child. Dallas and Burrell lived in a unit in Lurline Bay about ten minutes from Davis's house. In November 1993 Burrell left a note for the owner of an ocean-facing house in their street, expressing an interest in buying the house. The owner, however, did not want to sell. Three months later Dallas was diagnosed with cancer. In mid-1994 Burrell again wrote to the owner of the ocean-facing house and this time a deal was reached to buy the house for $600,000.

Davis's husband had died in 1984, leaving her a wealthy woman. In July 1994 Davis wrote a cheque for $500,000 in favour of Burrell. Three days later the bank manager phoned Davis and drew her attention to the fact that she had only $114,000 in her account. Davis explained that the cheque was 'a short term loan to a friend' and gave instructions to stop the cheque. A month later Davis wrote another cheque in favour of Burrell, this time for $100,000. When depositing the cheque in Burrell's account, Davis told the bank manager the funds were to be used as a deposit on a property. A week later Burrell withdrew $90,000 in cash from his account.

Davis explained to her daughter, Maree, that Burrell had told her Dallas was desperate to buy the Lurline Bay house, but that the owner had demanded a larger than usual deposit. Davis had agreed to help by writing Burrell a cheque for $500,000. When the cheque was stopped, Burrell told her the owner was prepared to accept a smaller deposit; Davis had then written the second cheque.

Burrell said nothing to Dallas about the 'loan' from Davis until several months later, when he gave a very different story to Davis's. In Burrell's version Davis wanted to conceal certain things from her children and had asked for his help. Davis had written him a cheque for $100,000, which was deposited into his account. A few days later he withdrew the cash and gave Davis $90,000. At her suggestion, Burrell said, he kept $10,000 for his trouble.

In August Burrell bought the ocean-facing house. The purchase price was covered by a bank loan; there was no need to use Davis's money.

According to Burrell's former business associate, Peter Grace, Burrell claimed that Davis had lent him money and asked for it back, threatening legal action, but Burrell had been unable to repay the loan. In fact, Burrell was broke and had been for some years. He had been only sporadically employed since at least 1992 and had been sacked several times, he received no social security benefits, had no source of income, was dependent upon the earnings of his wife until they separated, could not meet the repayments on either the Lurline Bay house or his Bungonia property, and had been living on money borrowed from his parents. Burrell had also been living off the proceeds of cars he stole and then sold, property he had stolen from Bernie and any other money he could 'con'. The money Davis lent him in July 1994 was spent before the house in Lurline Bay was even bought.

A month-long inquest into the disappearances of Whelan and Davis began in May 2002. After the inquest, the coroner referred the papers to the director of public prosecutions, and ex officio indictments were subsequently filed against Burrell over the disappearance of Kerry Whelan and Dorothy Davis. Burrell's trial for the murder of Whelan had been due to start in January 2003, but Burrell's poor health caused delays. The trial eventually got underway two and a half years later, on 10 August 2005, and continued for ten weeks. On 2 November, after ten days of deliberations, the jury failed to reach a verdict and was discharged. The retrial began four months later and lasted ten weeks. This time, after nine days of deliberation, the jury found Burrell guilty. He was gaoled for life for the murder of Kerry Whelan and for sixteen years for her kidnapping, both sentences to be served concurrently. An appeal against the severity of those sentences was dismissed in 2007.

On 30 July 2007, thirteen months after being convicted of murdering Kerry Whelan, Burrell faced trial for Davis's murder. He pleaded not guilty, but was convicted and gaoled for 28 years.

The strike force investigation revealed Burrell to be a man with few redeeming features. Casual acquaintances often mistook him as affable, outgoing, well connected and independently wealthy. Those who knew him better regarded him as an inveterate name-dropper; an idle, untalented bully who stood over women to do work that he would take credit for; a bullshit artist with an evil temper who could become violent when things did not go his way; a liar and a sleazebag who was always conning money from others.

Burrell also had an obsession with a notorious criminal: Ivan Milat. When hosting parties at Bungonia he would often talk at length about the backpacker murders and the stash of weapons seized by police when they arrested Milat. Pointing to the forested national park that bordered his property, Burrell would tell his guests, 'You could hide a body so easily out there and no one would ever find it,' adding that he knew the area 'like the back of my hand'.

Perhaps there was more to Burrell's comments than just an obsession. Neither Dorothy Davis's nor Kerry Whelan's body has ever been found; Burrell is believed to have buried both in a forest somewhere near his property.

18 GRIEF

Rita and Peter O'Malley had a good life together in Sydney's eastern suburbs. Rita ran a bridal and dressmaking shop at Double Bay, and the two of them performed as the 'Singing O'Malleys', often turning up to entertain the residents at local nursing homes. Nothing connected them to the horrors of the Belanglo State Forest. But this changed in April 1991 when Rita, who was born in Germany and spoke fluent German, received a phone call from a friend. The friend asked Rita to help look after Manfred and Anke Neugebauer, who were flying to Sydney to search for their missing son, Gabor, and his girlfriend, Anja Habschied. Anja's brother, Norbert, would accompany them to help with the search. While the Neugebauers' search for Gabor and Anja proved fruitless, their meeting with Rita at Sydney Airport marked the beginning of a deep friendship.

Manfred and Anke flew home disappointed, but they stayed in contact with Rita by phone and letters. After hearing that Gabor's and Anja's bodies had been found in the Belanglo State Forest, Anke and her elder son, Tibor, returned to Australia. Rita met them at the airport, spent time with them in Sydney, and went with them to the forest to visit the site where Gabor and Anja had lost their lives, before Anke and Tibor flew back to Germany with the bodies of Gabor and Anja.

In February 1994 the premier, John Fahey, unveiled a plaque in memory of the murdered backpackers in the Belanglo State Forest, close to the former site of the police command post. Pat Everist, Ray and Peggy Gibson, and Ray and Gill Walters attended the memorial service, together with the police commissioner, Tony Lauer, local police and members of Task Force Air, including me. The Clarke family was unable to attend but sent a letter of support and encouragement that was read out at the service. Rita represented the families of Gabor and Anja and of Simone Schmidl.

The memorial and service had been organised by the Reverend Steven Davis. 'I felt it was a good opportunity for the parents, for the local community in which I live and for the police to tie a whole lot of things together,' he said. 'In the midst of death—even such violent and tragic deaths as these—I want to stand up and hold out a word of hope and light.'

After the memorial we all returned to Bowral Police Station. Recalling her meeting with Pat Everist and Peggy Gibson, Rita told Steve Meacham of *The Sydney Morning Herald*, 'That first day we met, we all formed this special friendship. It was the oddest thing. Here we were, a group of strangers drinking tea and eating sandwiches in a police station. We all felt we had known each other for years. We shared this common horror.' Pat told Meacham, 'Rita made it bearable for us, in unbearable circumstances . . . It has become a wonderful friendship. Not just with Rita, and the other parents, but with the police. They were so compassionate. They became friends, like family. I never knew you could have a relationship with the police.'

Most of the victims' families were in Sydney for the committal hearing and the trial. It was while Rita was attending Ivan's committal at Campbelltown Court that she became friends with the Schmidls. 'I helped him [Simone's father, Herbert] get through every day as he has no knowledge of English. He spent a good portion of time with myself and my husband at our home . . . he was so glad to have someone he could talk to in German and of course to relate many stories about his beloved daughter Simone.' Rita also spent a lot of time with Herbert during Ivan's trial: 'It must have taken all his strength to walk into that courtroom and face the man who had destroyed such a part of his life.'

Norbert Habschied also returned to Australia for the committal proceedings, together with his and Anja's mother, Olga. Speaking no English, Olga relied on the Neugebauers and on Rita to explain the trial to her.

The O'Malleys again caught up with the families of the victims at the trial but, not expecting it to continue for as long as it did, had booked a trip to Germany and were overseas during its final weeks. During the trip the couple spent several days at the Neugebauer home with Anke while Manfred was at the trial in Sydney. Gabor was never far from Anke's thoughts, Rita said. 'Every night she [Anke] takes the dog for a walk and then visits Gabor's grave . . . Gabor's room is practically as he left it and I have no doubt it will stay this way forever.' They also stayed with Herbert Schmidl, who had had to return home for personal reasons, and his second wife, Helene, and with Olga and Guenther Habschied. While Guenther remained very withdrawn, Olga seemed to be coming to terms with the loss of Anja, believing her daughter was 'in another place, a rose garden . . . very close to her'.

During Ivan's trial the families had stayed at Ebony House in Waterfall, a bushland property operated by the Homicide Victims' Support Group (HVSG). The concept of Ebony House came about after Christine Simpson identified the need for some kind of 'recovery' centre for people affected by the murder of a loved one. Christine's daughter, nine-year-old Ebony Jane, had been murdered. The Simpson family lived in Bargo, a small town about 100 kilometres south-west of Sydney. On 19 August 1992 Ebony left her school bus and was abducted and killed by 29-year-old Andrew Garforth, who was sentenced to life imprisonment, never to be released. Ebony House officially opened in December 1995 after a grant from the government. Although named in memory of Ebony, the house is a memorial to all murder victims.

The executive director of the HVSG, Martha Jabour, had some years earlier lost her second child, seven-week-old Michael, to sudden infant death syndrome (SIDS). Finding little in the way of support or empathy from the police, Martha saw a need for police training in grief and trauma counselling. After undergoing formal training, Martha became involved with other families, such as the Simpsons, who were campaigning for victim support services. Their efforts led to the establishment of the HVSG.

'For many people experiencing the trauma of the death of a loved one through homicide,' Martha said, 'there is sometimes a need to get away from everyday things. Ebony House provides an opportunity for families and friends of homicide victims to get together and provide care and support for each other. All seven families of Ivan Milat's murder victims stayed here at some point during the trial.'

Accommodation at Ebony House is free of charge, which made it especially valuable in the backpacker murder case, for which several families had to travel from overseas to attend the trial. Martha said, 'The families of the backpacker murder victims needed to be in the court to represent their murdered child. They didn't want people thinking about their child just as a victim of the backpacker murderer; they wanted people to know it was their son or daughter who was part of a loving family and to understand that their children were good, down-to-earth, loving kids.' Due to the length of the trial, the HVSG received a one-off grant of $10,000 from the New South Wales government to help it meet the costs of supporting the families.

Most days Martha herself accompanied the families to court. At the end of each day the families would be briefed on the type of evidence that would be given the next day, particularly where it related to their child. Martha pointed out that 'evidence regarding the circumstances of the murders and post-mortem results were very graphic, as were the pictures that were tendered during the proceedings. Being warned about this evidence allowed the families to make a decision as to whether they wanted to be present or not and, if they did, to prepare themselves for what was to come.'

When Ebony House was established in 1995 there were 270 members in the HVSG. Twenty years later, there are more than 3100 members. The group has helped bring about significant changes in the criminal justice system, making it more 'victim-oriented' and less 'offender-oriented'. It has lobbied successfully to prevent convicted prisoners from receiving compensation; to expand the definition of those entitled to make victim impact statements; to introduce a Victims' Compensation Act, a Charter of Victims' Rights and a Victims' Rights Act; to have prisoners' assets seized to pay for victims' compensation; and to change the knife laws. John Laycock, a former assistant commissioner with 37 years' experience in the New South Wales Police, commented, 'At least some of these changes would not have occurred and a lot of families would not have received the support they needed if it hadn't been for the efforts of the Homicide Victims' Support Group.'

Laycock first met Martha in 1994 when she made a presentation to senior police, seeking support for the families and friends of victims of homicides. For the next ten years Laycock strongly supported the HVSG and, after retiring from the police in 2004, became a policing consultant to the group. Along with Martha and other members, Laycock regularly participates in presentations on victim support at the Goulburn Police Academy. Martha sits on the New South Wales State Parole Authority, the Sentencing Council and the Domestic Violence Review Team.

Due in part to the group's efforts, the culture of the police and the courts has changed significantly in the two decades since the HVSG was established. Both Martha and Rita

O'Malley spoke out in praise of the officers in Task Force Air—especially Rod Lynch, Bob Godden and Steve Leach—who supported the victims' families in court and in their own time after work and at weekends.

As a matter of practice, the police now formally advise the HVSG of all murders, enabling it to communicate both with the contact officer and the victim's family.

Rita O'Malley and her husband had been together for more than 60 years when Peter passed away in March 2011. After Rita died ten months later, Detective Inspector Andy Waterman of Task Force Air delivered a speech in which he expressed the task force's appreciation of Rita's efforts to comfort and support the families of Ivan's victims.

19
DREAMS OF ESCAPE

It was never Ivan Milat's intention to live out his days quietly in gaol. His incarceration has been marked by self-harm, tantrums, appeals against his conviction and attempts to escape.

In March 1997, eight months after his conviction, Ivan met a fellow Maitland gaol inmate, 56-year-old George Savvas. Both men were serving long sentences and both were desperate to break out of the maximum-security gaol. They quickly became friends and began plotting their escape.

Savvas was a major figure in Sydney's underworld and had played a significant role in the Sydney gang war of the mid-1980s. At the time, Savvas sat on the Marrickville Council as an independent and described himself as 'King of Marrickville', claiming to have police protection. He was in business with another long-time criminal, Barry James McCann, who had been a partner with the notorious former police officer and drug importer, Murray Stewart Riley, in the infiltration of organised crime into licensed clubs in the 1960s. McCann later trafficked heroin with the Mr Asia syndicate before teaming up with Savvas. During an eighteen-month period in the mid- to late 1980s the pair imported more than 100 kilograms of heroin, much of which made its way onto the streets of Cabramatta in Sydney's west.

Their operation was beset by greed, drug and cash rip-offs, and violence. Savvas himself was under remand for fraud. Someone who criticised Savvas's continued role on the Marrickville Council while under remand on criminal charges had his life threatened. Within hours of receiving the threat, his car yard was firebombed. A witness in the fraud case was murdered—shot three times in the back of the head—while the victim, Savvas's former business partner, was threatened. Savvas was acquitted.

Around September 1987 more than $2 million worth of heroin belonging to McCann went missing. McCann accused Savvas of stealing it and wanted compensation. Three months later McCann's body was found in a Marrickville park. He had been shot 25 times. A year later Savvas was charged with the murder, drug importations and trafficking. He beat the murder charge, but was sentenced to 25 years' gaol for drug trafficking and fined $200,000. In March 1994 Savvas was found guilty of conspiring from Long Bay gaol to import up to 40 kilograms of cocaine from Brazil and 20 kilograms of heroin from Asia, and sentenced to another eighteen years, bringing his total sentence to more than 30 years. After eight years Savvas escaped from the Goulburn Correctional Centre. He was recaptured eight months later and met Milat while both were held in Maitland gaol.

Their escape plan was a crazed fantasy. They planned to overwhelm their guards, tie them up, steal their uniforms and scale an 8-metre prison wall topped with razor wire and under constant electronic surveillance; they would then slip through gates flanked by armed guards to reach accomplices waiting outside to drive them to freedom. Unfortunately for Savvas and Milat, the gaol authorities got wind of their plan and on 16 May 1997 the men were arrested as they made their move. Savvas hanged himself in his cell later that night: it was the only escape route he had left. The head of Corrective Services, Ron Woodham, told *The Sun-Herald*, 'They were prepared to injure or kill anyone who got in their way.'

While planning his escape, Milat had lodged an appeal, arguing that the photographic evidence against him should have been excluded. In November 1997 he once again dismissed his legal team, telling the court he didn't want to be represented. The matter was adjourned and, a few months later, the appeal was dismissed.

In 1999 prison officers searching Milat's cell found a hacksaw blade hidden in a biscuit packet. Two years later he swallowed razor blades, paper staples and a small metal chain from a pair of nail clippers. Later the same year he swallowed part of the flushing mechanism from the toilet in his cell. In early 2003 he deliberately broke his hand. The same year he complained that the head of Corrective Services, Ron Woodham, was 'orchestrating' the media by telling them that 'only the most dangerous prisoners are housed in here [the Supermax at Goulburn Correctional Centre]' and that 'I['m] in here . . . which means I['m] regarded as a dangerous prisoner.' As with all his letters since entering gaol, Milat signed his complaint with his name, followed by a drawing of the sign of The Saint—a stick figure of a man with a halo—from the television series of that name.

In July 2005 John Marsden, Milat's former lawyer, told *The Daily Telegraph* that he believed Milat's deceased sister, Shirley Soire, had been an accomplice in the backpacker killings. As we know, she had been living with Milat at his Eagle Vale home at the time of his arrest. Inevitably, Marsden's sensational claims made headlines and I was bombarded with requests for comment. My own opinion was that Ivan would not have trusted either Shirley or any of his brothers to help with the murders. Ivan was a loner, determined to be in control of his own destiny; an accomplice would have been too much of a risk.

I knew Marsden was suffering from terminal cancer. When I rang him at home, he told me groggily, 'Clive, I can't even remember the interview and I don't know who I was talking to. I was so doped up on morphine and other things I was out of my mind.' Marsden said virtually the same thing to *The Sydney Morning Herald*'s Kate McClymont: at the time he named Shirley he was 'doped to the gills with a double hit of morphine' and thought he was 'speaking to a police officer'.

In late 2005 I visited the Goulburn Supermax. While being taken through the complex by a senior Corrective Services officer, I bumped into Ivan. He was in his day room, which he shared with another prisoner and which was connected to his cell. Ivan's cell was 4 by 3 metres with a sink, an open shower and a stainless-steel toilet. The bed was a concrete slab with a foam mattress. At the back of the day room was a tiny caged exercise yard.

I was surprised by the deterioration in his physical and mental condition. Ivan bore little resemblance to the person we had arrested a decade earlier. His unkempt hair was thinning and had turned grey. He was not the fit and wiry man who had stood up in court confidently denying his guilt, but a skinny, stooped figure who looked very fragile. His conversation and mannerisms were those of someone who seemed to know he was no longer in control.

At first Ivan didn't appear to notice me as he complained to the officer about conditions in the gaol. I saw him glance in my direction a couple of times, then he turned and looked directly at me.

'I know you,' he said. 'You're Clive Small.'

I said, 'Yes, I am, Ivan.'

Ivan immediately began to protest his innocence. 'The DNA in the hair. Nothing to do with me,' he said, referring to strands of hair found in the right hand of Joanne Walters. (At first the hair had been identified as belonging to a man, but further examination identified it as Walters' own hair.)

Before I could answer, Ivan said, 'Why are you and your mate Marsden saying Shirley was involved?'

'I never said that,' I replied.

'You did,' said Ivan, shaking his finger. 'You and your mate Marsden. I know what you're doing.'

'You're wrong, Ivan,' I told him. 'I have never said that Shirley was involved. In fact I know she wasn't. You killed them all yourself.'

Ivan hesitated for a moment. 'Yes,' he said. 'So why are you telling them she was involved?'

It was as close to an admission of guilt as I had ever heard from Ivan. As soon as he finished speaking his whole demeanour changed, as if he had suddenly realised the significance of what he had said. He was silent for a few moments. Then he turned back to the Corrective Services officer and resumed his rant about conditions in the gaol.

Ivan's main complaint was that he was not being given enough time in the outdoor exercise yard. He said that the air conditioner was giving him a rash on his forehead and that it would only heal if he was allowed more time in the open air. Ivan's forehead was raw and covered with scratches, but it had nothing to do with the air conditioner; Ivan had been scraping his forehead against the rough cement wall of his cell.

Milat filed another appeal in the New South Wales Supreme Court. Representing himself, Milat sought to have his case referred to the Court of Criminal Appeal for an inquiry into his convictions. Such referrals can occur only if there appears to be doubt over the convicted person's guilt, over mitigating circumstances or over the evidence. A doubt over the guilt of an applicant would arise if there was unease over the material relied on to obtain a conviction. In October 2005 Ivan's application was refused.

A few weeks later, Chris Masters and a crew from the ABC's *Four Corners* spent several days filming at the Goulburn Supermax. While in the gaol they saw Milat several times in his cell. Milat had also seen them and demanded that prison authorities stop the filming, threatening to set himself on fire if it continued. Masters was told of Milat's protests, but filming continued. Ivan never carried out his threat.

Seven months later Milat was again embroiled in controversy when it was found that he had a television and toaster in his prison cell. They were rewards for 'good behaviour', for not engaging in acts of disobedience or self-harm and for not being likely to escape. Martha Jabour, executive director of the Homicide Victims' Support Group, described the privileges as 'an insult to the families of his victims'. *The Daily Telegraph* quoted Caroline Clarke's father, Ian, saying from his home in Northumberland that Milat did not deserve any privileges. 'He didn't give any privileges to any of our children. As far as I'm concerned, he can rot,' Clarke said. 'I wouldn't agree to him being given anything. It's a joke.'

Within hours of the media furore erupting, Ivan lost his television and toaster and the New South Wales Premier, Morris Iemma, suspended all other rewards. A review of the reward system in the Supermax system was ordered. After his privileges were withdrawn, Milat again threatened suicide. He was moved to a 'safe cell' and placed under 24-hour video surveillance.

Even as Milat complained about his lack of privileges, he was already preparing his next appeal, which was heard in the Supreme Court in December 2006. Essentially it was a repeat of his earlier application, with Ivan arguing that there was unease over the trial judge and his conduct of the trial. Only Ivan felt the unease. The court noted that each of the grounds raised by him had been cited in his earlier petition and fully dealt with. The application was refused.

Milat lodged yet another appeal. Once again, he wanted his case referred to the Court of Criminal Appeal for an inquiry into his convictions. This time Milat referred to a television program 'in which Mr Clive Small, a police officer apparently in charge of the investigations of Mr Milat's crimes, made comments about the matter. Mr Small allegedly said that there was no police evidence to suggest that Mr Milat acted with another person in committing the murders. The Crown prosecutor gave an interview on the same program. He apparently said that it was no part of the Crown case to prove that any person other than Mr Milat was involved in the murders.'

Milat complained that the trial judge had erred in ruling that the Crown did not have to prove whether Milat acted alone or in company. If the Crown couldn't prove whether or not another person or persons had been involved, he said, then he shouldn't have been convicted. Milat also complained that he had been denied procedural fairness during the trial. The court found his submissions were without merit and his application to appeal was refused.

On 26 January 2009 Milat cut off the little finger on his left hand just below the knuckle with a plastic knife, and placed the finger in an envelope padded with newspaper and addressed to New South Wales Supreme Court's Justice Peter McClellan, who had twice denied his application to appeal. At lock-up time Milat handed the envelope to a prison officer. Four guards escorted him to Goulburn Base Hospital, where he was handcuffed and shackled to a bed, but doctors decided that surgery to reattach the finger was not possible. The next day Milat was returned to the Supermax. Australian Associated Press reported Ron Woodham telling Macquarie Radio, '[W]hen you cut a finger off it does hurt . . . He's back in an observation cell this morning, dressed in a gown, feeling sorry for himself. We believe he's starting another hunger strike. But he likes his food so it will only last a day or two . . . when he does take his next meal he won't be getting a knife with it.'

The Daily Telegraph reported that in a letter to his brother Bill, Milat wrote, 'I don't regret it [cutting off my finger], though it was a stupid act . . . in here acts like that is [sic] regarded as normal . . . I wonder if I will have enough time to prove my innocence as time flies, but it takes a long time to get a reply from the authority-courts-government . . . That was a big factor in severing the finger off, to highlight the difficulties of a prisoner who wishes to appeal his case.'

Corrective Services' South-West Region assistant commissioner, John Dunthorne, told the media, 'It's the work of a desperate man and Ivan Milat is in the top echelon of desperate people . . . Ivan is a control freak and his moods will fluctuate if he thinks he's not in control.' Dunthorne noted that Ivan would be 'back in the Supermax by midnight tonight'. Woodham explained that he thought Milat was 'very close to losing his marbles', while others saw it as part of a plan by Milat to be shifted to a medical facility from which he could organise an escape.

In November 2010 the Supreme Court handed down its finding on Milat's fourth application for an inquiry into his conviction and sentencing. The handwritten application raised various issues: unease over the reliability of the Crown's primary evidence; the availability of new evidence; the fact that at his trial DNA evidence did not implicate him in the crime; and 'cogent evidence' of an alibi. Again, Justice McClellan found that he could not be 'satisfied that there are special facts or circumstances that justify the taking of further action' and refused Ivan's application.

In May 2011 Milat went on a nine-day hunger strike after his request for a Sony PlayStation 'to exercise his mind' was refused. His weight fell from 85 to 60 kilograms. Commissioner Woodham told *The Sunday Telegraph*, 'There's no inmate on my watch who would ever get anything close to a PlayStation, particularly Australia's worst serial killer.'

20 COPYCAT

Ivan Milat's notoriety goes far beyond the murders he is known to have committed. The most famous image of him—sitting on a sofa in a black hat, holding a shotgun, with a rifle resting beside him—remains a potent symbol not just of what Ivan has done, but of what he might have done, and of what others might have done to emulate him.

On the evening of 12 July 1980 Deborah Balken and Jillian Jamieson, both aged twenty, went to meet friends at the Tollgate Hotel at Parramatta. They left about 7.30 p.m. Around 9 p.m. Balken called their Dundas flatmate, Sue Gilchrist, to say that she and Jamieson were in Wollongong with some of Jamieson's former workmates, including the 'gardener fellow'. Balken asked Gilchrist to call in sick for them. Jamieson worked at Ryde District Hospital and Balken at a local nursing home; neither has been seen or heard from since.

At first there were no serious concerns for their safety, but after they had been missing for a few weeks Eastwood Police and the Homicide Squad began an investigation. Inquiries revealed that both women were heavy drinkers and occasional drug users; that they led active social lives and were sexually involved with several men; and that they were regulars at the Tollgate Hotel. It was thought that both women had planned to attend a party on the night they disappeared. An employee of the Tollgate told police that on the night they went missing she saw them speaking to a man and heard them discussing a party in Wollongong. The women left with this man, who was a regular drinker at the hotel and 'always wore a black felt hat with a broad brim'. Three months later, the employee said she saw the same man back at the hotel with two other men. After a minor disagreement, the man had threatened the employee, who told police that she was 'terrified'. The man was known to be a gardener who lived on a property where large parties involving drug use were said to be held.

The police focused their investigation on the 'gardener fellow', but they were unable to discover either his identity or the address in Wollongong where the party had taken place. Known friends of the women were interviewed and reported sightings were followed up, but after about two years the investigation petered out.

In March 1998 a Parramatta resident contacted local police. She said that in 1980, when she was fifteen years old, she was in Marsden Street, Parramatta, with her mother when she saw a white sedan parked outside a doctor's surgery. Inside the car were two women who appeared drugged or dead. Two men (she had a clear view of one) were leaning against the driver's side. The woman said she not reported the incident because her father—who had since left the family home—didn't want her having anything to do with the police. The mother made a statement confirming her daughter's version of events. Under hypnosis, the woman was able to provide a detailed description of the car, the girls and the men, but the date she gave for the incident was the day she was admitted to hospital for an operation. A check of hospital records showed this to be three weeks after the day the girls were last seen.

Detective Philip Denmeade was put in charge of the reopened investigation. He interviewed Peter Flood, a person of interest in the original investigation, who was at Bathurst gaol serving a sentence for sexual assault. Flood subsequently wrote a letter to the police requesting a reopening of the investigation into the disappearance of the two women, who were old schoolfriends of his. Flood was said to be obsessed with Balken, although nothing was found to connect him with her disappearance.

Throughout 1998 Denmeade pursued the investigation, reinterviewing some witnesses and interviewing several new witnesses. He discovered that Jamieson and Balken socialised with a group that included several men known to be violent (at least one was violent towards women), as well as drug suppliers and drug users. By late 1999 Denmeade began looking further afield for people who might have information useful to the investigation.

Over three days in March 2001, Denmeade visited Sue Gilchrist, the missing women's former flatmate, at her home in Lennox Head. *Sydney Morning Herald* journalist Eamonn

Duff reported that Denmeade had instructed Gilchrist to pick him up from Byron Bay railway station, explaining that he didn't have a police car because 'the boys upstairs are not being helpful and the budget's not there'. After questioning Gilchrist about the women and their sex lives, Denmeade asked to take a shower in her bathroom. Later he broke off the interview to 'lie down' because his computer was causing his 'eyes to hurt'. He also told Gilchrist he was writing a book about the disappearances. An internal police inquiry revealed there were no records of Denmeade's visit or the trips, and that these had not been 'authorised by any person in authority'; at the time of the visits Denmeade had been taken off criminal investigation duties and placed on general duties at Parramatta. The inquiry found Denmeade's behaviour to have been 'unauthorised . . . inappropriate and unprofessional'. He resigned from the police in 2002.

In 2003 Parramatta Police reopened the investigation into the disappearance of Jamieson and Balken, with Detective Sergeant Ian McNabb taking over the case. In 2004 Ivan Milat was interviewed about the disappearances, but he denied having met the nurses or even having visited the Tollgate Hotel in Parramatta. He admitted, however, to having worked at Granville, about 2 kilometres from Parramatta, around the time the women went missing. Two years later McNabb referred the case to the New South Wales deputy state coroner, Carl Milovanovich, who in May 2006 conducted an inquest into the disappearances at the Westmead Coroner's Court. The coroner observed that despite what had been said about the women's social lives, 'there is nothing to suggest that they were not close to their family and their friends and their work commitments.

And it is highly unlikely even if they fibbed a little bit about being sick and going to a party, it is highly unlikely that they would not have returned back to work . . . And there is no way in the world in my view that they would have just simply disappeared off the face of the earth.'

Ivan Milat was named during the proceedings as a person of interest, causing Milovanovich to comment, 'There has been a little bit of media frenzy about the fact that Ivan Milat is a person of interest. Unfortunately, his name comes up in every missing person's case that I deal with.' Milat was not considered a serious suspect. The coroner found that Jillian Jamieson and Deborah Balken 'died sometime on or after 12 July, 1980' but as to the place of death, manner and cause of death, from the evidence adduced he was unable to say.

After leaving the police in 2002, Denmeade moved to Queensland where he became a charter-boat skipper on the Great Barrier Reef. In early 2009 he approached Dr Rod Milton, the now retired profiler who had worked for Task Force Air on the backpacker investigation. Denmeade told Milton he been investigating the disappearances of Jamieson and Balken and was convinced they had been killed by Ivan Milat. After being shown an endorsement from a senior police officer, Milton agreed to help.

Denmeade used Milton's name to persuade Corrective Services to let him speak to Ivan in gaol. The head of Corrective Services, Ron Woodham, later told *The Sun-Herald*, 'A decision to grant access was made following verification from both police and a leading forensic psychologist [Milton] who worked on the Milat case. That clearance was granted as an act of decency to two grief-stricken families desperately searching for answers.' According to Duff, Denmeade's application had included 'words of support' from a senior homicide officer. Between April 2009 and May 2010 Denmeade visited Ivan half a dozen times.

Denmeade told Duff that during his interviews with Ivan, 'He now calls me a friend. That's a development and I believe there is a very strong chance of getting a result.' However, in a letter to a member of his family, Milat wrote, '[He] never gives me anything of substance, promises plenty, gave me two photographs of Mum & Dad and headstone.' Milat was also talking about Denmeade to gaol staff and fellow prisoners. While he complained that Denmeade was conning him, the truth is that he was conning Denmeade. Ivan had no intention of confessing to anything.

Denmeade's access was stopped when it became clear that he was not working with the police but was gathering material for a book. Having previously denied he planned to write a book, Denmeade now claimed to be 'hoping it would generate publicity that might help crack the case'. In fact no Homicide Squad investigator supported Denmeade having access to Milat; those he had approached rejected him outright.

At no time during Denmeade's investigations as a police officer had he raised the issue of Milat being a suspect. His suspicions about Milat appear to have originated with the man at the Tollgate Hotel who wore a black hat. Hearing about him had reminded Denmeade of the photograph of Milat sitting on a lounge wearing a black hat with shotgun in hand and a rifle at his side. The problem was, the man in the black hat at the Tollgate had been identified in 1980, not long after the women disappeared. It was not Ivan.

The Tollgate disappearances were reviewed by Task Force Air but, as with the Newcastle disappearances, while Ivan almost certainly had the opportunity, there was no evidence that he was involved.

■ ■ ■

On the afternoon of Sunday, 29 August 2010, ten trail bikers were riding through a heavily wooded area of the Belanglo State Forest just off Brethren Point Road, near a place known as Dalys Waterhole, when they came across some human bones. Emmett Hudson spotted a skull lying a few metres off the track. The group stopped, had a look and walked further into the bush, where they found more human remains and some clothing tucked away behind a log. The group had ridden the trail numerous times in the past without noticing anything.

They contacted Goulburn Local Area Command and local police arrived to secure the scene. The next morning the investigation was taken over by the Homicide Squad. Police and the media were already asking whether these were the remains of Ivan Milat's eighth victim.

Forensic and other police spent several days searching the area, recovering the skull and numerous other bones, along with a clump of long hair. As speculation increased, Goulburn's Superintendent Evan Quarmby refused to be drawn. Specialist officers sifted through soil 'grain by grain' (soil was put through a sieve, while sticks and leaves were sorted by hand) in the hunt for further evidence. Line searches collected items from around the area where the remains were found. 'As our investigation proceeds and as we get evidence back from the experts in relation to sex, age and how long the body's been there, that will allow us to narrow down some of those inquiries,' Quarmby told the media.

Once again, journalists contacted me for comment. The initial reports made me doubtful that the remains had anything to do with Ivan. The body had been found in a part of the forest well away from the site of Ivan's killings. Further, the physical conditions of the forest were different from those in which the backpacker bodies had been left, and the area did not have the isolation of the backpacker murder sites.

An examination at the Glebe morgue revealed that the remains were those of a female aged between thirteen and 25 years. A partly decomposed and discoloured T-shirt found with the bones still had enough fabric available to enable forensic officers to establish its original colour and pattern and its brand. It was possible the T-shirt held clues about the DNA of the victim or her killer, or even both. Potentially, it could play a crucial clue in identifying the remains, police told the media.

The bones were reckoned to have been in the forest for up to twelve years. Further investigation of the T-shirt found that it had been manufactured by the bicycle and garment company Chain Reaction and had been available for sale only between 2003 and 2006. On the front it had a rose and heart with wings and the word 'Angelic' in pink text. From this, the victim was given the name 'Angel'. Police released an artist's impression of the shirt, hoping it might jog someone's memory, but nobody came forward.

Both the dating of the bones and the T-shirt ruled out Ivan as a suspect: at the time of death Ivan had been in gaol for several (perhaps as many as nine) years.

As the police combed missing persons and other records in several states, they turned to Dr Susan Hayes, a facial anthropologist from the University of Western Australia. Flown to Sydney, Dr Hayes examined Angel's skull and used a sophisticated computer graphics program to reconstruct an image of Angel's face. In December 2012 the Homicide Squad released the image, asking, 'Do you know her?' By this time police knew quite a bit more about Angel: she had most likely been a teenager when she died; she had been in the forest for seven years or less; she had shoulder-length hair; her remains showed significant signs of trauma—she had been murdered. 'We're hoping someone might remember her as being a friend or a neighbour, or even someone they recognise as having been a member of their local community,' Detective Superintendent Willing, the officer in charge of the Homicide Squad, told the media.

In New South Wales alone, more than 50 women listed on the missing persons register matched Angel's age range. After several of these were eliminated, police began to suspect the victim might be from interstate or overseas. In November 2012 Western Australia police announced that 'Information received by police indicates the woman may have been a backpacker or worked in a vineyard [in the Margaret River region], and may have been of German or European background,' but there was no firm evidence to back these claims and no new leads emerged. One theory was that Angel's murderer had studied Ivan's career and was a copycat killer.

■ ■ ■

On the evening of 20 November 2010, Ivan Milat's grand-nephew, seventeen-year-old Matthew Milat, eighteen-year-old Cohen Klein, David Auchterlonie, who had turned seventeen that day, and his friend Chase Day, aged eighteen, drove into the Belanglo State Forest. Milat stopped the car and he and Klein then killed Auchterlonie and hid his body, covering it with branches and surrounding debris, just as Ivan had done almost two decades earlier.

The next day Chase Day told his father what had happened and his father took him to Picton Police Station, where he told police about the murder of his mate. Day led police to Belanglo and Auchterlonie's body. A day later Milat was arrested. He declined to participate in a recorded interview. Later the same day Klein was also arrested. In a recorded interview he admitted to driving with Milat and the others to the forest on the Saturday night, but claimed not to have known what Milat was planning. Later Klein changed his story, saying that Milat had been talking about wanting to kill Auchterlonie but insisting that he had paid no attention, believing that Milat was merely 'bullshitting'.

When police arrested Klein they seized his mobile phone. At first there appeared to be nothing of significance on it, but when the forensic team examined it they discovered a deleted video recording of the murder. Both youths were charged with murdering Auchterlonie. Both were refused bail.

It emerged that Matthew had been living in Newcastle with his then partner and their young daughter and working full time until September 2010, when he lost his job and moved into his grandparents' home in Bargo, south of Sydney. Now unemployed, Matthew spent his days smoking cannabis—he had been using drugs since the age of fourteen—and drinking alcohol. He had a new girlfriend, Rachael, and spent much of his time with Klein, Auchterlonie and Day.

Milat spent Saturday, 20 November the same way he spent most days, smoking cannabis with his mates. But on this day something was different. Several times Milat declared that he, Klein and possibly others were going to the Belanglo State Forest that night to kill someone, that 'someone' being Auchterlonie. Milat told Rachael, 'Me, Cohen and someone else are going to kill Auchto [Auchterlonie's nickname]', to which Rachael replied, 'Don't be stupid. Stop joking, no you're not.' Milat and Klein, who was standing beside him, laughed. When Rachael asked who the third person was, Milat told her it was Chase Day. Later, when Milat, Klein and Rachael were sitting in Milat's car, Milat rubbed his hands together and said, 'We're going out to Belanglo. Someone's going to die.'

Saturday was Auchterlonie's birthday and he spent it celebrating with friends and family. In the evening Auchterlonie went to visit Day. Auchterlonie had spoken several times on the phone that day with both Milat and Klein. That evening Milat called Auchterlonie and persuaded him to accompany them to the Belanglo State Forest to have a few drinks and a bit of fun. Around 9 p.m. Milat and Klein picked up Auchterlonie and Day and drove in Milat's car to the service station at Sutton Forest, a small village in the Southern Highlands. Auchterlonie had brought some cannabis with him. After buying a pair of scissors to cut up the cannabis, they bought something to eat at McDonald's, then drove to the Belanglo State Forest. Klein was in the front passenger seat, Auchterlonie and Day in the back seat. A short distance into the forest Milat stopped the car. He and Klein got out and went to the back of the car, while Auchterlonie got into the front seat and started cutting up the cannabis.

Auchterlonie was playing music on his phone. Klein picked up his own phone and switched on the video camera. He filmed Auchterlonie sitting in the front seat. There was some discussion about 'rolling a joint' and Klein was heard to say, quietly: 'Yeah, go it,' and Milat asked, 'Can you feel the adrenaline?' Klein then suggested to Auchterlonie that there might be a bong in the boot of the car and that he should go and have a look. As he walked towards the back of the car, Milat took a double-bladed axe from the boot and struck Auchterlonie in the torso.

Day got out of the car but was ordered by Klein to get back inside, which he did. Klein used his phone to record every moment of the murder. Auchterlonie was clearly in great pain as Milat struck him again with the axe. After Auchterlonie began running around the car Milat screamed at him to lie on the ground. When he did, Milat stood over him, accusing him of 'spreading stories about him [Milat] and sticking his nose into his business'. Milat then swung the axe again and struck Auchterlonie in the back of his head. Auchterlonie died instantly and Klein stopped recording.

Day then got out of the car and helped Milat drag the body into the undergrowth, where they covered it with branches and debris. The three then drove back to Bargo. On the way Milat said, 'That [the killing of Auchterlonie] was such an adrenaline rush.' Klein replied, 'I told you that you're going to go down the same path as your uncle.' The handle of the axe had been wrapped in electrical tape so it could be ripped off, removing all fingerprints, Milat boasted. After dropping off Day and Klein, Milat picked up another friend, who was given the pseudonym 'Damien' by the courts, and drove to yet another friend's place where they watched movies until around 2 a.m.

The day after the murder Milat cleaned his car to remove all traces of the killing and was heard gloating, 'You know me, you know my family. You know the last name Milat. I did what they do.' He talked about having stuffed his clothes and the axe into a bag weighed down with bricks and thrown it into the river. The next day Milat said to Damien, 'Guess who I killed?'

'Who?' Damien asked.

Milat replied, 'Nah, don't worry about it.'

'Nah, who?'

'Auchto,' Milat said.

Damien asked, 'What did you kill him with?'

'I hit him in the head with an axe.'

'Who did you get it off?'

Milat answered, 'Ken [a pseudonym for a friend who was not involved in the killing].'

Asked if he was serious, Milat replied, 'I'm serious. Don't tell anyone. If Ken finds out that I told anyone he will kill me because the axe has Ken's DNA on it. If I find out you told anyone I will kill you.'

In the hours after the killing Milat told almost everyone he met what he had done, while also warning them that if they told anyone, he would kill them.

Matthew Milat and Cohen Klein pleaded guilty in the New South Wales Supreme Court to the murder of David Auchterlonie. On 8 June 2012 Acting Justice Mathews accepted prosecution submissions that the killing by Milat and Klein was a senseless, brutal, cold-blooded and premeditated 'thrill kill' with no mitigating factors. Twelve months before his guilty plea and while in his cell, Milat wrote several poems. He put them in an envelope addressed to his mother, asking her to put them somewhere safe, but the poems were intercepted by Juvenile Justice authorities and passed on to police. Mathews referred to three poems written by Milat when handing down her sentence. One, entitled 'Your last day', reads (spelling as in original):

Click-clack,
hear that,
stopping in the, middle of the track,
Are you Getting Nervous in the back,
Should be Cxxt your getting wActed,
talk shit here, talk shit there,
No-one'z really gunna care,
but talk shit with every breath,
You just signed away your health,
I can see you start to sweat,
Wanderin what your gunna get,
hopin 4-1 in the head,
Cxxt ILL Put it in Your Leg,
tell me, ARE YA HAVIN FUN,
get up Cxxt, And start to run,
how fAr are ya gunna get,
Your Match Cxxt you have just Met,
stumblin all OVA the place,
Hear the crunch of leaves and feet,
feel your heart, skip a beat,

Are ya gunna get away,
No hope kid this is your day,
The day that you wont be found,
Six feet under Neath the ground.

Another poem, entitled 'Cold Life', ends with the following lines:

I am not fazed by blood or screams
Nothing I do will haunt my dreams
Maybe they might scare you
Cold blooded killer that's me not you.

Acting Justice Mathews concluded that 'the circumstances of this case . . . clearly falls within the worst category of cases of murder . . . The choice of location itself is a significant matter . . . The Belanglo Forest has assumed a form of notoriety in this State, as being the site where Milat's great uncle, Ivan Milat, lured a number of people and murdered them.'

Her Honour noted that there was evidence before the court that, when Matthew Milat was about fourteen years old, he had sexually abused a three-year-old female relative, but the charges were not proceeded with. She then sentenced Matthew Milat to 43 years' gaol and Cohen Klein to 32 years' gaol for the murder of David Auchterlonie.

Chase Day had only been charged with being an accessory after the fact to the murder of Auchterlonie. Nine months earlier, on 11 September 2011, at the Campbelltown Local Court, the charge against him had been dropped by the Crown prosecutor.

When Angel's remains were discovered in the Belanglo State Forest two months before Auchterlonie was murdered, many speculated that Ivan Milat might have been her killer. But Ivan was in gaol at the time of her murder. After Matthew Milat was convicted of murdering Auchterlonie, some wondered whether he might have murdered Angel. Matthew, however, would have been not much older than ten at the time Angel was murdered.

In October 2015 a 41-year-old man (not identified for legal reasons) was charged with the murder of Angel, identified as 20-year-old Karlie Pearce-Stevenson. Two months later he was charged with the murder of her two-year-old daughter, whose remains were found in South Australia.

21
IT WASN'T ME

In November 2004 John Stewart of the ABC's *Australian Story* program interviewed Ivan Milat by phone inside the Supermax facility at the Goulburn Correctional Centre. Ivan's sister-in-law, Carolynne, married to Ivan's younger brother Bill, was in regular phone contact with him. Carolynne told Stewart, 'Ivan gives me a phone call when he makes a request to use the phone and he has surprised me some mornings and he's rang me a couple of times during the week. We just have general chats and, with Ivan's permission, I have also recorded some of those conversations.'

Carolynne maintains that Ivan is innocent. 'I suppose life would be easier,' she told *Australian Story*, 'if we could accept that he has been found guilty and has done this crime, but that is not the case. He's, in our eyes, he is not guilty of it, and until the day that we find different, we will support him.'

Explaining why she, and at least some other members of the Milat family, believe Ivan to be innocent, she said, 'We believe that Ivan was framed. We believe that the stories that Ivan has told us, he saw one of the detectives taking two bags from the boot of his car. Those bags were taken inside his house and then all of a sudden parts were being found in the house.' Bill Milat also believes Ivan is innocent. He told *Australian Story*, 'I've never believed that Ivan had anything to do with this, right from the word go.'

In one of his conversations with Carolynne, Ivan denied that his brothers Richard or Walter were involved in the murders. Carolynne had asked Ivan, 'If you get a retrial, would you use the legal strategy that was used last time, of blaming your brother?' Ivan replied, 'I never argued that in the first place. I didn't know how that came into it. I was totally amazed when I was sitting down and I heard that, I had no idea. Because my basic defence in my trial was it wasn't me, I didn't know who did it. It was up to them to prove my guilt, not for me to prove my innocence.'

Ivan's lawyers were among those surprised by their client's claim that he was 'totally amazed' when he heard it suggested in court that his brothers were or could have been involved. Ivan's solicitor, Andrew Boe, responded that he had 'yet to be involved in a criminal trial where an assertion of fact was put to the Court without specific instructions from a client to do so and the Milat trial was no exception. The apparent suggestion that we did so in this case is a calculated falsehood. It is, however, not appropriate for us to publish Mr Milat's instructions on this or any other issue at this stage.' In effect, Ivan's own lawyers were calling him a liar.

Carolynne and Bill were not the only members of the family to defend Ivan. The following year, during an interview with *Crime Investigation Australia* for 'Ivan Milat: The backpacker murders', Richard declared Ivan to be innocent: 'No. I don't think he's guilty at all. Not by any evidence I've heard.' Later he added, 'As far as I'm concerned I think he's not guilty at all. I can't see no evidence against him.'

'So you stand by him?' the reporter asked.

Richard replied, 'Yeah until you've got more proof.'

In a 2010 interview with *Crime Investigation Australia* for 'Families of Crime: Backpacker bloodshed', Richard was asked what he thought about being dragged into the trial by Ivan as a suspect for the murders. He replied, 'Yep, Ivan would do anything, and I wouldn't blame him.' Later in the program Richard said, 'It was okay by me on that part because I knew it weren't me so I got no worries, no matter how much implication you can say . . . I knew why he was dragging me into it, trying to save himself.'

Richard's attitude towards the May 1994 police raids was also interesting: 'Fifty police officers come here, Channel 2 helicopters or Channel 10 helicopters, some, somebody's helicopters. Heaps of detectives come here and handled us like Gestapo—every sort of threat you could have. Other than that [it was] just a normal police operation.'

But not all members of the Milat family have been as supportive of Ivan. George, ten years younger than Ivan, made no secret of the fact that he believed him to be guilty. George explained that his father, Stiphan, had been angry that several of the children, including Ivan, could not stay out of trouble with the police and thought they should be locked up. He claimed that on one occasion his father was so furious that 'he tried to pay the police one day 50 bucks each, throw them in gaol and don't let them out . . . he didn't want them home'.

George had no doubt that Ivan committed the murders 'for the fun of it' and that 'he wouldn't have stopped if he didn't get caught'. Asked if he thought Ivan was sorry for what he did, George replied, 'No, he just doesn't care.' George then made a completely unexpected and startling claim: Ivan had admitted the murders to his mother, Margaret. 'She goes down [and visits Ivan in Supermax], comes back and I was having some lunch with Mum, across the table and I looked at her. I said "Mum, did he tell you something you didn't want to hear?" "He admitted he was guilty." I said, "How do you feel? . . . he's out of the way. You can rest up."' Despite Ivan's admission, his mother continued to protest his innocence until her death at the age of 81 in 2001.

Ivan's sister, Shirley, also maintained that Ivan was innocent until she died in 2003. But George offered an explanation for this. According to him, some members of the family knew 'there was trouble somewhere', but didn't know Ivan was murdering the backpackers. Later he appeared to contradict himself by adding that 'they reckon Shirley was in on it . . . I can't really say Shirley did [actually commit any of the murders], all I can do is say she was involved.' He explained that 'there was incest in the family': Ivan had been having an affair with Shirley since the early 1950s, when she was in her twenties. 'Shirley's gone, Ivan's gone and everything's just stopped.'

When asked about Ivan's relationship with Shirley, Ivan's brother Richard replied, 'what's the difference, one or the other, if you're doing it with your sister or your mate up the road?'

Boris, two years older than Ivan, was another brother who was convinced of Ivan's guilt. Asked when he first suspected Ivan, Boris replied, 'I woke up straight away . . . what I knew about Ivan, something was telling me strongly that something wasn't right.' He described Ivan as being 'a completely, completely evil person and I would say that if he never got caught he would have went on to more evil things . . . I'd see 10,000 Ivans die before I'd see one of them [backpackers] die. I just hate him for what he's done . . . He's probably sitting in gaol right now thinking he shouldn't be there, and that's, that's the truth.'

After Ivan's conviction another brother, Alex, became active in the gun lobby. In 1998 he announced that he was going to stand as an independent member in the Queensland Parliament on a pro-gun, pro-knife-carrying and anti-political-correctness ticket. Everyone should be given a .303 calibre rifle to protect Australia, he said.

In 2007 Wally Milat's wife, Lisa, ran for the ACT Senate as a member of the Liberal Democratic Party. The next year she ran for the Wingecarribee Council in the Southern Highlands of New South Wales and two years later, again as a member of the LDP, she ran for the lower house seat of Hume, south of Sydney. Among other things, the LDP sought a relaxation of gun laws. Asked about Ivan, she replied, 'You can't choose your relatives.' Wally also defended a relaxation in gun laws, saying, 'Guns in themselves are harmless, aren't they? It's only the people you put behind them, same as in a car.'

A decade after the trial the Crown prosecutor, Mark Tedeschi, commented that Paul Onions was 'the most important witness in the prosecution case . . . He was the only person who had . . . been the subject of an attempted abduction by Ivan and got away . . . he not only gave evidence which positively identified Ivan Milat as the man who had . . . attempted to abduct him, but he also gave a very good description of his car . . . and . . . the only description of his method.' In addition there was all 'this circumstantial evidence and forensic evidence . . . there was an enormous amount of evidence . . . his possession of the guns was unexplained'.

Tedeschi noted that Ivan 'was asking the jury to accept that all of this evidence was . . . just some terrible coincidence . . . and I think at the end of the day the jury must have felt that it's a little bit like the coincidence that . . . you have a whole lot of pieces of metal lying around . . . and a big wind comes up and just happens to blow it into a jumbo jet . . . a fully functioning jumbo jet'.

22
DID IVAN ACT ALONE?

While the jury answered the question of whether Ivan Milat murdered the seven backpackers in the Belanglo State Forest, it left another unresolved: did Ivan act alone?

Some evidence appeared to point strongly in the direction of there being more than one killer. In three cases two victims were abducted at once, raising the question as to how one offender could control two victims. Two different types of weapons—a knife and a firearm—were used in the murders of Anja Habschied and Gabor Neugebauer, and of Caroline Clarke and Joanne Walters. Two .22 calibre rifles, one a 10/22 Ruger and the other an Anschutz, had been used to fire up to a total of around 100 bullets 165 metres from the Neugebauer crime scene. Richard was supposed to have remarked that 'Stabbing a woman is like cutting a loaf of bread', that 'There are two Germans out there, they haven't found them yet', that 'I know who killed the Germans', and that 'There's more bodies out there, they haven't found them all.' The comment about 'the Germans' was said to have been made before the bodies of Anja and Gabor were found, while the comment about there being 'more bodies out there' was said to have been made before the last bodies were discovered. Justice Hunt himself told the jury that 'as a matter of common sense and experience, it is obvious that more than one person would be needed, particularly when more than one hitchhiker had been picked up, to subdue them and to ensure that there would be no trouble in killing both of them'.

Why, then, am I so sure that Ivan committed the murders by himself?

At law the prosecution was not required to prove whether Ivan acted alone or in company. The fact that he was involved in each of the murders and the abduction was sufficient. As Justice Hunt observed during the trial, 'The Crown says it does not have to prove in this case whether or not the accused acted alone in the course of these killings. The Crown says either the accused did it himself, did the acts himself, or alternatively, the acts were done by him with others in a joint enterprise in which he was responsible for the acts of those others.' By avoiding the argument over whether or not he acted alone, the Crown blunted many of the defence's claims and minimised the opportunities for the defence to sidetrack the jury by taking the focus off Ivan and raising hypothetical scenarios that could have created confusion or doubt. It was a successful strategy, as Ivan's conviction proved.

The strongest evidence that he acted alone is not in the court record but in the story of Ivan's life. His first known 'abduction' occurred in 1971, when he picked up two female hitchhikers, bound them both and had sex with one of them. They escaped when Ivan stopped at a petrol station on the Hume Highway. Ivan was arrested after a police chase, but he subsequently beat the charges. The next documented case, involving Therese and Mary, occurred six years later. They also escaped Ivan's clutches. Again, Ivan was alone when he attempted to abduct them. In 1990, when he attempted to abduct Paul Onions, Ivan was again alone. In all three cases Ivan was by himself, showing that he was confident of subduing either one or two hitchhikers without the help of an accomplice.

The third part of the lone killer argument relates to the 'souvenirs' and weapons seized in the police raids. A large amount of property belonging to the backpacker victims was found in the Eagle Vale house shared by Ivan and his sister, Shirley. Property belonging to the backpackers that was found in the homes of Ivan's mother, Margaret, and his brothers William, Walter and Alex all came from Ivan and no other member of the family. Equipment and weapons used in the murders were either under Ivan's control when found by police, or had been given by Ivan to another member of the family. They included rags similar to those used to bind and gag some victims; electrical tape; cords with blood stains from Caroline Clarke; guns, including the Ruger rifle parts used in several of the murders, found in the Eagle Vale house; and weapons and ammunition, belonging to Ivan, found in the homes of Walter, Richard and Margaret. In addition, the 4WD vehicle described by Paul Onions was Ivan's.

Fourth is the character of Ivan himself. He had no close long-time friend. Even among his family there was dysfunction and distrust. Ivan's demand for control extended to giving clothes and property he had taken from his victims to family members and others, such as his girlfriend Chalinder Hughes, and obtaining gratification and a form of control from watching them wearing the clothes and using the property. These items were strewn around the house in Eagle Vale so that they could be seen, and even used, by visitors. The gratification he derived from these objects came from being able to play the killings over and over again in his mind. They enabled him to relive the violence and the pleasure it gave him.

Ivan's self-confidence reflected a belief that his control was so absolute he would never be caught. That confidence did not extend to taking others into his confidence by making them accomplices to his crimes. Nothing in Ivan's behaviour indicated that he would ever have been willing to put his life and freedom in the hands of another person. Except for the inadvertent partial confession he made to me when I met him inside the Goulburn Supermax, the only person Ivan is said to have admitted his crimes to is his mother, who continued to protest his innocence until the day she died.

There are some indications that with each successive murder Ivan's killings were becoming more ritualistic, and that he was spending more and more time at the crime scenes. Some have taken this to suggest the presence of an accomplice. I suggest the opposite—that the more often Ivan killed, the more self-absorbed and self-possessed he became, asking himself, 'What could I do to make it better, to get more satisfaction?' The answer was to make the killings more ritualised and to take more time carrying them out. This was the psychological scenario Dr Rod Milton had proposed in 1994, before the arrest of Ivan.

In the debate about whether or not Ivan had an accomplice it is essential to distinguish between an accomplice—that is, a person (or people) who participated directly in the abductions and murders—and someone who knew what Ivan was doing but played no part in committing the crimes. I suggest that there is no compelling argument for any person other than Ivan having committed the crimes. There are indications, however, that some members of the Milat family knew Ivan was doing something bad without knowing exactly what it was. Given their knowledge of Ivan's character and behaviour (especially towards his wife, Karen) it seems likely that they would have suspected his bad behaviour involved the abuse of women. Ivan's brother, George, certainly seemed to believe 'there was trouble somewhere'. George also seemed convinced that 'Shirley was in on it'. If anyone in the family knew what Ivan was doing, it seems likely to have been Shirley, since the house she shared with him was full of unexplained property belonging to the murdered backpackers. If she didn't know before his arrest, she knew enough afterwards to attempt to cover up Ivan's crimes once he had been charged with the murders. At Ivan's request, Shirley removed a revolver he had hidden in the backyard so that the police would not find it. While that makes her guilty of concealing a crime, it does not make her an accomplice in the crime.

If Ivan acted alone, how was he able to abduct, subdue and kill more than one victim at a time? We have seen that on at least three occasions—in 1971, 1977 and 1990—his victims were able to escape. Each of those incidents helps build up a picture of how Ivan gained control of his victims.

Having picked up his victims, Ivan engaged them in conversation in order to relax them and ensure that they were suitable for abduction. For example, in the case of Paul Onions, Ivan asked whether he had been in the military (if so, Onions might have learnt skills that made it difficult for Ivan to overpower him) and whether he had relatives or friends nearby (if nobody knew where he was, he would not be missed and his disappearance might go undetected for longer).

Near the Belanglo State Forest, Ivan would make an excuse to stop his car and get out, intending to retrieve his pistol from under the seat and take control. He would tell the victim (or victims) that he intended to rob them and if they followed his instructions then no one would get hurt, but if they tried to resist he would kill them. His purpose was both to enforce cooperation and to confirm his sense of being in control. The next step was to have them bound. He would do this, particularly in the case of a male and female victim, by telling the female to bind her boyfriend with electrical ties that he would give her, reassuring them that it was only to prevent them doing anything silly so that he could rob them without harming them. Having secured one victim, Ivan would then use the tie to bind the second victim himself. Keeping them calm and encouraging them to believe that they would soon be released would have added to Ivan's excitement. Once both victims were bound, Ivan had complete control and from this point he could enjoy the fear experienced by both victims as they realised he had no intention of releasing them, and the terror experienced by the first victim as his or her partner was murdered in front of them. (Not every abduction followed the same pattern, but the evidence given by those who escaped Ivan supports the scenario described above.)

One question remains: why did Ivan's killing spree end?

Over a period of more than two decades, Ivan's violence appeared to have been triggered either by instability in his relationship with a woman or by his lack of a relationship. When he was charged with abduction and rape in 1971, Ivan was not in a relationship with any woman. He met his future wife, Karen, in 1975 and used threats of violence to control their relationship. The marriage is believed to have been going through a bad spell before the attempted abduction of Mary and Therese in 1977. Ivan's wife left him in February 1987 and told him she wanted a divorce. The disappearance and murder of Peter Letcher in November 1987 coincided with a time when Ivan had lost control of his family. According to some members of the Milat family, Ivan had several affairs after separating from his wife and during the period of the backpacker murders (from December 1989 to April 1992), but any such affairs were short-term and insecure: they did not give Ivan the control he needed.

I would argue that by introducing Ivan to her friend Chalinder Hughes, Shirley—either wittingly or unwittingly—put Ivan into the kind of stable relationship that tended to mitigate his impulse to kill, and that Chalinder, by entering into that relationship, took away his need to seek gratification by abducting and murdering hitchhikers. I believe it was those two women who saved more hitchhikers from becoming Ivan's victims.

AFTERWORD

Ivan Milat's record of violence towards women dates back many years before the backpacker killings. In the wake of his conviction for those murders, a number of other unsolved killings and disappearances were reinvestigated. Milat has been named as a person of interest in connection with almost every unsolved disappearance to have occurred in New South Wales in the two decades before his arrest. It is possible that murders Milat himself could not have committed were committed by others copying his methods.

Many thought the Belanglo murders would never be solved. Proving the doubters wrong meant following every clue and logging every piece of information. The experiences gained and lessons learnt during the two and a half years of Task Force Air's existence would lead to significant changes and improvements in the management of major investigations, including the development of the E@gle.i information management system (which, at the time of writing, holds more than 12,200 major investigations and more than 8500 briefs of evidence); the introduction of cold case homicide reviews and the establishment of the Unsolved Homicide Squad; and the systematic review of long-term missing person cases. Several unsolved homicides and missing person cases that had been allowed to languish, sometimes for decades, have been solved as a result. A number of killers have been gaoled.

While much has been achieved, much still needs to be done. Since 1970 no trace has been found of more than 600 long-term missing persons in New South Wales. Of these, around 130 have been classified as 'suspected homicides', but have not been referred to the Unsolved Homicide command. While they continue to be categorised as long-term missing persons rather than suspected murder victims, these cases will be denied the full resources of a homicide investigation. Their families and friends and the community at large deserve more.

■ ■ ■

The murder of seven backpackers in the Belanglo State Forest between December 1989 and April 1992 cast a shadow that did not lift with Ivan Milat's conviction. While Milat is destined to spend the rest of his life in gaol, he has continued to haunt the popular imagination. He is a personification of evil that will not go away. Nobody has suffered more from the legacy of Milat's crimes than the families and friends of the seven young backpackers whose lives he cut short. It is fitting that this book should end with the words of those families and friends.

Frank and Angela Klaassen, who live in Sydney's eastern suburbs, knew the Neugebauer family through their nephew, Arthur Priem, in Holland. They recall how, in April 1992:

> Arthur rang to let us know that Gabor's parents, Manfred and Anke would be coming to Australia with Anja's brother, Norbert, to look for Gabor and Anja. He asked if we could meet them at the airport and give them any assistance they needed. We asked our longtime friends Rita and Peter O'Malley to come with us to the airport as Rita was German and could help with translations, if necessary. Unfortunately, their inquiries in Sydney and travels around Australia were to no avail and the three left Australia coping with the despair of not finding any evidence of Gabor and Anja.

Manfred and Anke would return to Sydney several more times during the investigation. 'During these visits Manfred and Anke stayed with us and so did Herbert Schmidl, Olga Habschied and her son Norbert,' the Klaassens recall, 'and Rita became invaluable in helping the police with translating documents and making phone calls to Germany.'

Rita's godchild, Kim Shipton, remembers: 'Rita and Peter offered their time and energy voluntarily and as a priority, which reflected their caring and giving nature. Their lives were deeply enriched by their experiences and by the friendships built with the victims' families.'

On behalf of his wife, Anke, and himself, Manfred Neugebauer writes:

It was Christmas Eve 1991 when we last talked with our son Gabor in Sydney by telephone. Every year, it is still a time of grief for us. The days are short and the nights are long and the snow covers the ground around our home in Germany. We remember the familiar sound of his voice. His final resting place is now in the cemetery, only a five-minute walk from here, and Anke visits and cares for the grave almost daily.

When Anke visits Anja Habschied's mother, Olga, near Munich, 650 kilometres away, both mothers drive to Anja's grave to think of Anja and Gabor, the young couple whom Ivan Milat denied the right to live a full life.

The Australian authorities have done their best to discover the facts, but Milat has still not confessed to his crimes, so we can only imagine what happened in the Belanglo Forest on Boxing Day 1991. Milat's failure to confess means there are many questions still unanswered. Part of Anja's body has not been recovered. Did he act alone?

Besides our youngest son Gabor, we have two other children, a son, Tibor, and a daughter, Ilka. Both are married and have children. They were totally devastated by the death of their brother. Ilka immediately made a clay sculpture of Gabor's head which still looks from outside the window into the room that was Gabor's bedroom as a child. Tibor named one of his twin sons Gabor, thus we have not a son but a grandson, Gabor Neugebauer. Each year Tibor meets with classmates and friends of Gabor to remember him. Some of his old classmates still visit his grave, so Gabor is not forgotten. A few

> days ago I met the mother of a classmate of Gabor. We spoke and she said to me that when she talks with me she feels like she is looking at the face of Gabor. She reminded me of the saying, 'A man is not dead until he is forgotten.' Gabor is not dead.

Manfred also pays tribute to the Klaassens and Rita O'Malley for their emotional support and for their help in acting as intermediaries between the families and the police task force, particularly Bob Godden and Steve Leach.

Deborah Everist's brother, Tim, writes:

> Our father, Frank, passed away after Deborah had been reported missing but before her remains were found, so he never knew what had happened to her nor had he heard the name Ivan Milat. Our mother, Pat, died in 2009, never having gotten over the murder of Deborah.
>
> I didn't believe what was happening when it first started. You always think, 'It won't happen to me!' I thought Deb would walk through the door one day. But as things developed I guess I was in shock for quite a few years. Friends and other people would find it hard to say anything but 'sorry'. I tended to deal with it by not confiding in anyone, choosing at times not to believe what had happened. On learning that I would be called to give evidence and on facing Milat I had an unearthly feeling of rage, torment and disbelief that someone could have absolutely no respect for innocent human life.
>
> My mother had to endure a life sentence of hell over this horrific event. Having to hear in court the detail of

> what had happened to her daughter was nearly unbearable in itself.

For Olga and Guenther Habschied, 'Time goes by, but it does not heal all wounds. Despite all the years passed, we still have incredible difficulties writing about our children. We are not able to talk about our losses and pain to people outside.'

Ray and Gillian Walters recall Joanne being 'very happy picking grapes in the Capogreco Winery in Mildura', and how, 'after our own visits to the winery we forged a great friendship with all the Capogreco family, which has lasted throughout these past years'. And yet, they write, 'We meet people now, perhaps when we are away from home where people do not know us, perhaps on holiday, and they ask the inevitable questions, "Have you any children?" Any conversation about Australia will include questions like, "Have you been to Sydney?" "Have you seen the Opera House?" We still find this very difficult.'

> We met a number of people in Australia, people who have become good friends, and we have received a lot of support from the Welsh Societies and Victim Support Groups, but by far we are most grateful to the Police out there over the years who have looked after us and kept us informed throughout. It would be unfair to name individuals, for they have all been tremendous, but we would like to make a special mention of Detective Sergeant Steve Leach, who is no longer with us, and who became a special friend.

In a final remark that could speak for all the families and friends, Ray and Gillian write: 'There is only one man/monster responsible for this tragic case and that is Ivan Milat. We would like to thank everyone who had a hand in his capture and prosecution.'

Milat is a story of unfathomable cruelty, a portrait in terror. But it is also a story about the small kindnesses of strangers, about the value of friendship, and about the everyday acts of courage and determination that make a huge difference to the lives of us all.

APPENDICES

Appendix 1: Summary of circumstances implicating Ivan Milat in the seven backpacker murders and the attempted abduction of Paul Onions

James Harold Gibson and Deborah Phyllis Everist: Disappeared 30 December 1989

Items located and claims against Ivan	Comments
Green sleeping bag found on shelf in walk-in wardrobe in bedroom 1 at Ivan's house in Eagle Vale.	1. Found in same plastic bag as Salewa sleeping bag identified as belonging to Simone Schmidl. 2. Identified by Timothy Everist, brother of Deborah, as having been borrowed by Deborah. 3. Photograph located by police in search of William Milat's house at Bargo depicts Ivan with a similar sleeping bag. Picture has caption 'Wombeyan 29.3.91'.
Ivan carried a knife in his car. Gibson, Everist, Schmidl, Habschied, Clarke and Walters had stab wounds and/or clothing cut.	1. A camouflage-handled Bowie knife in a brown leather pouch was found inside a 'Triple M' bag in bedroom 4 at the Eagle Vale house. 2. Ivan said he carried the camouflage knife in his work bag. 3. Witness Johanna Breitkopf, who worked with Ivan, saw the knife on the floor of Ivan's car. 4. Anthony Sara, a workmate of Ivan's, identified the knife as being carried by Ivan.

Items located and claims against Ivan	Comments
	5. Craig Gandy, work associate of Ivan, identified the camouflage-coloured knife as being very similar to the one carried by Ivan.
Ricoh XR-2 camera, serial number 32103005, lens serial number 110731.	1. Found on 31 December 1989 west of bridge on side of Galston Road, Galston. 2. Identified as belonging to Gibson. 3. Ivan was working at Dural (near Galston) during week of 12–18 December 1989.
Berghaus 'Cyclops Echo' backpack, red with blue trim and green suede, first seen on side of Galston Road, Galston, west of bridge, in January 1990. Picked up from side of road on 13 March 1990 by local resident and handed to police a fortnight later.	1. Identified as belonging to Gibson. 2. Name cut out, as with Schmidl's water bottle and pouch found in bedroom 4 of Ivan's house. 3. Ivan was working at Dural in week of 12–18 December 1989.

Simone Loretta Schmidl: Disappeared 20 January 1991

Items located and claims against Ivan	Comments
Red size 12 T-shirt with Loquat Valley School emblem cut down the back found about 50 metres from Schmidl's body.	1. Cut rag. Cut the way it was, the T-shirt was consistent with industrial recycled rags found at Ivan's house.
Green water bottle and pouch found with Ivan's imperial telescopic sight in 'F15E Seymour Johnson' model plane box on bed in bedroom 4 of Ivan's house.	1. Name 'Simi' scratched in two places on the water bottle and patch torn out in pouch. 2. Identified as having been purchased by Schmidl in New Zealand with witness Jeanette Muller, who purchased identical water bottle and pouch. 3. Admitted by Ivan as belonging to Schmidl.
Green and pink/purple Salewa sleeping bag in white plastic bag found in same plastic bag as green sleeping bag and identified as being owned by Everist, found in walk-in robe in bedroom 1 at Ivan's house.	1. The Salewa sleeping bag matched the blue Salewa cover found in the garage of Ivan's house. 2. Admitted by Ivan as belonging to Schmidl.
Blue Salewa nylon sleeping bag cover containing: green Vaude Hogan tent bag with tent and fly, green peg bag with pegs and cords, and green bag with aluminium tent frame; found on shelving in garage at Ivan's house.	1. Blue sleeping bag cover belonging to Schmidl's Salewa sleeping bag found in bedroom 1 of Ivan's house. 2. Ivan admitted sleeping bag cover and contents belonged to Schmidl.
Compact-o-mat headband found wrapped around Vaude Hogan tent in Salewa sleeping bag cover.	1. Identical band found around Schmidl's head in forest. 2. Jeanette Muller said Schmidl had a pair of these headbands. 3. Ivan admitted the headband belonged to Schmidl.

Items located and claims against Ivan	Comments
Arno multicoloured strap in 'Cadpac 5' bag with shotgun parts and straps located on shelf in garage of Ivan's house.	1. John Timmins identified the 'Cadpac 5' bag as being identical to those used by Readymix where Ivan worked. 2. Ivan admitted the 'Cadpac 5' bag and contents were his, but denied any knowledge of the Arno strap. 3. Ivan admitted the Arno strap belonged to Schmidl.
Envelope containing three NZ $20, one NZ $10 and other banknotes located on bedside table in bedroom 3 of Ivan's house.	1. Ivan had not been out of Australia in the relevant period. 2. Schmidl had travelled to New Zealand on 20 November 1990 and returned to Australia on 19 January 1991.
Markill cooking set with Edelrid stove and Kayser cups located by police in kitchen pantry in Ivan's house.	1. Kristine and Doris Murphy identified cooking set and stove as belonging to Schmidl. 2. Jeanette Muller identified Kayser cups as belonging to Schmidl.
Salewa 'Canyon SH 60/75' multicoloured backpack handed to police by Elizabeth 'Joan' Milat, sister-in-law of Ivan and married to Alex, at West Woombye, Queensland.	1. Joan Milat said Ivan had given her the backpack before she and Alex moved to West Woombye in January 1993. 2. Ivan admitted the backpack belonged to Schmidl.
One yellow grandfather T-shirt with one cut piece of green cloth stamped 'Linen Service Public Hospital', five cut pieces of green cloth and two cut pieces of light-blue cloth located on garage bench at the Guildford house of Ivan's mother, Margaret.	1. John Walls identified the T-shirt as being manufactured for and only available from Hallenstein stores in New Zealand during the latter part of 1990.

Items located and claims against Ivan	Comments
	2. Schmidl purchased four of these T-shirts on 20 December 1990. 3. The cut rags were consistent with being industrial recycled rag.
E. W. Groening bag containing a quantity of rags located in garage of Ivan's house.	1. Similar to rags found at and near crime scenes in the forest. 2. Identified as being supplied to the Central Asphalt Depot. 3. Ivan admitted that he obtained the bag of 'jumbo' rags from work.
Blue High Sierra day pack with contents including: two camouflage-coloured SKK rifle magazines; four cartridge adaptors containing 24 .45 calibre PMC, Winchester and Norma cartridges; five packets of Winchester 30/30 cartridges, and seven packets of Hushfire .22 calibre cartridges, batch number '52392', located in an apple box in the alcove under Walter Milat's house at Hill Top.	1. Ivan admitted that the day pack belonged to Schmidl. 2. Ivan admitted that the two SKK magazines belonged to him. 3. The five packets of Winchester 30/30 cartridges were suitable for use in the Winchester 30/30 repeating rifle located in the alcove under Walter's house, and consistent with a packet of cartridges in a photograph of Ivan holding a Winchester 30/30 rifle. Photograph dated '16.1.94'. 4. The seven packets of Hushfire .22 calibre cartridges have the same batch number—'52392'—as packets found in yellow haversack marked 'Ivan' found in the alcove under Walter's house (one empty packet), and in the pockets of green

Items located and claims against Ivan	Comments
	jacket with the name 'Preston' in Ivan's Holden Jackaroo number QBY-388 (two packets), and ten other packets found in the alcove under Walter's house.
Ivan carried a knife in his car. Schmidl and others suffered stab wounds.	1. A camouflage-handled Bowie knife in brown leather pouch was found inside a 'Triple M' bag in bedroom 4 of Ivan's house. 2. Ivan admitted that the knife was his and that he carried it in his work bag. 3. Johanna Breitkopf identified the knife as similar to the one she had seen in Ivan's car. 4. Anthony Sara identified the knife as the one carried by Ivan. 5. Craig Gandy identified the knife as being very similar to the one carried by Ivan.

Gabor Kurt Neugebauer and Anja Susanne Habschied: Disappeared 26 December 1991

Items located and claims against Ivan	Comments
Two pieces of material. One piece of material knotted and wrapped around head of Neugebauer. The second piece of material was used as a gag and covered mouth of Neugebauer.	1. Both pieces of material came from one garment, a dress. 2. The knot was of similar configuration to knotted pink cloth found with pink jeans belonging to Habschied found 165 metres from Neugebauer.
A leash-type device made of a length of black electrical tape wound into two loops, with brown leather strap, a length of white sash cord and black cable tie, all intertwined, located 61 metres from Neugebauer.	1. The cable tie, electrical tape and sash cord were similar to items found at Ivan's house. 2. Karen Milat identified the cord as being of a type used by Ivan.
Length of black electrical tape located 62 metres from Neugebauer.	1. Six small pieces stuck together compared with tape in 'leash' and tape at Ivan's house. Jim Gothard, a senior analyst from the NSW Health Department's Division of Analytical Laboratories, identified the tapes as being of the same composition as that found in the forest. The surface was different, but this could have been caused by weathering.
Piece of pink cloth with knot located with folded pink jeans belonging to Habschied 165 metres from Neugebauer.	1. Cloth with knot consistent with use as a blindfold. 2. Matches strip of pink cloth and buttons found nearby with a pair of underpants.

Items located and claims against Ivan	Comments
	3. Professor Michael Pailthorpe said both pieces of pink cloth were part of the same garment, possibly a shirt or blouse.
Length of yellow and blue rope located 165 metres from Neugebauer.	1. Rope had two loops, one loop measured at 70 centimetres long, the other at 12 centimetres. 2. Identified as being similar to rope used by Telecom and rope in boot of green Datsun Bluebird number RJF-631, at Hill Top, the property of Richard Milat, but printing ink on tape inside rope a different colour. 3. Karen Milat identified the rope as being the same type as that used by Ivan.
Small-sized singlet cut down the back from the neck to the waist located in vicinity of Habschied.	1. Professor Pailthorpe described the cut and material as being consistent with being cut industrial recycled rags.
Ebbtide sloppy joe located in vicinity of Habschied.	1. Consistent with being an industrial recycled rag.
Empty Winchester 'Winner' .22 calibre cartridge case box and plastic tray located 165 metres from Neugebauer.	1. Boxes with same batch number 'ACD1CF2', manufactured on 2 June 1988, found in alcove under Walter's house.
Empty Eley .22 calibre cartridge box located 165 metres from Neugebauer.	1. Batch number of box is 'J23CGA' or 'J26CGA', manufactured on 23 or 26 March 1979.

Items located and claims against Ivan	Comments
	2. Boxes with batch number 'J23CGA' were found by police in bedroom 4 in Ivan's house and in the alcove under Walter's house.
Twenty-three of 27 Winchester .22 calibre cartridge cases, twenty Winchester .22 calibre cartridge cases, and four unfired Winchester .22 cálibre cartridges, all located 165 metres from Neugebauer.	1. Forty-seven cartridge cases and the four unfired cartridges are consistent with Winchester 'Winner', 'H' head stamp. 2. Thirty-eight packets of Winchester 'Winner' cartridges were found by police in the alcove under Walter's house. 3. Cartridges, consistent with Winchester 'Winner' brand, were found in bedrooms 3 and 4 of Ivan's house. 4. One Winchester cartridge was found by David Gill in the silver Nissan Patrol that he owned and that had been previously owned by Ivan. 5. One cartridge case with Winchester 'Subsonic', 'W' head stamp and five packets of Winchester 'Subsonic' cartridges, batch number 'AED1FE32', found in alcove under Walter's house.
Twenty-six of 30 Eley .22 calibre cartridge cases; one Eley .22 calibre cartridge case; eleven Eley .22 calibre cartridge cases; and four Eley .22 calibre cartridge cases located 165 metres from Neugebauer.	1. Detective Superintendent Prior identified two Eley cartridge cases as having been fired through the Anschutz rifle located in the alcove at Walter's house.

Items located and claims against Ivan	Comments
Six bullet fragments in two trees 165 metres from Neugebauer.	1. Four of the six fragments were consistent with having been discharged from a Ruger 10/22. 2. A Ruger and parts were found at Ivan's house. 3. The other two fragments were consistent with having been discharged from an Anschutz rifle. 4. An Anschutz rifle was located in the alcove at Walter's house.
Ruger trigger assembly, bolt assembly, spring and guide, 50-shot Ram-Line magazine with two pieces of cloth in white plastic bag and Ruger ten-shot rotary magazine located in wall cavity of Ivan's house. Ruger receiver serial number 120-15357 located in Hytest boot in hallway cupboard of Ivan's house. Ruger barrel band broken into two located in the 'Sarnia' box in bedroom 4 of Ivan's house. Ruger black gun butt end (plate) located on shelf in garage at Ivan's house.	1. All parts are suitable for use in a .22 calibre Ruger model 10/22 rifle. 2. The trigger mechanism (item 1) and receiver (item 3) have camouflage paint indistinguishable from paint on paintball mask and magazine engraved 'I M' and 'TEXAS' with other model paints found in bedroom 4 of Ivan's house. 3. Ivan said he used model paints to paint the mask. 4. The receiver is part of a Ruger model 10/22 rifle sold to the Horsley Park Gun Shop with two other firearms in early 1988. 5. The Ruger model 10/22 does not appear in the records of the gun shop. When sold to the gun shop the rifle had no camouflage paint on it.

Items located and claims against Ivan	Comments
	6. Records of the Horsley Park Gun Shop indicate that a Winchester 'Defender' pump-action shotgun, serial number L2015051, found in the alcove at Walter's house was purchased from the shop on 12 December 1987 by someone using the shooter's licence of Norman Chong. A receipt for the transaction was found in the drawer of the dressing table in bedroom 4 at Ivan's house. 7. Walter Milat said Ivan had access to the Chong licence and that he had a Winchester shotgun. 8. Ivan said he purchased a Winchester shotgun using the Chong licence. 9. Records of the gun shop indicate that a Baikal .22 calibre rifle (not located) was purchased from that shop on 5 January 1988 by someone using the Chong licence. 10. The gun shop records indicate that a Ruger Mini-14 .223 calibre self-loading rifle, serial number 180-81020, found in the alcove at Walter's house was purchased on 27 May 1988 by someone using the Chong licence.

Items located and claims against Ivan	Comments
	11. Walter Milat said Ivan had access to the Chong licence and that he had a Ruger Mini-14 rifle. 12. Ivan said he purchased a Ruger Mini-14 rifle using the Chong licence.
Book, *Ruger 10/22 Instruction Manual*, located inside *Bituminous Surfacing* book on dressing table in bedroom 4 of Ivan's house.	1. '4 4 92' written on front cover. Karen Milat said this was Ivan's handwriting. 2. The 'unused' Ruger model 10/22 rifle, serial number 234-11733, found in the alcove at Walter's house was purchased on 4 April 1992 in the name of Pittaway from the Horsley Park Gun Shop. 3. Walter Milat said he purchased the rifle from the gun shop using the Pittaway licence, which had been left at their mother's address, using money provided by Ivan. 4. Walter Milat said that some time later he took the rifle to Ivan's house and left it there for the accused. 5. Ivan disputed Walter's version of events and knowledge of the weapon. 6. Ivan admitted that the instruction manual was his.

Items located and claims against Ivan	Comments
Book, Desert Publications, *Select Fire 10/22*, located on shelf in family room of Ivan's house.	1. Relates to a Ruger model 10/22 rifle and its internal workings and includes conversion of the rifle to fully automatic. 2. The book has Ivan's fingerprints on it. 3. Ivan admitted that the book was his.
One pair of worn size 7 Hytest boots with plastic located in cupboard in hallway of Ivan's house, and one pair of new size 7 Hytest boots in shoebox located in wardrobe in bedroom 4 of Ivan's house.	1. The shoes are of a type issued to Ivan by the RTA and Readymix. 2. The Ruger receiver was wrapped in plastic in one of the boots. 3. Ivan admitted that the boots in the hall cupboard were his.
Anschutz .22 calibre rifle, number 1053118 (minus bolt) located in the alcove at Walter Milat's house. Anschutz .22 calibre rifle bolt located wrapped in red checked material inside the yellow haversack marked 'IVAN' in a Sanyo box in the same alcove as the rifle.	1. The barrel on the Anschutz rifle had been threaded to fit a silencer. 2. The rifle was wrapped in the same blanket as a Winchester 30/30 repeating rifle, serial number 4111732. 3. Ivan is seen holding a Winchester 30/30 rifle in photographs dated '16.1.94' taken at his house. 4. The red checked material has the same pattern as the material on the bed in bedroom 4 in Ivan's house. 5. Karen Milat identified the red checked material as part of a shirt she bought Ivan.

Items located and claims against Ivan	Comments
	6. The yellow haversack also had one empty packet of Hushfire .22 calibre cartridges, batch number '52392'. The same batch number on packets of Hushfire bullets found in High Sierra A day pack, in pockets of green jacket with name 'Preston' found in the accused's Holden Jackaroo number QBY-388 and in ten other packets found in the alcove at Walter's house. 7. Ivan said that he purchased the Anschutz rifle from a workmate at Boral in late 1989 or early 1990.
Threaded barrel cap located in console of Ivan's red Holden Jackaroo number QBY-388.	1. Suitable for use on the Anschutz .22 calibre rifle found in alcove of Walter's house.
Four boxes of Eley subsonic .22 calibre cartridges located inside 'Sarnia' IA box in bedroom 4 of Ivan's house, and twelve packets of Eley .22 calibre cartridges located in a cardboard box in the alcove at Walter's house.	1. The cartridges at both houses have batch number 'J23CGA', manufactured on 23 March 1979. 2. The batch number on the Eley cartridge found in the forest 165 metres from Neugebauer was either 'J23CGA' or 'J26CGA' and manufactured in 1979.

Items located and claims against Ivan	Comments
Brick (with six packets) of Winchester 'Winner' .22 calibre cartridges located in apple box, and three bricks (ten packets each) and two packets of Winchester 'Winner' .22 calibre cartridges, all located in alcove at Walter's house.	1. All packets had batch number 'ACD1CF2', manufactured on 2 June 1988, the same batch number as on the Winchester 'Winner' box located 165 metres from Neugebauer.
One Winchester .22 cartridge case with Ruger impression located in plastic bag with .45 and .32 calibre ammunition, inside cardboard box on bed in bedroom 4 at Ivan's house.	1. The cartridge case is consistent with having been fired by a Ruger 10/22 that had fitted the Ruger bolt assembly found in the wall cavity at Ivan's house.
Brick (with five packets) of Winchester 'Subsonic' .22 calibre cartridges located in cardboard fruit box in alcove at Walter's house.	1. The five boxes of Winchester 'Subsonic' cartridges have batch number 'AED1FE32', manufactured on 23 May 1991. 2. The cartridges are consistent with the single Winchester cartridge case with 'W' head stamp found in forest 165 metres from Neugebauer.
Thirty-eight .22 calibre cartridges including Winchester cartridges with 'H' head stamps located loose in a tin in the wardrobe of bedroom 3 at Ivan's house. Fifty Winchester .22 calibre cartridges with 'H' head stamps, loose in black plastic tray located with model paints and brushes in cardboard box under window of bedroom 4 in Ivan's house.	1. The Winchester cartridges in both groups are consistent with the Winchester cartridges found at the Clarke crime scene in the forest.

Items located and claims against Ivan	Comments
Four Winchester .22 calibre cartridge cases found at the Wombeyan Caves Road property owned by Walter and Richard Milat.	1. The cartridge cases were consistent with having been fired from a rifle to which the Ruger bolt assembly located in the wall cavity at Ivan's house had been fitted.
Three Winchester and one PMC .22 calibre cartridge cases located at shooting mound on property previously owned by Alex Milat at Buxton.	1. All four cartridges had been discharged from a rifle to which the Ruger bolt assembly found in the wall cavity at Ivan's house had been fitted.
Envelope containing two Indonesian 1000 rupiah, two Indonesian 500 rupiah, two Indonesian 100 rupiah and other banknotes located in bedside table of bedroom 3 at Ivan's house.	1. Ivan had not been out of Australia in the relevant period. 2. Habschied and Neugebauer arrived in Darwin after flying from Indonesia on 20 November 1991.
Roll of black electrical tape located on bedside table in bedroom 3 of Ivan's house. Roll of black electrical tape located in blue bag in bedroom 3 at Ivan's house, and roll of black electrical tape located on floor of garage at Ivan's house.	1. Similar to electrical tape located in the forest and elsewhere in Ivan's house.
Four black 'G' series cable ties, found with eight other cable ties located on shelving in garage at Ivan's house.	1. Ties compared with the cable tie in the 'leash device' found at the Habschied and Neugebauer crime scene. 2. Andrew Foster said the four 'G' series cable ties are the same as the cable tie marked 'G3' in 'leash device'.

Items located and claims against Ivan	Comments
	3. Foster said the cable ties were manufactured by Giantlok in Taiwan and imported by his company, Solterco. They are heavy-duty ties, not for domestic use, and his company has supplied this type of cable tie to the RTA.
Five lengths of sash cord in green striped pillowcase and single length of sash cord located on a shelf in the garage at Ivan's house.	1. Cords compared with sash cord in 'leash device' at Habschied and Neugebauer crime scene. 2. Karen Milat identified the sash cords as the type used by Ivan to tie minibike onto trailer. 3. Karen Milat identified the pillowcase as belonging to Ivan's mother. 4. Ivan said that he used this type of sash cord.
Bowie knife with camouflage-handle in brown leather pouch found inside 'Triple M' bag in bedroom 4 of Ivan's house.	1. Ivan carried a knife in his car. 2. Victims Everist, Gibson, Schmidl, Habschied, Clarke and Walters had stab wounds and/or clothing cut. 3. Drawing by witness Johanna Breitkopf of knife in Ivan's car. 4. Witness Anthony Sara identified the knife found as the one carried by Ivan. 5. Craig Gandy, work associate of Ivan, said Ivan had a knife very similar to the one found. 6. Ivan said that he carried the knife in his work bag.

Items located and claims against Ivan	Comments
Length of blue and yellow rope found in boot of green Datsun Bluebird number RJF-631, owned by Richard Milat of Hill Top.	1. Telecom rope, similar to that found in vicinity of Neugebauer, but printing on tape inside rope different colour.
E. W. Groening bag containing a quantity of rags located in garage at Ivan's house.	1. Rags similar to items found in forest including: Neugebauer's gag, singlet and Ebbtide sloppy joe. 2. Type of bag and industrial recycled 'jumbo' rags supplied to the Central Asphalt Depot. 3. Ivan said that he got the bag of 'jumbo' rags from work.
Owner's manual for silver Nissan Patrol number OPO-172 (now number SPW-930) received from David Gill, owner of vehicle after Milat.	1. Contains two handwritten pages of service history of vehicle. Karen Milat identifies the handwriting as Ivan's. 2. One entry reads 'L H Door [left-hand door] Repaired 10/1/92 73200 K'. 3. Ivan left his Nissan Patrol vehicle with his neighbour, Mr El-Hallak, to repair the damage caused by a bullet having been discharged inside it just over a week after Anja Habschied and Gabor Neugebauer disappeared. 4. Ivan said that he discharged his rifle in his car at Wombeyan Caves about 29 December 1991. 5. Barry Winning of State Lotteries said that a registration card in Ivan's name was used at a Mittagong newsagency on 29 December 1991.

Caroline Jane Clarke and Joanne Lesley Walters: Disappeared 18 April 1992

Items located and claims against Ivan	Comments
Three sections of brown cloth, part of Gloweave shirt, wrapped around Walters' face and mouth. One piece knotted.	1. All pieces from one shirt, size 41. 2. One piece (shoulder section) compared in size and shape with piece of shirt material found with Ruger parts in the wall cavity of Ivan's house. 3. Also compared with a piece of shirt material found wrapped around a rifle bolt in the padlocked grey locker at the Guildford house of Ivan's mother, Margaret. 4. Professor Pailthorpe said the cloth in the grey locker was approximately the same width as the piece from the Walters' gag, but slightly longer. 5. Ivan said he may have bought Gloweave shirts, which range in size from 38 to 45.
Seven spent bullets removed from Clarke's head and head area and three metal bullet fragments sifted from soil under Clarke.	1. Markings on the bullets suggest the use of a silencer. 2. Homemade silencer found in garage at Ivan's place. 3. This silencer was tested by Sergeant Gerard Dutton, but blew out baffles inside silencer (could have fitted a modified Ruger model 10/22 rifle barrel). 4. Noel Wild, a workmate of Ivan, said he saw Ivan with a silencer fitted on a .22 calibre rifle.

Items located and claims against Ivan	Comments
	5. Witnesses Johanna Breitkopf and Walter Milat said that Ivan discussed silencers. 6. Rifles other than the Ruger, owned by Ivan, had threaded barrels to suit silencers.
Ten fired Winchester .22 calibre cartridge cases found within 5 metres of Clarke.	1. All cartridge cases could be reasonably expected to have been ejected from a rifle after it had been used to shoot Clarke. 2. All cartridge cases had been discharged from a Ruger 10/22 to which the Ruger bolt assembly found in the wall cavity at Ivan's house had been attached.
Ruger trigger assembly, bolt assembly, spring and guide, 50-shot Ram-Line magazine with two pieces of shirt in white plastic bag and Ruger ten-shot rotary magazine located in wall cavity in Ivan's house. Ruger receiver serial number 120-15357 located in Hytest boot found in hall cupboard in Ivan's house. Ruger barrel band broken in two located inside Sarnia box in bedroom 4 of Ivan's house, and Ruger black gun butt end (plate) located on shelf in garage at Ivan's house.	1. All items are suitable for use in a .22 calibre Ruger model 10/22 rifle. 2. Trigger mechanism and receiver have camouflage paint essentially indistinguishable from paint on paintball mask and magazine engraved 'I M' and 'TEXAS' and one paint with other model paints found in bedroom 4. 3. Ivan said he used model paints to paint the mask. 4. The receiver is part of a Ruger model 10/22 rifle sold in early 1988 to the Horsley Park Gun Shop with two other firearms. The Ruger does not appear in

Items located and claims against Ivan	Comments
	the records of the gun shop. The rifle had no camouflage paint on it when sold by Komarek. 5. Records of the Horsley Park Gun Shop indicate that a Winchester 'Defender' pump-action shotgun, serial number L2015051, found in the alcove at Walter's house was purchased from the shop on 12 December 1987 by someone using the shooter's licence of Norman Chong. A receipt for the transaction was found in the drawer of the dressing table in bedroom 4 at Ivan's house. 6. Walter Milat said Ivan had access to the Chong licence and that he had a Winchester shotgun. 7. Ivan said he purchased a Winchester shotgun using the Chong licence. 8. Records of the gun shop indicate that a Baikal .22 calibre rifle (not located) was purchased from that shop on 5 January 1988 by someone using the Chong licence. 9. The gun shop records indicate that a Ruger 'Mini-14' .223 calibre self-loading rifle, serial number 180-81020, found in the alcove at Walter's house

Items located and claims against Ivan	Comments
	was purchased on 27 May 1988 by a person using the Chong licence. 10. Walter Milat said Ivan had access to the Chong licence and that he had a Ruger 'Mini-14' rifle. 11. Ivan said that he purchased a Ruger 'Mini-14' rifle using the Chong licence.
Book, *Ruger 10/22 Instruction Manual*, located inside *Bituminous Surfacing* book on dressing table in bedroom 4 of Ivan's house.	1. '4 4 92' written on front cover of manual. Karen Milat said this was Ivan's handwriting. 2. The 'unused' Ruger model 10/22 rifle, serial number 234-11733, found in the alcove at Walter's house was purchased on 4 April 1992 in the name of Pittaway from the Horsley Park Gun Shop. 3. Walter Milat says he purchased the rifle from the gun shop using the Pittaway licence, which had been left at their mother's address, and using money provided by Ivan. 4. Walter Milat said that some time later he took the rifle to Ivan's house and left it there for the accused. 5. Ivan disputed Walter's version of events and knowledge of the weapon. 6. Ivan admitted that the instruction manual was his.

Items located and claims against Ivan	Comments
Book, *Select Fire 10/22*, Desert Publications, located on shelf of family room at Ivan's house.	1. Relates to a Ruger model 10/22 rifle and its internal workings and includes conversion of the rifle to fully automatic. 2. The book has Ivan's fingerprints on it. 3. Ivan said the book was his.
Size 7 worn Hytest boots with plastic located in hallway cupboard of Ivan's house, and size 7 unused Hytest boots in shoebox located in wardrobe in bedroom 4 of Ivan's house.	1. The shoes are of a type issued to Ivan by the RTA and Readymix. 2. The Ruger receiver was wrapped in plastic in one of the boots. 3. Ivan admitted that the boots in the hall cupboard were his.
Thirty-eight .22 calibre cartridges including Winchester cartridges with 'H' head stamps located loose in a tin in wardrobe of bedroom 3 at Ivan's house. Fifty Winchester .22 calibre cartridges with 'H' head stamps, loose in black plastic tray with model paints and brushes in cardboard box located under window of bedroom 4 in Ivan's house.	1. The Winchester cartridges in both groups are consistent with the Winchester cartridges found at the Clarke crime scene in the forest.
Four Winchester .22 calibre cartridge cases found at the Wombeyan Caves Road property owned by Walter and Richard Milat.	1. All four cases were consistent with having been discharged from a rifle to which the Ruger bolt assembly located in the wall cavity in Ivan's house had been fitted.

Items located and claims against Ivan	Comments
Three Winchester and one PMC .22 calibre cartridge cases recovered in shooting mound at Buxton property previously owned by Alex Milat.	1. All four cases were consistent with having been discharged from a rifle to which the Ruger bolt assembly located in the wall cavity in Ivan's house had been fitted.
One Winchester .22 cartridge case with Ruger impression located in plastic bag with .45 and .32 calibre ammunition, inside cardboard box on bed in bedroom 4 at Ivan's house.	1. The cartridge case is consistent with having been fired by a Ruger 10/22 to which the Ruger bolt assembly found in the cavity of the wall at Ivan's house had been fitted.
Two pieces of shirt with Ruger parts in white plastic bag located in wall cavity in Ivan's house.	1. One piece of cloth was the shoulder section of a shirt comparable in size and shape to one of the pieces of material in Walters' mouth gag.
Silver-coloured silencer located in box on shelf in garage of Ivan's house.	1. At least one rifle used in the killing of the backpackers was fitted with a silencer when seven or more bullets were fired. 2. This silencer was tested but blew out baffles inside silencer (could have fitted a modified Ruger model 10/22 rifle barrel). 3. Noel Wild, a workmate of Ivan, said he saw Ivan with a silencer fitted on a .22 calibre rifle. 4. Johanna Breitkopf, who worked with Ivan, and Walter Milat said that Ivan discussed silencers.

Items located and claims against Ivan	Comments
	5. Rifles owned by Ivan other than the Ruger had threaded barrels to suit silencers.
Ivan carried a knife in his car.	1. Victims Everist, Gibson, Schmidl, Habschied and Walters had stab wounds. Clarke and some others had cuts to their clothing. 2. A camouflage-handled Bowie knife in a brown leather pouch was found inside a 'Triple M' bag in bedroom 4 at the Eagle Vale house. 3. Ivan said he carried the camouflage knife in his work bag. 4. Johanna Breitkopf, who worked with Ivan, saw the knife on the floor of Ivan's car. 5. Anthony Sara, a workmate of Ivan's, identified the knife as being carried by Ivan. 6. Craig Gandy, work associate of Ivan, identified the camouflage-coloured knife as being very similar to the one carried by Ivan.
Five lengths of sash cord in green striped pillowcase and single length of sash cord located on a shelf in the garage at Ivan's house.	1. The pillowcase and one of the cords have blood on them consistent with blood of a child of Mr and Mrs Clarke. 2. Cords comparable with sash cord in 'leash device' at Habschied and Neugebauer crime scene.

Items located and claims against Ivan	Comments
	3. Karen Milat identified the sash cords as the type used by Ivan to tie minibike onto trailer. 4. Karen Milat identified the pillowcase as belonging to Ivan's mother. 5. Ivan said he used this type of sash cord.
E.W. Groening bag containing a quantity of rags located in garage of Ivan's house.	1. The rags were similar to Walters' gag and other rags recovered in the forest near crime scenes. 2. Identified as being supplied to the Central Asphalt Depot. 3. Ivan admitted that he obtained the bag of 'jumbo' rags from work.
Olympus 'Trip S' 35 mm camera, serial number 1259700, located in kitchen drawer at Ivan's house.	1. Identified as same type of camera owned by Clarke. 2. The serial number identified the camera as being manufactured in Malaysia and shipped to UK, where it was received on 29 June 1990. Clarke left UK for Australia in September 1991.
1989 English 20-pence coin located in console of Ivan's red Holden Jackaroo number QBY-388.	1. Clarke and Walters came from UK after 1989. 2. Ivan had no international travel movements during relevant period.

Items located and claims against Ivan	Comments
Two photographs of Chalinder Hughes, Ivan's girlfriend, in green and white Benetton top, located in album and photograph wallets on the coffee table in the family room at Ivan's house.	1. Mr and Mrs Clarke say that Caroline had a green and white Benetton top before leaving for Australia. 2. This type of top was sold in Europe before 1990. There was a Benetton shop near where Caroline had worked in Surrey, England. 3. A Benetton representative said that that all photographs of the Benetton top on Chalinder Hughes (Ivan's girlfriend) and Clarke appear to be of the genuine item and the same size, style and colour.
Piece of cloth (shirt) wrapped around a rifle bolt in the padlocked grey locker at the Guildford house of Ivan's mother, Margaret.	1. Professor Pailthorpe said the cloth was consistent with part of the back panel of a shirt and appeared to have been cut and torn. 2. The piece of cloth was comparable in size and shape with one of the pieces of material in the Walters' mouth gag and found to be similar. 3. Ivan said the grey locker and its contents were his.
Blue and lilac Caribee 'Blaze' sleeping bag located in cupboard inside garden shed at Richard Milat's Hill Top property.	1. Ivan admitted the sleeping bag belonged to Walters. 2. Found near a green and orange tent and green tent fly, which Ivan admitted belonged to him.

Items located and claims against Ivan	Comments
Blue and orange Ultimate sleeping bag in grey and red sleeping bag cover, Karrimat bed roll with Karrimor strap marks, blue tent with strip of computer label, and blue bag containing poles and accessories located in cupboard inside garden shed at Richard Milat's Hill Top property.	1. The blue tent was given to Clarke by Stephen Wright during their trip to Tasmania. Wright repaired a hole he had made in the tent with a strip from a computer label. 2. Wright also identified an elasticised camping clothes line in the blue bag as belonging to Clarke. 3. Ivan admitted the sleeping bag belonged to Clarke. 4. Ivan claimed the tent and tent fly belonged to him.
Green and orange tent in brown bag, green tent fly also in brown bag, tent supports and tent poles in two brown bags; hessian bag with tent pegs and ropes, and white plastic bag containing rags and other material located in cupboard in garden shed at Richard Milat's Hill Top property.	1. Property identified by Karen Milat as belonging to Ivan. 2. Karen Milat identified the tent as being the same tent shown in a photograph with Ivan. The green tent fly only is depicted in the photograph. 3. Carolynne Milat identified the tent in the photograph as the tent Ivan used during a camping trip at the Wombeyan Caves Road property. 4. A tent and accessories identified as belonging to Ivan were found on or near the same shelf where the camping equipment he admitted as belonging to Clarke and Walters was found. 5. Ivan said the tent and tent fly belonged to him.

Paul Thomas Onions: Attempted abduction and shooting January 1990

Items located and claims against Ivan	Comments
Small men's-size, long-sleeved blue cotton Next-brand shirt in red plastic box located on floor of garage at Guildford house of Ivan's mother, Margaret.	1. Onions identified the shirt as being identical to his shirt, which was in his backpack when taken by Ivan, except for some red stitching. 2. Anthony O'Connor of Next, England, identified photographs of a shirt being worn by Onions and the shirt found on the garage bench as being Next shirts of the same design and style. 3. The shirt was manufactured for Next and available for sale from Next stores in the UK during their 1986 season. 4. There were no overseas outlets for the sale of that shirt at that time. 5. Onions wore a small men's-size shirt, the same size at that found in the garage at Ivan's mother's house. 6. Found in the same red plastic box on the floor of the garage was a blue-checked short-sleeved shirt. 7. Karen Milat identified this shirt as belonging to Ivan. 8. Ivan said he had a shirt similar to the blue-checked shirt.

Items located and claims against Ivan	Comments
The accused had a revolver that matched the description of the one seen by Onions. Revolver 1: Colt .45 ACP revolver.	1. Grip plates suitable for Colt 'New Service' .45 ACP revolver and two PMC .45 calibre cartridges—one fired—located in left-hand drawer of dressing table in bedroom 4 of Ivan's house. 2. Quantity of .45 PMC and Winchester cartridges in a plastic bag with .32 calibre cartridges and a single fired Winchester .22 calibre cartridge case in a cardboard box, on the bed in bedroom 4 of Ivan's house. 3. Quantity of .45 PMC, Winchester and Norma cartridges found in plastic bag in milk crate on shelf in garage at Ivan's house. 4. Twelve cartridge adaptors (full moon clips) found in console of Ivan's red Holden Jackaroo number QBY-388. 5. All items suitable for use in a Colt 'New Service' .45 ACP revolver. 6. Photographs found at Ivan's house depict Ivan's Harley Davidson motorcycle number YYG-37 and revolver, which appears consistent with a Colt 'New Service' .45 ACP revolver loaded with copper-tipped cartridges. Written on the back of one photo are the words '17 Colt 45 ACP'.

Items located and claims against Ivan	Comments
	7. Also depicted in the photograph is Ivan's Franchi 12-gauge self-loading shotgun found in the alcove at Walter Milat's Hill Top house; camouflage-coloured 7.62 × 39 mm SKK rifle consisting of: • SKK barrel and receiver, serial number 8813143, with telescopic sight, found in the alcove • gun magazine, one of two SKK magazines owned by the accused, found inside Schmidl's High Sierra day pack, which was in the alcove • wooden rifle stock found in the alcove • bayonet, found in the left-hand drawer of the dressing table in bedroom 4 of Ivan's house. 8. The .45 calibre cartridges are the same brands and type as 24 .45 calibre cartridges in four cartridge adaptors found inside Schmidl's High Sierra day pack in the alcove. 9. The .45 calibre cartridges are copper-tipped, and Onions said Ivan used copper-tipped bullets in the revolver.

Items located and claims against Ivan	Comments
	10. The cartridge adaptors are the same style and type of manufacture as the four cartridge adaptors in the High Sierra day pack. 11. Detective Senior Constable Roach, Ballistics, said the barrel length of the Colt .45 ACP revolvers range from 4 to 7½ inches. 12. Onions said Ivan had a revolver with a barrel of 4–6 inches.
The accused had a revolver that matched the description of the one seen by Onions. Revolver 2: .38 calibre revolver.	1. Four Dominion 'Smith and Wesson' .38 calibre fired cartridge cases located in left-hand drawer of dressing table in bedroom 4 at Ivan's house. 2. Box of Dominion 'Smith and Wesson' .38 calibre cartridges with Canon 'Prima' instruction book and model parts in cardboard box located on bed in bedroom 4 at Ivan's house. 3. Dominion cartridges suitable for a .38 calibre revolver. 4. Anthony Sara, a workmate of Ivan, said Ivan had told him he had a .38 six-shot revolver. 5. The .38 calibre cartridges are copper-tipped and Onions says the accused used copper-tipped bullets in the revolver.

Items located and claims against Ivan	Comments
The accused carried a handgun in his car.	1. Browning, manufactured by Fabrique Nationale, 7.65 mm (.32 calibre) pistol, engraved, with nine cartridges, pouch and magazine with five cartridges (Winchester and Sellier & Bellot), with plastic bag, found under washing machine in laundry in Ivan's house. 2. Detective Senior Constable Roach, Ballistics, said the engraving on the pistol is by percussion engraver, as is engraving on .44 calibre black powder revolver found in alcove at Walter's property. 3. Karen Milat identified pistol and pouch as belonging to Ivan. 4. Karen Milat said Ivan used to carry this pistol in his sock and under the driver's seat of his car. 5. Ivan disputed that he carried his pistol in his sock and under the driver's seat of his car. 6. Walter Milat said Ivan had a pistol like the one recovered under the washing machine. 7. Ivan said the pistol was his, but he last saw it at Blackett in early 1987 when Karen Milat left. 8. Quantity of .32 (Winchester and Sellier & Bellot) cartridges found in plastic bag, with .45 calibre cartridges and a single fired Winchester .22 calibre cartridge case, inside cardboard box on bed in bedroom 4 at Ivan's house.

Items located and claims against Ivan	Comments
	9. The .32 calibre cartridges are suitable for use in the pistol. 10. A camouflage-coloured wooden box with .44 calibre black powder revolver marked 'Texas' with contents found in alcove at Walter Milat's property. 11. Detective Senior Constable Roach, Ballistics, said the engraving on the revolver is consistent with the type of engraving on the pistol found at Ivan's place. 12. Karen Milat identified the revolver and the wooden box as belonging to Ivan. 13. Karen Milat said Ivan would put the box with revolver in it under the back seat of the car when they went on trips. 14. Ivan denied putting the gun under the back seat of his car. 15. Ivan admitted that he owned the revolver.
The accused had a bag of dirty ropes similar to that seen and described by Onions.	1. Five lengths of sash cord in a green striped pillowcase were found on a shelf in the garage at Ivan's house. 2. Karen Milat identified the sash cords as the type used by Ivan to tie a minibike onto trailer. 3. Ivan said he used the type of sash cord found. 4. Karen Milat identified the pillowcase as belonging to Ivan's mother.

Items located and claims against Ivan	Comments
1989 English 20-pence coin found in console of Ivan's red Holden Jackaroo number QBY-388.	1. Onions left England about 8 December 1989. 2. Ivan had no international travel movements during relevant period.
When Ivan picked up Onions he called himself Bill.	1. Ivan used the name William 'Bill' Milat when he worked at Sweeping Services in late 1988. 2. New Zealand postcard addressed to 'Bill' from Graham 'Jock' Pittaway, postmarked 22 April 1992, found on bedside table in bedroom 3 of Ivan's house. 3. Tax declaration form in the name of William Milat from the RTA.
Ivan's vehicle matches the description given by Onions.	1. A number of photographs depict a camping trip at the Wombeyan Caves Road property during Easter 1991. They include photographs of Ivan's silver Nissan Patrol, number OPO-172, with sheepskin seat covers. 2. Onions' description of Ivan's vehicle describes lambswool seat covers on the front seats.

Appendix 2

MODEL 10/22

CLARKE BODY
1. 10 bullet entry wounds.
2. Seven bullets found with body and three bullets found in ground beneath body.
3. Bullets were engraved with rifling consistent with having been fired from a .22 Ruger 10/22 rifle.
4. Markings on bullets suggest the use of a silencer.

CLARKE BODY
1. 10 .22 Winchester fired cartridge cases found metres from the body.
2. Cases were fired by the Ruger 10/22 bolt assembly found in the wall cavity at , Eagle Vale.

NEUGEBAUER BODY
1. Six bullet wounds to head with possible seventh bullet wound.
2. Four bullets found in skull and one with upper body.
3. Three of the five bullets were .22 calibre (other two too damaged). All bullets damaged beyond specific weapon identification.
4. No cartridge cases found.

NEUGEBAUER BODY "AREA A"
1. 165 metres from body of NEUGEBAUER were one empty 50 round Eley aummuniton box and one empty 50 round Winchester Winner ammunition box.
2. Batch number of the Eley ammunition box matches the batch number of the Eley ammunition boxes found at Eagle Vale, and at Hilltop.
3. Batch number of the Winchester ammunition box matches the batch number of the Winchester ammunition boxes found at , Hilltop.

NEUGEBAUER BODY "AREA A"
1. 165 metres from body of NEUGEBAUER were numerous fired .22 cartridge cases.
2. All cartridge cases are Winchester (47) and Eley (46) brands of ammunition.
3. All 47 Winchester fired cartridge cases were fired from the same firearm used in the CLARKE killing.

NEUGEBAUER BODY "AREA A"
1. 165 metres from body of NEUGEBAUER were six bullets recovered from trees.
2. Four bullets could have been fired from a range of firearms including a Ruger 10/22 rifle.

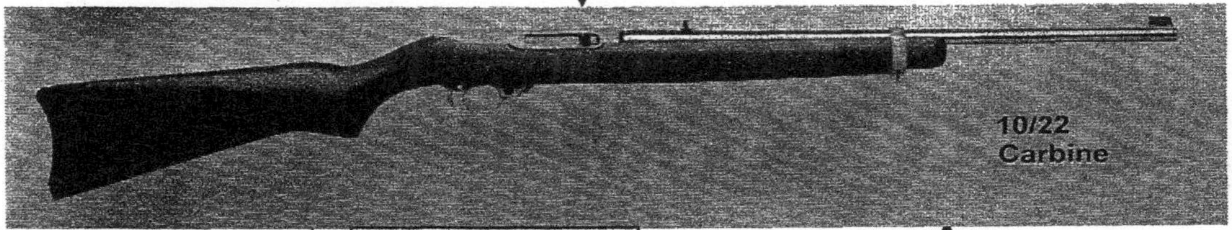

10/22
Carbine

FOUND IN WALL CAVITY AT EAGLE VALE
1. White plastic bag containing:
a. Trigger assembly
b. Spring and guide
c. Bolt assembly
d. .22 Magazine (50 cartridge capacity) designed for use with Ruger 10/22 rifle.
2. Ruger .22 rotary magazine.
All items from 1. and 2. are components of a Ruger 10/22 rifle.
3. Bolt assembly was test fired and found to have been used in the rifle that fired the 10 cartridge cases found near CLARKE's body.

FOUND IN FAMILY ROOM AT EAGLE VALE
1. Book titled "Select Fire 10/22".
2. Book has accused's fingerprints on it.

FOUND IN HALL CUPBOARD AT , EAGLE VALE
1. Ruger .22 calibre model 10/22 receiver serial No. 120-15357.

FOUND IN GARAGE AT , EAGLE VALE
1. Ruger butt plate.

FOUND IN BEDROOM 4 AT , EAGLE VALE
1. Ruger barrel band in two pieces.

FOUND IN BEDROOM 4 AT , EAGLE VALE
1. One .22 Winchester fired cartridge case.
2. Cartridge case is consistent with having been discharged in a rifle fitted with the bolt assembly found in the wall cavity at Eagle Vale.

FOUND AT HILLTOP
1. .22 Winchester Winner ammunition boxes.
2. Batch numbers of boxes match the batch number of the Winchester Winner box found in NEUGEBAUER/HABSCHIED "Area A" to the exact manufacturer's shift.

FOUND IN BUSHLAND AT WOMBEYAN CAVES PROPERTY
1. Quantity of cartridge cases and spent bullets.
2. Four of these cartridge cases are consistent with having been discharged in a rifle fitted with the bolt assembly found in the wall cavity at Eagle Vale.

FOUND AT BUXTON FIRING RANGE
1. Large quantity of fired cartridge cases and spent bullets.
2. Four cartridge cases were fired by a rifle fitted with the Ruger 10/22 bolt assembly found in the wall cavity at Eagle Vale.

HORSLEY PARK GUN SHOP
1. Ruger 10/22 rifle serial No. 120-15357 sold to Horsely Park Gun Shop by KOMAREK in early 1988.
2. Ivan Milat was a customer.

Appendix 3

ANSCHUTZ .22 CALIBRE REPEATING RIFLE MODEL 1441/42 SERIAL NO. 1053118

NEUGEBAUER/HABSCHIED "AREA A"

1. 165 metres from body of NEUGEBAUER were numerous fired .22 cartridge cases.
2. There were Winchester (47) and Eley (46) brands of ammunition.
3. The 46 Eley cartridge cases are consistent with having been fired from a rifle fitted with the Anschutz breech bolt found at Hilltop.
4. Two bullets recovered from trees could have been fired from a range of firearms, including the Anschutz rifle found at Hilltop.

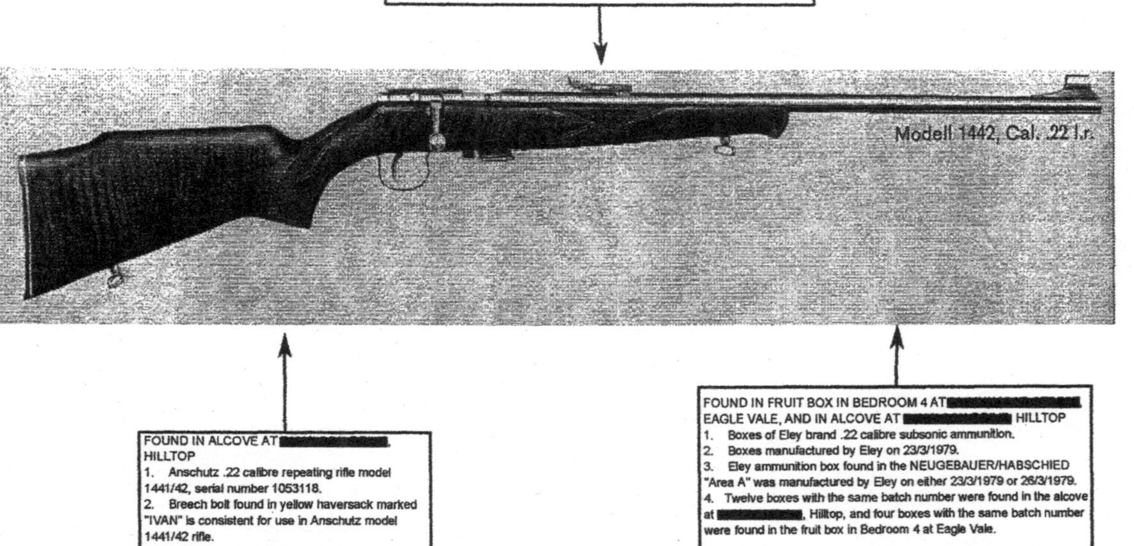

FOUND IN ALCOVE AT [redacted], HILLTOP

1. Anschutz .22 calibre repeating rifle model 1441/42, serial number 1053118.
2. Breech bolt found in yellow haversack marked "IVAN" is consistent for use in Anschutz model 1441/42 rifle.

FOUND IN FRUIT BOX IN BEDROOM 4 AT [redacted], EAGLE VALE, AND IN ALCOVE AT [redacted] HILLTOP

1. Boxes of Eley brand .22 calibre subsonic ammunition.
2. Boxes manufactured by Eley on 23/3/1979.
3. Eley ammunition box found in the NEUGEBAUER/HABSCHIED "Area A" was manufactured by Eley on either 23/3/1979 or 26/3/1979.
4. Twelve boxes with the same batch number were found in the alcove at [redacted], Hilltop, and four boxes with the same batch number were found in the fruit box in Bedroom 4 at Eagle Vale.

Appendix 4: Staff of Task Force Air

Rank, name and region	Duty	Dates attached
Superintendent Clive Small, South West Region	Commander	13.10.93 to 10.06.94
Detective Inspector Rodney Lynch, South West Region	Deputy Commander	21.10.93 to 10.06.94
	Commander	11.06.94 to 30.11.96
Detective Inspector Robert Godden, North Region	Chief Investigator (Operations)	13.10.93 to 31.01.95
Detective Senior Sergeant Robert Benson, South Region	Chief Investigator (Intelligence)	21.10.93 to 31.01.95
Detective Sergeant Royce Gorman, 5th Region	Investigator	1.11.93 to 31.12.94
Detective Sergeant Stephen McLennan, South West Region	Investigator	13.10.93 to 28.09.96
Detective Sergeant Stephen Leach, North West Region	Investigator	1.11.93 to 28.09.96
Detective Sergeant Darrel McIntyre, South Region	Investigator	2.01.94 to 23.04.95
Detective Sergeant Gaetano Crea, 5th Region	Investigator	7.11.93 to 30.04.95

Rank, name and region	Duty	Dates attached
Detective Senior Constable Paul Gordon, South West Region	Investigator	2.01.94 to 4.06.94
Detective Senior Constable Louise Donald, 5th Region	Investigator	10.01.94 to 28.09.96
Detective Senior Constable Andrew Waterman, North Region	Investigator	1.11.93 to 28.09.96
Detective Senior Constable Graeme Pickering, North Region	Investigator	2.01.94 to 05.08.95
Detective Senior Constable Mark Feeney, South Region	Investigator	2.01.94 to 31.03.95
Detective Senior Constable Stuart Wilkinson, North Region	Investigator	1.11.93 to 12.08.95
Detective Senior Constable Peter O'Connor, South Region	Investigator	2.01.94 to 30.04.95
Detective Senior Constable Howard Gumley, North Region	Investigator	2.01.94 to 31.03.95
Detective Senior Constable David McCloskey, South West Region	Investigator	2.01.94 to 31.03.95
Detective Senior Constable Andrew Richmond, North West Region	Investigator	2.01.94 to 11.02.95

Rank, name and region	Duty	Dates attached
Detective Senior Constable Michael Ashwood, South West Region	Investigator	13.10.93 to 26.08.95
Detective Senior Constable Timothy Seirlis, 5th Region	Investigator	26.04.94 to 29.07.95
Detective Senior Constable Geoffrey Hamment, South West Region	Investigator	13.10.93 to 21.10.95
Detective Constable First Class Reginald Miller, South West Region	Investigator	13.10.93 to 28.09.96
Detective Constable First Class Angelo Bilias, North West Region	Investigator	1.11.93 to 26.08.95
Detective Constable First Class Brett Anthony Coman, South Region	Investigator	1.11.93 to 28.09.96
Detective Constable First Class Tony Roberts, South West Region	Investigator	13.10.93 to 28.01.95
Plainclothes Constable John Kershler, North West Region	Investigator	2.01.94 to 11.02.95

Rank, name and region	Duty	Dates attached
Incident room and analysts		
Sergeant Catherine Urquhart, South West Region	Incident Room	13.10.93 to 26.08.95
Sergeant Christopher Clark, North West Region	Analyst	5.06.94 to 8.07.95
Detective Senior Constable Kristina Illingsworth, 5th Region	Analyst	7.11.93 to 15.06.96
Senior Constable Patrick Gagan, North West Region	Incident Room	7.11.93 to 30.11.96
Constable First Class Michael Rochester, North Region	Analyst	7.11.93 to 30.04.95
Constable Paul Martin (resigned)	Analyst	13.10.93 to 24.09.94
Bowral		
Detective Sergeant Vivien Little, South West Region	Investigator	13.10.93 to 30.07.94
Detective Sergeant Kevin Hammond, South West Region	Investigator	13.10.93 to 27.08.94
Sergeant Donald Hayes, South West Region	Investigator	13.10.93 to 30.07.94
Detective Senior Constable Stephen Ballard, South West Region	Investigator	13.10.93 to 7.05.94

Rank, name and region	Duty	Dates attached
Senior Constable Peter Vaughan, South West Region	Investigator	13.10.93 to 30.07.94
Detective Senior Constable Peter Lovell, South West Region	Investigator	13.10.93 to 11.2.95
Specialist Services support		
Sergeant Francois Helsen, 5th Region	Analyst	1.11.93 to 30.11.94
Sergeant Bernard O'Reilly, North Region	Analyst	15.11.93 to 15.01.94
Sergeant Christopher Wilesmith, 5th Region	Analyst	15.01.94 to 25.09.94
Detective Senior Constable Carmela Ohmenzetter, 5th Region	Analyst	1.11.93 to 24.11.94
Senior Constable David Powdrell, 5th Region	Analyst	1.11.93 to 24.11.94
Detective Senior Constable Andrew Grosse, Crime Scene Unit, South West Region	Crime scene examiner	8.03.94 to 16.09.94
Support Staff		
Susana Maria Correia, State Intelligence Group	Administration	18.04.94 to 10.02.95

Specialist NSW police who supported the task force but were not attached to it

Detective Sergeant John Goldie, Crime Scene Unit, South West Region	Crime scene examiner
Sergeant Gerard Dutton, Forensic Ballistics Unit, Operations Support	Ballistics expert
Detective Senior Constable Shaun Roach, Forensic Ballistics Unit, Operations Support	Ballistics expert
Senior Sergeant Edward Billett	Police Prosecuting Branch

Australian Federal Police

Detective Superintendent Ian Prior Firearms and Ballistics Branch	Ballistics expert

BIBLIOGRAPHY

Much of the information used in writing this book was obtained first-hand in the course of the police investigation of the backpacker murders, from court records and from personal interviews conducted with retired police and others by the authors. The authors are grateful to all the people, named and unnamed, without whose support and cooperation this book could not have been written.

Government publications

Abernethy, John, New South Wales State Coroner, 'Inquest into the deaths of Leanne Beth Goodall, Amanda Therese Robinson and Robyn Elizabeth Hickie', 5 July 2002

——, 'Inquest into the death of Debbie Rae Pritchard', 31 January 2003

Milovanovich, Carl, New South Wales Deputy State Coroner, 'Inquest into the deaths of Gillian Janine Jamieson and Deborah Susan Balken', 22 May 2006

Books

Marsden, John, *I Am What I Am: My life and curious times*, Melbourne: Penguin, 2005

Mercer, Neil, *Fate: Inside the backpacker murders investigation*, Sydney: Random House, 1997

Sutton, Candace & Connolly, Ellen, *Lady Killer: How conman Bruce Burrell kidnapped and killed rich women for their money*, Sydney: Allen & Unwin, 2009

Whittaker, Mark & Kennedy, Les, *Sins of the Brother: The definitive story of Ivan Milat and the backpacker murders*, Sydney: Macmillan, 1998

Television documentaries

Australian Story, 'Into the forest', Part 1, transcript, screened 1 November 2004, ABCTV

——, 'Into the forest', Part 2, transcript, screened 8 November 2004, ABCTV

——, 'Back into the forest', transcript, screened 30 May 2005, ABCTV
Crime Investigation Australia, 'Ivan Milat: the backpacker murders', Season 1, Episode 4, screened 25 September 2007, Crime & Investigation Network
——, 'Families of crime: backpacker bloodshed', Season 4, Episode 4, screened 30 November 2010, Crime & Investigation Network
Sunday, screened 28 July 1996, Channel 9

Newspapers and periodicals

Advocate (Hornsby)
The Australian Financial Review
The Daily Telegraph
Southern Highland News
The Sun-Herald
The Sunday Telegraph
The Sydney Morning Herald
Who Weekly

Letters

Newnham, Noel, Letter to Clive Small, dated 5 July 1996